# Teaching Reading to English Language Learners

## Differentiated Literacies

**Socorro G. Herrera**
*Kansas State University*

**Della R. Perez**
*Kansas State University*

**Kathy Escamilla**
*University of Colorado, Boulder*

## Allyn & Bacon

Boston ■ New York ■ San Francisco
Mexico City ■ Montreal ■ Toronto ■ London ■ Madrid ■ Munich ■ Paris
Hong Kong ■ Singapore ■ Tokyo ■ Cape Town ■ Sydney

*Executive Editor:* Aurora Martínez Ramos
*Editorial Assistant:* Kara Kikel
*Executive Marketing Manager:* Krista Clark
*Production Editor:* Janet Domingo
*Editorial Production Service:* Omegatype Typography, Inc.
*Composition Buyer:* Linda Cox
*Manufacturing Buyer:* Megan Cochran
*Electronic Composition:* Omegatype Typography, Inc.
*Interior Design:* Omegatype Typography, Inc.
*Photo Researcher:* Annie Pickert
*Cover Administrator:* Linda Knowles

For related titles and support materials, visit our online catalog at www.pearsonhighered.com.

Between the time Website information is gathered and then published, it is not unusual for some sites to have closed. Also, the transcription of URLs can result in typographical errors. The publisher would appreciate notification where these errors occur so that they may be corrected in subsequent editions.

**Library of Congress Cataloging-in-Publication Data**

Herrera, Socorro Guadalupe.
  Teaching reading to english language learners : differentiated literacies / Socorro G. Herrera, Della R. Perez, Kathy Escamilla.
     p.  cm.
  Includes bibliographical references and index.
  ISBN-13: 978-0-205-49217-6 (pbk.)
  ISBN-10: 0-205-49217-7 (pbk.)
  1. English language—Study and teaching—United States—Foreign speakers.
2. Reading—United States.   3. Linguistic minorities—Education—United States.
4. Multiculturalism—United States.  I. Perez, Della R.  II. Escamilla, Kathy.
III. Title.
  PE1128.A2H4676   2010
  428.2'4—dc22
                                           2008045138

Printed in the United States of America

10  9  8  7  6  5  4  3  2  1     13  12  11  10  09

**Credits appear on page 288, which constitutes an extension of the copyright page.**

**Allyn & Bacon**
is an imprint of

www.pearsonhighered.com

ISBN-10: 0-205-49217-7
ISBN-13: 978-0-205-49217-6

*With love, to my husband, Gilbert,*
*and my children, Dawn, Kevin, Jesse, & Isamari.*

*—Socorro*


*To my mother, Ruth,*
*who inspired me to love reading,*
*and to my daughter, Ruth Dea,*
*to whom reading is a joy!*

*—Della*


*Con amor para mi esposo Manuel,*
*mis hijos Alexandro, Sonya, Amanda, y Ruben,*
*y mi querida nieta Victoria.*

*—Kathy*

### Dr. Socorro G. Herrera

Dr. Herrera serves as a professor of elementary education at Kansas State University and directs the Center for Intercultural and Multilingual Advocacy (CIMA) in the College of Education. Her K–12 teaching experience includes an emphasis on literacy development. Her research focuses on literacy opportunities with culturally and linguistically diverse students, reading strategies, and teacher preparation for diversity in the classroom. Dr. Herrera has recently published two books with Allyn and Bacon: *Mastering ESL and Bilingual Methods: Differentiated Instruction for Culturally and Linguistically Diverse Students* (2005) and *Assessment Accommodations for Classroom Teachers of Culturally and Linguistically Diverse Students* (2007). Dr. Herrera has authored articles for numerous nationally known journals, such as the *Bilingual Research Journal, Journal of Hispanic Higher Education, Journal of Research in Education,* and the *Journal of Latinos and Education.*

### Dr. Della R. Perez

Dr. Perez serves as an assistant professor of elementary education at Kansas State University and is the Associate Director of Undergraduate Programming at the Center for Intercultural and Multilingual Advocacy (CIMA) in the College of Education. Her research has focused on literacy development and instruction for culturally and linguistically diverse students and parental involvement. Dr. Perez has published *The Five Components of Reading Development: A Classroom Teacher's Guide to Scaffolding Reading Instruction for ELL Students* (2006) and *ELL Literacy Interventions: Accommodations and Acceleration for Reading Success* (2005). Dr. Perez also has co-authored a book chapter for *Culturally Responsive Teacher Education: Language, Curriculum, and Community* (2008).

### Dr. Kathy Escamilla

Dr. Escamilla is a professor of education at the University of Colorado, Boulder. She has been a bilingual teacher, program administrator, and professor for over 37 years. She helped to develop the Spanish reconstruction of Reading Recovery (Descubriendo la Lectura), which was published in the book *Instrumento de observación de los logros de la leco-escritura inicial* (Heinemann). She has done extensive research in the area of literacy for Spanish-speaking children in the United States and has authored over 40 journal articles in this area. She served two terms as the President of the National Association for Bilingual Education (NABE) and works as a technical assistant and consultant for bilingual/ESL programs nationwide.

# ■ contents

## ▪ chapter 3

## Rethinking Phonemic Awareness: A Cross-Linguistic Transfer Perspective      40

## ■ chapter 6

# Strategies-Based Comprehension Instruction: Linking the Known to the Unknown        132

## chapter 7

## chapter 8

# chapter 9

# chapter 10

## ■ The Need for a New Perspective on Second-Language Literacy

The reader might ask, Why do we need another book about literacy instruction and why one that is specific to second language learners? Bernhardt (2003) states that 80 percent of all reading research in the world has been done in four countries—the United States, England, New Zealand, and Australia—all of which are English-speaking countries. This research, while instructive, has been conducted largely by monolingual English researchers on monolingual English-speaking students and then applied to second language learners without question and, in many cases, without modification. Bernhardt adds that the preponderance of this monolingual English view of how children learn to read is exacerbated by state and federal policies regarding best practices for reading instruction, which rely solely on this monolingual research base.

Further compounding the issue is the production of commercial reading programs that are also based on this monolingual view and that are purchased by states and local school districts and used with diverse populations of children, assuming that the research base applies across languages and cultural groups. This deeply entrenched approach toward literacy has left little space for biliteracy and mutiliteracy development or guidelines for how teaching literacy in English may need to be modified for culturally and linguistically diverse (CLD) students (Moll, 2001; Moll & Dworin, 1996; Perez, 1998; Reyes, 2001; Schwarzer, 2001).

This situation has resulted in a call for a new perspective on teaching literacy to second language learners that emphasizes approaches and strategies specific to the needs of CLD learners. The chapters in this text address some of the gaps in research surrounding literacy instruction for second language learners so that English as a second language (ESL) teachers and grade-level/mainstream teachers can bridge theory to practice as they develop a culturally responsive pedagogy. ESL teachers are encouraged to continue providing ESL services if a CLD student qualifies for them via a solid oral ESL program that takes place daily and is explicit in its focus on literacy development. Grade-level/mainstream classroom teachers are encouraged to provide a comprehensive second-language reading program that takes place in addition to and not instead of ESL. This text provides grade-level/mainstream classroom teachers with the information they need to support second-language literacy development with their CLD students, in addition to whatever ESL program the school has in place.

Our research has found that teachers and schools who incorporate the languages and cultures represented by their CLD students have far greater success in supporting literacy development than those that do not. This success is further enhanced when ESL teachers and grade-level/mainstream classroom teachers work together to create a comprehensive literacy development program. Each of the chapters in this text provides concrete suggestions and hands-on strategies for both ESL and grade-level/mainstream teachers to implement in their daily instructional practice. Following these suggestions and applying these strategies will help ensure that children's languages and cultures are the cornerstone of their literacy development.

## ■ Beginning to Develop a New Pedagogy

Chapter 1 sets the stage for this text by exploring what *literacy* means for CLD students. This chapter then introduces the five elements of literacy instruction that the National Reading Panel (NRP, 2000) views as critical to any reading program: phonemic awareness, phonics, vocabulary, comprehension, and fluency. Chapter 1 also details current approaches to reading instruction for alphabetic languages, which include analytic or top-down approaches (whole to part), synthetic or bottom-up approaches (part to whole), and interactive approaches. The NRP (2000) findings were synthetic (bottom-up) in their recommendations. This text proposes that rather than a focus on learning to crack the code, literacy instruction for second language learners must focus on meaning.

Chapter 2 presents an introduction to the CLD student biography and its role in literacy development. Central to this discussion is the need for educators to consider the whole child by exploring each student's sociocultural, linguistic, academic, and cognitive dimensions to best use his or her assets to further the abilities to read and write in a second language. Too often, these dimensions are overlooked, viewed as problems to be solved, or seen as sources of interference in learning to read in English. Suggestions for getting to know students and using their languages and cultures in instruction are presented.

At the core of this text is a focus on the five core elements of reading instruction that were introduced by the NRP (2000). Chapter 3 begins this exploration by proposing a reexamination of phonemic awareness with CLD students. Traditionally, the development of phonemic awareness in monolingual English reading programs is based on instruction in phonemic awareness tasks. The challenge for CLD students is that these tasks are often decontextualized drills of isolated English letter sounds. For CLD students who are learning English and who do not yet know these letter sounds, this decontextualized approach to phonemic awareness instruction often results in a disconnect. The reexamination in Chapter 3 is centered on research that found that CLD students can engage in cross-linguistic transfer by accessing existing phonemic awareness skills in their native language and transferring these skills to reading and writing in English. In an analysis of the word recognition view and sociopsycholinguistic view of reading, this chapter identifies which view is most beneficial for CLD students. This chapter proposes multiple strategies for teaching phonemic awareness tasks by modeling a contextualized approach to instruction that emphasizes cross-linguistic transfer.

Chapter 4 takes a historical look at the role of phonics in reading instruction. Building on the presentation of the word recognition view and the sociopsycholinguistic view of reading presented in Chapter 3, this chapter contextualizes phonics instruction from a sociopsycholinguistic viewpoint. Phonics instruction in the sociopsycholinguistic view incorporates three cueing systems to support the learner: the graphophonic, semantic, and syntactic cueing systems. Using authentic literature, Chapter 4 suggests possible ways educators can build from their prescribed reading programs to provide integrated phonics lessons for CLD students. Founded on a student-centered approach to phonics instruction that supports and builds on CLD students' existing phonics skills, this chapter also identifies specific strategies that promote the use of linguistic investigations as the starting point from which educators can develop phonics skills with CLD students.

Chapter 5 explores the implications of current approaches to vocabulary development in instruction with CLD students. Building from these current approaches, this chapter highlights the importance of providing vocabulary instruction within meaningful linguistic and cultural contexts. To support teachers in the development of these meaningful contexts, this chapter provides specific examples of how vocabulary development can be linked to each of the four dimensions of the CLD student biography (sociocultural, linguistic, academic, and cognitive). Central to this discussion is a focus on differentiating vocabulary for CLD students at different stages of English language acquisition. Chapter 5 also explores how to tap into students' prior and background knowledge before the lesson to bridge and connect the known to the unknown. Multiple strategies for promoting student interaction, practice, and application of academic vocabulary are provided. Furthermore, authentic assessment of students' understanding of academic vocabulary is discussed and modeled through student samples.

Cognizant of the fact that vocabulary development underlies reading comprehension, the text moves from a discussion of vocabulary instruction to comprehension instruction in Chapter 6. Building on current research, this chapter proposes that central to comprehension instruction are the schematic connections students make while reading. CLD students who bring different life experiences than those of their monolingual English-speaking peers frequently make schematic connections that differ as well. Chapter 6 explores this juxtaposition by illustrating how teachers can tap into the CLD student biography to promote the use of schematic connections in practice. Additionally, Chapter 6 provides teachers with three types of hands-on reading comprehension strategies that have been specifically designed to support CLD students' schematic connections to text. The first type of strategy is metacognitive in nature and promotes CLD students' monitoring of their own thought processes while reading. The second type, cognitive strategies, provides CLD students with concrete tools they can use individually or with peers. The third type, social/affective strategies, promotes student interaction and cultural connections to text.

Chapter 7 brings together the aspects of phonemic awareness, phonics, vocabulary, and comprehension development by identifying how they work in unison to support fluency development. Traditionally, fluency instruction for CLD students has focused largely on *surface constructs* of fluency development, in which accuracy, speed, and prosody are the emphasis (Pikuiski & Chard, 2005). Chapter 7 introduces key considerations for promoting surface constructs of fluency development. Additionally, this chapter explores how teachers can transition CLD students to *deep constructs* of fluency development, in which the ultimate goal is comprehension. Numerous strategies are introduced to support teachers in providing fluency instruction that guides CLD students to develop these deep constructs of fluency. The emphasis of each of these strategies is on the power of collaboration and modeling. Through the use of interactive grouping configurations at the partner and small-group level, these hands-on strategies provide the reader with a new twist on fluency development.

Often, literacy books are about reading and not about writing. Chapter 8 specifically addresses the need to modify writing instruction for second language learners. As with reading instruction, writing instruction with CLD students is frequently approached in the same manner as writing instruction for monolingual English-speaking children. We propose that teachers adopt the perspective that what students know about writing in one language can be used to help teach the second language. For example, conducting a minilesson in which CLD students contrast languages might be more effective than asking students to correct grammar errors in written English sentences.

Chapter 9 challenges teachers to look "outside the lines" of traditional literacy assessment when working with CLD students by building from the multiple dimensions of the CLD student biography when approaching assessment. This chapter provides an overview of some of the most common assessments currently used in classrooms to identify students' language proficiency levels and reading proficiency in the following areas: phonemic awareness, phonics, vocabulary, comprehension, and fluency. Building from an authentic approach to assessment, this chapter explores the ways teachers can assess CLD students' knowledge in each of these areas by going back to the CLD student biography. Formative assessments are presented as one of the key ways for educators to apply authentic assessments in practice. Strategies for extending questioning that advances CLD students' thinking, learning, and application are also introduced. The chapter concludes by presenting two student case studies that illustrate how to bring together the CLD student biography, reading instruction, and authentic assessment.

Chapter 10 brings the text to a close by examining how the information learned in the previous chapters aligns with two sets of standards: the *Standards for the English Language Arts* of the International Reading Association and the National Council of Teachers of English (IRA/NCTE, 1996) and the *ESL Standards for Pre-K–12 Students* of the Teachers of English to Speakers of Other Languages (TESOL, 1997). Using both standards as a theoretical foundation, this chapter discusses how educators can maintain fidelity to the core curriculum they are required to teach yet still make accommodations within their reading curriculum to support their CLD students' academic success. The chapter provides specific strategies that demonstrate how teachers can blend what they already do in their daily instruction with the new information they have learned so that they are able to maintain fidelity yet approach literacy instruction with a new lens rooted in the CLD student biography.

In sum, this text is organized around the principles that reading and writing instruction for CLD students begins with the CLD student biography and should have at its core a focus on meaning. Consequently, the languages and cultures of second language learners are considered resources to be used in teaching, rather than problems to be solved. Throughout this text, teachers are guided to modify literacy instruction in ways that address both the assets and needs of CLD students. Modification does not mean doing the same thing only slower, more frequently, after school, or on Saturdays. Modification means doing something differently and changing our habits of mind!

## ■ Additional Features

To support readers' understanding, additional features are included in each chapter of this text. These features have been designed to reflect the various learning styles of readers and to highlight critical concepts.

### *Chapter Outlines*

Every chapter begins with a chapter outline, which serves as a graphic organizer by providing the reader with an overview of the key content to be presented.

### Critical Considerations

After each chapter outline, questions are posed for teachers and practitioners working with CLD students. The Critical Considerations prompt the reader to reflect on the issues to be explored in depth in the chapter.

### Strategies in Practice

These boxes provide the reader with detailed instructions for implementing the strategies introduced in each chapter. Special emphasis is given to the adaptations included with each strategy that are specific to CLD students. Driven by the strategy itself, these adaptations reflect the specific sociocultural, linguistic, academic, and cognitive dimensions of the CLD student biography.

### Samples of Student Work

Select samples of student work have been included in this text and incorporated in several of the Strategies in Practice to depict student products. The student samples have been gathered from multiple classrooms in multiple states and reflect a wide range of CLD students. Not only are these students culturally diverse, but they are also linguistically diverse in that they represent multiple language groups in addition to Spanish speakers.

### Teacher Voices

In our work with public school teachers, we have been fortunate to see and share in the successful implementation of literacy instruction modified specifically for CLD students. We have included quotations from teachers throughout the text to share the insights gained by teachers from their various experiences and to highlight critical concepts. From the teachers' voices, readers can learn firsthand how literacy instruction that targets the multiple dimensions of the CLD student biography not only significantly impacts the academic success of CLD students but also helps create powerful communities of learners with monolingual English students in grade-level classrooms.

### Vignettes

Vignettes are included in selected chapters to provide the reader with specific classroom scenarios that highlight critical concepts. Using the vignettes, readers are prompted to critically reflect on how these concepts directly impact their daily instructional practice.

### Key Theories and Concepts

Each chapter provides a theoretical orientation and defines critical concepts relevant to the chapter content. At the end of each chapter, these key theories and concepts are presented via a list of key vocabulary terms, which serve as a reminder to the reader of the theoretical foundation on which the chapter was based.

## Professional Conversations on Practice

These prompts provide readers with topics for discussion about the key issues presented in each chapter. This feature guides educators to elaborate on the concepts presented and to engage in critical reflection on the application of this content in their own professional practice.

## Questions for Review and Reflection

At the end of each chapter, questions are provided to engage readers in self-reflection on key content. The prompts further challenge teachers to consider their own readiness for implementing what they have learned in their professional practice.

PEARSON
**myeducationlab**
**Where the Classroom Comes to Life**

MyEducationLab (www.myeducationlab.com) is a research-based learning tool that brings teaching to life. Through authentic in-class video footage, interactive simulations, rich case studies, examples of authentic teacher and student work, and more, MyEducationLab prepares you for your teaching career by showing what quality instruction looks like.

MyEducationLab is easy to use! At the end of every chapter in the textbook, you will find the MyEducationLab logo adjacent to activities and exercises that correlate material you've just read in the chapter to your viewing of multimedia assets on the MyEducationLab site. These assets include:

- **Video:** The authentic classroom videos in MyEducationLab show how real teachers handle actual classroom situations.
- **Case Studies:** A diverse set of robust cases illustrates the realities of teaching and offers valuable perspectives on common issues and challenges in education.
- **Simulations:** Created by the IRIS Center at Vanderbilt University, these interactive simulations give you hands-on practice at adapting instruction for a full spectrum of learners.
- **Lesson Plans:** Specially selected, topically relevant excerpts from texts expand and enrich your perspectives on key issues and topics.
- **Classroom Artifacts:** Authentic preK–12 student and teacher classroom artifacts are tied to course topics and offer you practice in working with the actual types of materials you will encounter daily as teachers.
- **Lesson & Portfolio Builders:** With this effective and easy-to-use tool, you can create, update, and share standards-based lesson plans and portfolios.

### Glossary

This feature is designed to aid readers in their understanding of this text as well as in their future applications of content in practice. Attention has been given to acronyms readers are likely to be unfamiliar with and terms that are essential to literacy instruction for CLD students.

### References

A complete list of works cited in American Psychological Association (APA) bibliography style is included at the end of the text. This reference list documents the multiple sources used to provide the theoretical foundation and the research-based and practical applications of content suggested by the authors throughout this text. Additionally, this feature can be used as a resource for educators of CLD students at the preservice and inservice levels.

## ■ Starting the Journey

This text has been written to support educators in navigating the precarious task of teaching CLD students to read and write. Literacy instruction that is modified to be relevant and meaningful for second language learners provides these children with a solid path to academic success.

As we navigate the never-ending tides of politics that drive what happens in schools, we urge educators to let the following proverb guide their steps:

> Not to let a word get in the way
> Of its sentence,
> Not to let a sentence get in the way
> Of its intention,
> But to send your mind out to meet
> The intention as a guest,
> That is understanding.

Understanding the unique aspects of literacy development for CLD students needs to be the goal if we are to educate the children who sit before us. We must understand literacy development from a new perspective where pedagogy is important but the unique aspects of students' cultures and languages and their interaction with learning to read and write are more important. This text is intended to provide educators with the necessary information to move one step beyond their current practice to ensure more intentional accommodations for their CLD students.

# ■ Acknowledgments

Perhaps the greatest gift a teacher can give a child is to instill a passion for reading and writing. With the support of many colleagues and educators, we have shared our passion for educating culturally and linguistically diverse students so that they can receive this gift and become passionate readers and writers of English.

In particular, we thank Melissa Holmes for her support, encouragement, and expertise. Without her valuable insights and feedback, this book would not have become a reality. Among the many gifts Melissa brought to this effort were her editorial expertise, attention to detail, focus on the reader, and vigilance in seeing this project through to the end. To her, we owe our sincerest gratitude and heartfelt appreciation.

We also give special thanks to Sheri Meredith. Her steadfast attention to detail, voice, and formatting has resulted in a product we can proudly share. We thank her for keeping us organized, structured, and on task. Without her, this project would not have been completed.

We wish to acknowledge, too, the many teachers across the United States who contributed valuable insights and examples in practice to contextualize critical concepts throughout this text. Each of these educators exemplifies what it means to go above and beyond for culturally and linguistically diverse students and families in and out of the classroom. Thank you for inspiring us through your example and sharing with us a piece of your heart.

We would like to thank the following reviewers for their comments on the manuscript: Kimberley Kreicker, Emporia State University; Paula M. Selvester, California State University, Chico; and Cheryl A. Slattery, Shippensburg University.

Finally, we extend a special thanks to the many colleagues with whom we work. Shabina Kavimandan was a great advocate and resource throughout the production of this text. Her insights, support in collecting strategies in practice, and examples were outstanding. Additional thanks goes to Stephanie Wessels, who provided us with many valuable contributions and practical examples from her personal and professional experiences in elementary classrooms. Dr. Seong-Shin Kim, Miki Loschky, Dominika Ornatowska, Jennifer Brunenn, Gisela Nash, and several of our preservice undergradutate students also deserve our thanks for their support and contributions.

# Literacy and the Culturally and Linguistically Diverse Student

Ms. Gilbert has 24 children in her third-grade class. Thirteen of these children are classified as culturally and linguistically diverse (CLD). Eight of the CLD students are Spanish speaking; however, they are hardly homogeneous. Four of these children have been in Ms. Gilbert's school since kindergarten; their instruction has been all in English, and they have had English as a second language (ESL) classes. Two of the children arrived at her school this year. They are beginning-level ESL students, but they can both read and write in Spanish. The other two children have moved back and forth between Mexico and the United States over the past four years and, in the process of moving, have missed many days of school in both countries. Three of the five remaining CLD students are Vietnamese children born in the United States. All three have attended school since kindergarten and speak English, but they struggle with reading and comprehension tasks. The final two students are Hmong and have recently immigrated to the United States. While one has some basic English skills, the other Hmong student is classified as a non-English speaker; both have been placed in an ESL class for part of the school day. This is the first time Ms. Gilbert has had any Hmong students in her classroom.

Ms. Gilbert has just returned from a district-mandated literacy workshop, where she was told that the basic reading program that was purchased for the monolingual English children should be "just fine" for her CLD students. Because the program is research based, she just may need to repeat lessons for her CLD students. Ms. Gilbert is frustrated because she has observed that none of the 13 CLD students is progressing well in English; they have different needs than monolingual English children, and they are not "all the same." The seven students who have been in the United States since kindergarten are good decoders, but they have poor comprehension in English reading and have very weak writing skills. The two Spanish-speaking newcomers try very hard and use their knowledge of Spanish to read and write in English, but they cannot read English text at the third-grade level. The two Hmong newcomers are having difficulty transferring their knowledge of Hmong to English because a number of phonological features in Hmong are unfamiliar to English speakers. The two children with interrupted schooling are simply lost in this curriculum.

Using the mandated reading program for CLD students as it was meant to be used with native English speakers is not working for half of Ms. Gilbert's class. Ms. Gilbert has observed that the program needs to be modified for her English language learners and realizes that there is no one type of CLD student.

The dramatic demographic changes in the United States over the past decade have been well documented. In the year 2000, over 11 percent of the U.S. population was foreign born, with more than 51 percent of that populace originating from Latin America (U.S. Census Bureau, 2006). Out of the more than 400 languages represented in U.S. schools, Spanish-speaking students comprise 77 percent of the total kindergarten through grade 12 (K–12) CLD student population. Of the remaining languages spoken, Vietnamese, Hmong, Haitian Creole, and Korean are among the top four, and each comprises 1 to 3 percent of this remainder (USDE, 2002).

Given the diversity of languages and cultures represented by students across the country, our preferred term to describe the students for whom this book is targeted is *culturally and linguistically diverse (CLD)*. However, when discussing instruction and learning processes unique to second language learners, we frequently will use the term *English language learner (ELL)*.

CLD students are not only located in urban school districts, but they are also increasingly present in small town schools and rural school districts. In addition to those areas that historically have had large immigrant populations, more and more areas that have never had immigrant populations are now home to CLD students. The impact of this new population is particularly apparent in K–12 public schools. Nineteen percent of U.S. schoolchildren speak a language other than English at home, and 28 percent of these students are limited in English proficiency (NCES, 2006). By 2025, an estimated one out of every four students will be an English language learner (Spellings, 2005).

Despite the growing numbers of students who bring diverse language experiences to school, just 26 percent of all public school teachers and only 27 percent of teachers teaching English language learners feel well prepared to meet the needs of students with limited English skills (NCES, 2001). At the same time, 90 percent of U.S. teachers are white (National Education Association, 2003), and 97 percent are estimated to be monolingual in English (Darling-Hammond & Sclan, 1996). Frequently, those who work with CLD students have little experience adapting to a new culture or learning a second language. While they may be caring teachers and want to be effective with all their students, many have no knowledge of what students are experiencing culturally or linguistically and have few concrete strategies and approaches for teaching this population. In short, most teachers will have second language learners in their classrooms, yet few will have the preparation to teach them.

Nowhere is this more evident than in the instruction of literacy. Of the public school teachers across the United States, only 12.5 percent of those who have CLD students in their classrooms have had eight or more hours of professional development targeting the needs of these students (NCES, 2002). Moreover, only a small portion of this training has focused on literacy development. Yet teachers need this explicit training to support English literacy development among students who are second language learners of English.

As in the case of Ms. Gilbert, the majority of teachers care about the children they teach and want to be effective in teaching them. However, these teachers often are frustrated by the "one size fits all" reading programs they are given and the misguided advice that suggests that good methods will be equally effective with all students. Good teachers know that all children do not learn in the same way and at the same pace, and they are well aware that children who do not speak English need different methods to help them learn English and be successful readers and writers in U.S. classrooms. This book explores how teachers can provide differentiated literacy instruction that addresses the specific linguistic and cultural needs of their CLD students by proposing an interactive literacy design.

## ■ Interactive Literacy: Defining Literacy for CLD Students

The *Newbury House Dictionary of American English* defines *literacy* as "the ability to read and write." In this book, we propose that literacy is much more than simply the ability to read and write. Literacy, as defined in this text, is biographical, fundamental, and research based. For CLD students, the biographical dimensions that define literacy are sociocultural, linguistic, academic, and cognitive in nature. The fundamental domains that define literacy are listening, speaking, reading, and writing. The research-based elements that define literacy are phonemic awareness, phonics, vocabulary, comprehension, and fluency. Figure 1.1 identifies each of these components and illustrates the interactive nature of these elements during instruction as teachers continually move back and forth between them when teaching literacy to CLD students.

■ **figure 1.1**    Interactive Literacy Design

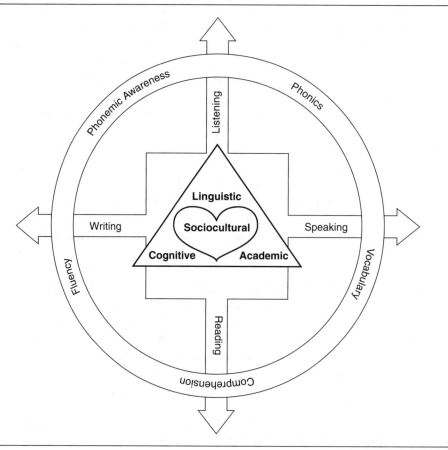

## Literacy Is Biographical

From the time a child is born, he or she is developing literacy. The family, home, and community are the foundations of literacy development in the life of the child. Therefore, we propose that literacy is first and foremost biographical in nature. The sociocultural, linguistic, academic, and cognitive dimensions of CLD students are critical. Although each of these dimensions plays a role in shaping how CLD students view and approach literacy, the sociocultural dimension lies at the heart.

Socioculturally, the family and community in which the CLD student is being raised define literacy. Consider the following example:

> It is bedtime, and Jesse (7 years old), Isa (5 years old), and Ruth (4 years old) sit outside on the porch with their *abuelita* (the Spanish name for *grandmother*). The air is

humid, and cars speed down the road in front of the house. But the children don't notice the heat or the noise, for this is their special time with *Abuelita*. It is just before 10 o'clock, and it will be several hours before their parents get home from work. Knowing that it is almost bedtime, Isa asks *Abuelita* to tell them the story of "La Llorona." At the mention of her name, Ruth grabs *Abuelita's* hand and squeezes it tightly. She smiles in anticipation, even though she is scared.

In this example, these Mexican American children are engaged in an act of literacy development that is rooted in their sociocultural background. "La Llorona" ("The Weeping Woman") is a traditional story told to children so they do not stray from home at night in fear that the weeping woman will mistake them for her own children and take them away with her. The children here are being exposed to a form of storytelling that is culture-specific and unlike more traditional examples of bedtime stories, in which a book is read aloud while the child is tucked snugly into bed. Instead, the children in this example are sitting outside on a porch late at night, listening to their grandmother tell the story orally. However, other CLD students are not exposed to these specific kinds of literacy at all. Rather, they come to school never having had a book read to them or a story told to them, making their socialization to literacy very distinct from that of their peers.

Building on the previous example, the children's *abuelita* told the story of "La Llorona" in Spanish, the family's native language. For many CLD students who enter school with a native language other than English, literacy is defined by their native language, making language the second way in which literacy is biographical. Some of the key language factors that shape literacy development are as follow:

- *Phonology:* the sounds of the native language, which may or may not exist in the English language
- *Syntax:* the order in which words are put together in the native language, which can be very different from English word order
- *Morphology:* the structure of words and the meanings of word parts
- *Semantics:* the meanings of words in context

Knowing about these language factors can support educators as they approach literacy instruction with CLD students.

Equally important for educators to know is the academic biography of the CLD student. *Academic literacy,* as defined by Gipe (2006), is the instructional literacy children have been exposed to through personal experiences with books and other forms of written or spoken language. For CLD students, exposure and access to books or text may or may not have been part of their academic literacy. Therefore, the academic literacy biographies of CLD students may not necessarily match those of peers encountered in a public school setting.

The final dimension that makes literacy biographical is the cognitive dimension. *Cognition* refers to "the nature of knowing, or the ways of organizing and understanding our experiences" (Gipe, 2006, p. 5). The experiences that CLD students bring to the classroom shape the way they view and understand information. These experiences may or may not match those of their monolingual English-speaking peers.

Within this text, the biographical nature of literacy is the foundation on which literacy instruction is based. Understanding the impact of the sociocultural, linguistic, academic, and cognitive dimensions on CLD students' literacy development informs educators by providing a holistic picture of each CLD student. Knowing the biographical literacy backgrounds of their CLD students empowers educators as they build on students' assets to promote their literacy development and academic success.

## Literacy Is Fundamental

The fundamental domains of literacy are listening, speaking, reading, and writing. When CLD students begin to receive formal instruction in literacy at school, these are the four areas targeted. Consider the following examples:

- *Listening:* First-grade students are asked to listen to a story being read aloud by the teacher in English.
- *Speaking:* Second-grade students are asked to share with partners what they think a book will be about after looking at the cover.
- *Reading:* Third-grade students are asked to read a story from a basal.
- *Writing:* Fourth-grade students are asked to write a short story.

Each of these fundamental domains of literacy is emphasized and taught to CLD students from the day they enter school. However, for teachers to successfully guide students to perform these fundamental acts of literacy in English, they must begin by looking at CLD students' biographies, which set the stage for learning.

## Literacy Is Research Based

Research-based literacy is defined by five key elements: phonics, phonemic awareness, vocabulary, comprehension, and fluency. According to the National Reading Panel (NRP, 2000), these five research-based elements need to be present in any reading approach or program designed to develop the skills necessary for children to become successful lifelong English readers. For CLD students, acquiring these research-based elements of literacy is central to becoming literate; therefore, a foundation of research comprises the final characteristic of literacy. In fact, it is the acquisition of these research-based elements of literacy that provides the framework for this text.

The characteristics of literacy, as discussed in this text, are interactive in nature, such that no single aspect should be considered in isolation when working with CLD students. Throughout this text, we illustrate how teachers can continually build on CLD students' biographical literacy to foster and promote fundamental and research-based literacy in English.

## Essential Elements of Literacy Development

Teachers in today's classrooms must focus on literacy. As previously shared, the NRP (2000) identified five research-based elements that need to be present in any reading approach or program designed to develop the skills necessary for children whose first language is English to become successful lifelong readers. These elements are phonemic awareness, phonics, vocabulary, comprehension, and fluency.

The NRP made a conscious decision *not* to include the scientific literature available on the development of language and literacy for those students learning to read in English for whom English was not their first or native language (NRP, 2000). Furthermore, the NRP focused solely on reading, although by definition, literacy includes both reading and writing. The NRP did not address, in any way, what research says about learning to write in English for native English speakers, thereby giving no direction to policymakers and practitioners about the potential best practices for teaching writing. If little is known about how to teach writing to native English speakers, then even less is known about teaching writing in English to students who are second language learners.

In 2006, a second report on literacy that specifically addressed second language issues was published. That report, titled *Developing Literacy in Second-Language Learners* (August & Shanahan, 2006), examined and reported on the research regarding the development of literacy in children whose first language is not the societal or majority language (i.e., English). This second report sought to determine whether the principles set forth by the NRP report might apply to English language learners and specifically to Spanish-speaking children. While the report concluded that little quality research is available on how to best teach literacy to English language learners, it did discuss several noteworthy trends.

First, August and Shanahan (2006) report that bilingual instruction has a positive impact on English reading outcomes. That is, children who learn to read and write in their native or first language either before or while they are learning to read and write in English have better outcomes in English literacy than children in English-only or English immersion classrooms. The reality in current policy and practice is that most second language learners are in English medium classrooms and are learning literacy only in English. Regardless of the language of instruction, however, a student's first language is a resource for learning to read and write in English, not a barrier or a problem. The relationship between the first language and the second language and how teachers can use both languages to enhance literacy learning are dominant themes throughout this text.

Second, August and Shanahan (2006) report that English oral proficiency is closely associated with reading comprehension skills in English. Thus, literacy programs for second language learners need to include a strong oral language component that builds on the students' existing oral language skills and supports the transfer of those skills to English. The relationship between oral language and literacy, although important for monolingual English learners, is *critical* for second language learners. This text includes suggestions for promoting oral language development and the transfer of oral language skills from the CLD student's native language to English.

Third, August and Shanahan's (2006) findings suggest that elements of literacy instruction that help monolingual English-speaking students learn to read and write are advantageous for second language learners as well. However, these authors caution that the strategies, routines, and approaches used with monolingual English speakers need to be modified for second language learners to make them effective as well as linguistically and culturally relevant.

Finally, although August and Shanahan (2006) call for modifications to basic literacy elements for second language learners, they do not provide concrete direction for practitioners in terms of *how* such instruction should be modified. This text strives to provide practitioners with concrete strategies for modifying the elements of reading instruction for second language learners.

## ■ The Theoretical Foundations of Reading

As literacy instruction has evolved over time, so have the methods of literacy instruction used in classrooms across the United States. To better understand this historical evolution and the impact it has had on instruction, this section will discuss three of the most prevalent research-based reading process models: bottom-up, top-down, and interactive. Each of these reading process models presents a specific theoretical framework that explains how monolingual English-speaking children learn to read.

These models were chosen for their strong research base, historical significance, and historical prevalence. However, such historical models are not part of the research base on teaching reading to CLD students. Therefore, as each model is introduced, the instructional implications for teachers working with CLD student populations will be explored. Having an understanding of each reading process model is important, as educators select models that reflect their beliefs about the reading process, the reader's role in this process, and how reading instruction is contextualized in daily literacy instruction (Leu & Kinzer, 2003).

## Reading the Symbols and Sounds of English: The Bottom-Up Reading Process Model

One of the first reading process models that emerged from the research is the *bottom-up reading process model*. This model depicts reading as a process of decoding written symbols into sounds (Gunning, 2000; Kuder & Hasit, 2002; Marzano, Hagerty, Valencia, & DiStefano, 1987; Reutzel & Cooter, 2000, 2005; Vacca, Vacca, Gove, Burkey, Lenhart, & McKeon, 2006). Figure 1.2 provides a visual demonstration of the steps readers go through for acquiring literacy proficiency in the bottom-up reading process model.

Figure 1.2 illustrates how the reader sequentially processes information to decode text. Each level and the prerequisite skills associated with that level are defined on the left-hand side of Figure 1.2. In the bottom-up reading process model, it is only after achieving mastery of the first level that the reader can move on to the next level. To get to the whole, the reader must pass sequentially from the smallest unit of meaning to the largest unit of meaning (Vacca et al., 2006). The right-hand side of Figure 1.2 identifies the implications of each level for CLD students. Because the bottom-up model was developed around monolingual English readers, such implications were not made an integral part of the original model. For educators working with CLD students, consideration of these implications supports the contextualization of literacy instruction within the classroom.

### *Literacy Instruction via the Bottom-Up Reading Process Model*

Educators who use the bottom-up reading process model as the foundation for literacy instruction view literacy as a series of skills to be mastered in a sequential order (Gunning, 2000; Marzano et al., 1987; Reutzel & Cooter, 2005; Vacca et al., 2006). However, when consideration is not given to the broader issues associated with mastery of each level for CLD students, this sequential approach to literacy development may hinder rather than support these students' literacy development.

This process model is most commonly associated with phonics-based reading programs. In phonics-based programs, the initial emphasis is on identifying the individual sounds and symbols found in text. Educators who approach instruction in this manner emphasize a structured approach to literacy instruction by focusing on teaching students to blend sounds to form words. As these skills are mastered, the student is then taught how to combine these words into phrases and clauses and finally to develop phrases and clauses into sentences.

■ **figure 1.2**    The Bottom-Up Reading Process Model

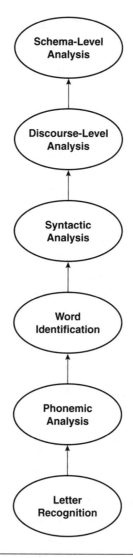

| Definition | | Implications for CLD Students |
|---|---|---|
| At the final stage of schema level analysis, readers understand that text is an organized whole (Marzano, 1987). | **Schema-Level Analysis** | Schema-level analysis requires the CLD student to connect what was read to personal experience, background knowledge, and/or events from his or her background. |
| "Discourse level processing is the recognition of the format and organization of a paragraph or an entire passage rather than of a single sentence" (Marzano et al., 1987, p. 173). | **Discourse-Level Analysis** | Discourse structures vary across languages. CDL students need to be taught what discourse structure to look for when reading in English, as well as how to identify markers within the discourse structure. |
| Syntactic analysis describes the reader's ability to understand "the way words fit together in sentences" (Marzano et al., 1987, p. 165) | **Syntactic Analysis** | Syntactical patterns may vary across languages. Therefore, CLD students need to be explicitly taught the syntactic patterns of the English language (e.g., adjective, noun, verb etc.). |
| Word identification is "the ability to recognize words and their meanings as distinctive units" (Marzano et al., 1987, p. 33) | **Word Identification** | CLD students need to develop the skill of automaticity through repeated practice with words in meaningful contexts so that they can readily decode the words and focus on interpreting their meanings in text. |
| Phonemic analysis is "the act of translating printed symbols (letters) into the sounds they represent" (Marzano et al., 1987, p. 33). | **Phonemic Analysis** | English has 26 individual letters but more than 40 sounds associated with those letters. In addition, many of the letters may not exist in the CLD student's native language, or if they do, they may represent different sounds. |
| Letter recognition is "the child's ability to recognize and name the letters of the alphabet" (Marzano et al., 1987, p. 135). | **Letter Recognition** | Depending on the native language of the CLD student, cross-language transfer of letters to English is not guaranteed, particularly for those students whose native languages use non-Roman symbols. |

The drawback to using this phonetic approach with CLD students is that identifying letters and their corresponding sounds is considered a prerequisite to reading. As a result, before being exposed to authentic text, CLD students often end up enduring hours of drill and practice to master isolated letter names and sounds that have no meaning. This approach also assumes that the primary obstacle readers must overcome, particularly CLD students who do not speak English, is an inability to decode the English text. According to Reutzel and Cooter (2005), this assumption explains why teachers using phonics-based approaches believe that readers "must be taught phonics first via the letters of the alphabet and the sounds these letters represent before beginning to read books" (p. 8). However, by contrast, studies have shown that when these phonics skills are taught via authentic experiences with text, students acquire and master letter names and sounds much more quickly (Escamilla, 2004; Krashen, 2002). This is particularly true for CLD students, who benefit greatly by having a meaningful context to draw from when learning letters and sounds of the English language.

*Decodable books* are also based on the bottom-up reading process model and typically comprise words that follow phonic generalizations or patterns readers are expected to learn, such as short vowel families (e.g., *sit, fit, bit*) (Ruetzel & Cooter, 2005). These books are meant to provide repeated practice on specific letter/sound patterns; however, they rarely emphasize meaning. This type of text, while repetitive in nature, does not help CLD students make schematic connections to existing background knowledge, and without these schematic connections to text, little if any comprehension takes place (Gunning, 2000; Nunan, 1999). For CLD students, reading comprehension is highly dependent on schematic connections to text that are made before, during, and after reading. These schematic connections provide CLD students with the meaningful connections they need to successfully understand and interpret the text. The importance of these schematic connections is explored in more detail in the second model, the top-down reading process model.

## Schematic Connections to Text: The Top-Down Reading Process Model

The *top-down reading process model* "assumes that reading begins at the schema level and works down to the letter level" (Marzano et al., 1987, p. 46). Accordingly, the process of reading in the top-down model is the exact opposite of that presented in the bottom-up model. As seen in Figure 1.3, the top-down model highlights the central role of schematic connections in the reading process.

To understand how reading within the top-down model begins with schema-level analysis, let us take a moment to discuss what a *schema* is and what role schematic connections play in this reading process model. Rumelhart (1980) developed a theoretical model known as *schema theory* to describe how knowledge of objects, events, and situations is categorized and retained in the reader's memory. In a sense, a *schema* is a mental, representational storage facility for experiences.

The top-down reading process model proposes that the reader accesses these stored experiences (or schemas) for making sense of the information encountered while reading. Thus, proponents of the model argue that using schematic connections

■ **f i g u r e   1 . 3**     The Top-Down Reading Process Model

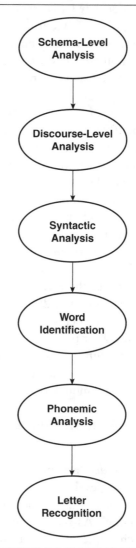

enables a reader to manipulate existing concepts and knowledge for comprehending text (Gregory, 1996). When educators begin reading instruction by bringing students' schemas to the surface, the cultural and linguistic backgrounds of CLD students are not only acknowledged but also built on to promote meaningful connections to text.

The top-down reading process model also aligns with a theory of second language acquisition known as *transfer theory.* Developed by Cummins (2000), transfer theory is built on the idea that the literacy and language skills a CLD student has in the native language are transferable and can aid in his or her acquisition of second-language literacy skills. Instrumental to this theory are the connections CLD students make to existing schemas when reading. It is important to consider that words by themselves do not have meaning. Rather, the reader constructs meaning from a personal understanding of the words, along with the schematic connections that accompany this understanding. (The concept of linguistic transfer will be discussed in greater detail in Chapter 2.)

### *Literacy Instruction via the Top-Down Reading Process Model*

Educators who use the top-down reading process model are most often described as "whole language" teachers. A primary reason for this characterization is that teachers using this approach see it as their responsibility to guide understanding of the reading process and text by tapping into students' prior knowledge (Williams & Snipper, 1990). As such, the CLD student continually draws on prior experience while reading in an effort to create meaning. This approach to instruction provides learning leverage by ensuring, as Rutherford (1987) aptly notes, that the CLD student "does not embark upon his/her second-language learning experience as a *tabula rasa* or in total ignorance" (p. 7).

In addition, teachers using the top-down reading process model contextualize literacy instruction by using authentic texts rather than predictable and decodable texts, which are constructed to provide repeated practice of phonemic skills. Authentic reading materials represent naturally occurring patterns of language. For example, in the story "The Three Little Pigs," readers learn repetitive patterns such as "I'll huff, and I'll puff, and I'll blow your house down." Such patterns of language can be linked to CLD students' schemas and work to support their development of the sounds and patterns of words in authentic contexts.

## Reading as a Circular Process: The Interactive Reading Process Model

The more research focused on the bottom-up and top-down models, the more theorists came to believe that neither model adequately explains the complexity of the reading process (Reutzel & Cooter, 2005). As a result, researchers proposed the *interactive reading process model*. This model defines the reader's role as a constructor of meaning, whereby the reader simultaneously makes schematic connections *and* decodes letters and words, thus moving fluidly between the skills and processes defined in the bottom-up and top-down models. Thus, the interactive reading process model combines the theoretical perspectives of the bottom-up and top-down models (Kuder & Hasit, 2002; Marzano et al., 1987; Reutzel & Cooter, 2000, 2005; Vacca et al., 2006). Figure 1.4 illustrates the interactive reading process model, showing how readers use top-down and bottom-up skills concurrently during the reading process.

■ **figure 1.4**   The Interactive Reading Process Model

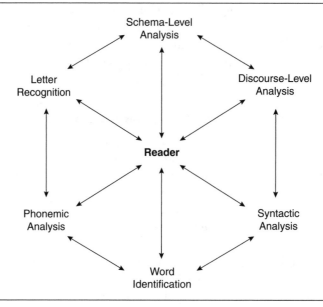

The interactive view of reading assumes that the reader proceeds cognitively from both whole to part and part to whole. Readers navigate among multiple processes to comprehend text in the most efficient manner. Readers take an active role when they possess a relevant schema about the information presented. For example, when a student is reading a text about birds and already knows a lot about birds, he or she can more actively engage in reading and comprehending the text. If, however, the student is reading a text for which he or she has no relevant schema to draw from, he or she will spend more time decoding the text to understand the author's message. Thus, the reader takes on a more passive role. According to this model, a CLD student uses schematic connections to comprehend text while simultaneously decoding letter sounds and word meanings as necessary to comprehend the text by taking on both *active* and *passive* roles (Vacca, Vacca, & Gove, 1995).

### *Literacy Instruction via the Interactive Reading Process Model*

Teachers who use the interactive reading process model approach reading from a skills-based perspective. Skills-based reading instruction comprises three components: decoding, vocabulary, and comprehension. As such, "children are expected to integrate their knowledge of decoding and their background knowledge, vocabulary, and experiences as needed to construct meaning from text" (Reutzel &

Cooper, 2005, p. 16). Many teacher editions of basal readers used in U.S. classrooms are structured to follow this format:

- Basal readers traditionally guide teachers to draw out students' background knowledge before reading the text.
- Teachers are also encouraged to preteach vocabulary before assigning a reading.
- During reading instruction, teachers are guided to teach decoding and vocabulary skills as well as comprehension strategies.
- After reading, students are assessed to determine their comprehension of the story.

The benefits of this model for CLD students relate to the interactive nature of the reading process. For example, the interactive model teaches CLD students to draw on relevant schemas and background knowledge to support text comprehension. Equally relevant in this model are the decoding skills that are contextually taught as students interact with text. Finally, this model recognizes that each child is unique and brings different sets of skills and knowledge to the reading process.

Each of the reading process models presented in this section has a strong theoretical foundation on which it was developed. This information can be used to support educators as they perform these tasks:

- critically reflect on their own beliefs about literacy development and instruction
- articulate the theoretical foundations on which their instruction is based
- adapt the mandated curriculum to support and foster literacy development for their CLD students

Educators' socialization influences their initial views on literacy development. This socialization involves not only the ways they were taught to read but also the ways they were trained to teach reading. For educators working with CLD students, it is important to understand how their own literacy instruction can affect CLD students' success in learning to read English.

## ◼ Conclusion

In this chapter, we defined *literacy* as interactive. The biographical, fundamental, and research-based aspects of literacy are intertwined. For CLD students, the biographical dimensions of literacy are sociocultural, linguistic, academic, and cognitive in nature. The fundamental domains of literacy are listening, speaking, reading, and writing, and the research-based elements of literacy are phonemic awareness, phonics, vocabulary, comprehension, and fluency. Together, these aspects communicate to educators the necessity of keeping the whole child in mind as they develop instruction that targets the research-based aspects of literacy, while maintaining an emphasis on communication for meaning.

The chapter also identified and discussed the theoretical foundations of three dominant reading process models. This discussion articulated the impact of teachers' philosophical foundations and personal beliefs on their daily literacy instruction. Teachers' ability to maximize the assets CLD students bring to literacy endeavors is enhanced by knowing how they define literacy and understanding the ways their literacy instruction and practices can directly affect how CLD students learn to read.

## key theories and concepts

- authentic text
- biographical dimensions of literacy
- bottom-up reading process model
- culturally and linguistically diverse (CLD)
- fundamental domains of literacy
- interactive reading process model
- literacy
- research-based elements of literacy
- schema
- top-down reading process model
- transfer theory

## professional conversations on practice

1. This chapter defined *literacy* as biographical, fundamental, and research based. Talk about your own definition of literacy and how the information presented in this chapter might affect your definition.

2. Central to the definition of literacy presented in this chapter was the proposition that literacy is first defined via the biographies of your students. Think of a CLD student you know and identify considerations for him or her related to the biographical dimensions of literacy (i.e., sociocultural, linguistic, academic, and cognitive).

3. This chapter explored the theoretical foundations of three models of literacy instruction for monolingual English-speaking students. Discuss the implications of each model for CLD students' literacy development.

## questions for review and reflection

1. How is *interactive literacy* defined in this chapter?

2. In what ways do you address biographical, fundamental, and research-based aspects of literacy in your own instruction?

3. What are the key components of the bottom-up reading process model, and what are the implications of this model for CLD students?

4. The top-down reading process model argues that background knowledge is central to reading comprehension. What are the implications of this model for CLD students whose background knowledge differs from that of their monolingual English-speaking peers?

5. What are the key components of the interactive reading process model? In what ways does this model support CLD students' literacy development?

6. How does access to authentic text (or lack thereof) impact the acquisition of key literacy skills for CLD students?

**Where the Classroom Comes to Life**

Now go to the Herrera, Perez, and Escamilla MyEducationLab course at www.myeducationlab.com to:

- read and connect with the chapter Objectives;
- use the Study Plan questions to assess your comprehension of the chapter content;
- study chapter content with your Individualized Study Plan;
- engage in multimedia exercises to help you build a deeper and more applied understanding of chapter content.

- How are the multiple dimensions of the CLD student biography addressed within literacy lesson planning and delivery?

- How can teachers access CLD students' sociocultural needs to support literacy development?

- What cross-language transfer occurs between a CLD student's native language and English to support literacy development?

- How is the academic knowledge of CLD students built on during literacy instruction?

- How can CLD students' existing cognitive assets be built on to promote literacy development?

# Contextualizing Literacy Development for the CLD Student in the Grade-Level Classroom

When describing her approach to literacy instruction, one elementary teacher explained as follows:

> *When I first started teaching, I approached literacy instruction in a very systematic and structured way, as prescribed by the district-mandated curriculum. However, as the biographies of my CLD students became increasingly diverse, I found that this structured approach no longer worked. So I began to pull from a variety of resources and instructional methods that complemented and enhanced my mandated curriculum so that I could better meet the needs of my CLD student populations.*

As demonstrated by this excerpt, effective educators of CLD students not only base their literacy instruction on scientifically based research methods, but they also adapt existing curricula to address the multiple dimensions of the CLD student biography. In this chapter, we explore in depth the sociocultural, linguistic, academic, and cognitive dimensions of the CLD student biography. Each dimension helps to inform educators about the diverse assets, as well as the differential learning needs, that CLD students bring to the literacy process.

## ■ The CLD Student Biography

CLD students bring multiple knowledge reserves to the classroom (Moll, Armanti, Neff, & Gonzalez, 1992). Thus, the more teachers know about these existing knowledge bases, the more accurately they can structure literacy lessons to reflect students' needs. The following conversation between two teachers, Mrs. Ramirez and Mrs. Dye, illustrates how information gathered about a fifth-grade CLD student, Yamin, can support literacy instruction in the classroom:

**Mrs. Ramirez:** Hello, Mrs. Dye. I wanted to see how things were going with Yamin. It has been a week since he moved from my ESL pullout class into your classroom for literacy instruction. Do you have any questions?

**Mrs. Dye:** Thanks for coming to see me. As a matter of fact, I do have some questions. I've noticed Yamin is having difficulty with the story we are reading this week: *The Wall,* by Eve Bunting.

**Mrs. Ramirez:** I love that story! It's a really powerful example of the impact of war. It is so sad that the little boy never got to meet his grandfather, who died while fighting in the war. But I love the fact that the father could take his son to the Vietnam Memorial, where he could see his grandfather's name inscribed on the memorial with the names of all the other soldiers who died fighting.

**Mrs. Dye:** I agree. The story really has grabbed the interest of the class, and I thought Yamin would connect with it as well. But he really doesn't seem engaged when we read the story.

**Mrs. Ramirez:** Actually, I think the content may be a little too real for Yamin. When he first enrolled in school, I did a home visit and talked to his parents. They shared with me that the whole family had recently moved from Iraq to escape the war. They talked about losing their oldest son in the war and how they wanted to give Yamin a chance at a better life. They have only been in the United States five months.

**Mrs. Dye:** Wow! I didn't know that! No wonder Yamin is having a hard time. His English is a little weak, but overall, it's pretty good, so I assumed he had been here longer than that.

**Mrs. Ramirez:** Yes, his grasp of conversational English is deceptive, making him appear to know more English than he does.

This conversation illustrates the central role the CLD student's biography plays in instruction, as well as some key considerations teachers should explore as they meet the literacy needs of CLD students. These considerations go beyond language acquisition issues, which educators often foresee as the primary obstacle in teaching CLD students to read. The *prism model,* which is based on the research of Thomas and Collier (Collier, 1987; Thomas & Collier, 1997), is depicted in Figure 2.1 and identifies the four interrelated dimensions of the CLD student biography that impact students' success in the classroom.

## The Sociocultural Dimension

Central to the CLD student biography is the *sociocultural dimension,* which consists of the social and cultural factors that influence student learning. As depicted in Figure 2.1, this dimension is the heart of the prism model. The sociocultural dimension also represents the heart of CLD students—what they love, what makes them laugh, and what shapes and defines their lives to make them who they are as individuals. It is difficult to overstate the importance of sociocultural influences in shaping CLD students' lives, particularly when it comes to literacy instruction.

**■ figure 2.1**    The Prism Model

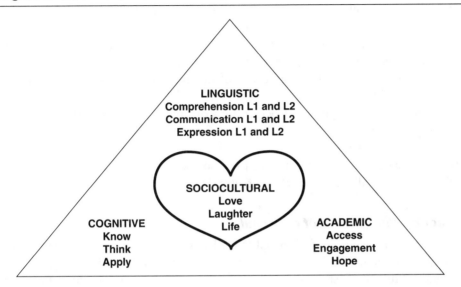

**Questions to Consider**

**SOCIOCULTURAL DIMENSION:**
   **Love, Laughter, Life**

- How has the student been socialized to literacy based on culture/family background?
- What type of resources and literacy experiences has the student had within the home?
- How is reading perceived/defined, and how does this fit the teacher/school definition?

**LINGUISTIC DIMENSION:**
   **Comprehension L1 and L2, Communication L1 and L2, Expression L1 and L2**

- How is the native language used as a resource to support the CLD student's literacy development in English?
- What stage of language acquisition is the CLD student in, and how is literacy instruction accommodated to meet the CLD student's language level?

**ACADEMIC DIMENSION:**
   **Access, Engagement, Hope**

- What literacy skills does the student bring to the classroom based on his or her prior academic experiences?
- In what ways is the CLD student immersed in academically challenging tasks to promote grade-level literacy acquisition?

**COGNITIVE DIMENSION:**
   **Know, Think, Apply**

- How is instruction designed to build on existing cognitive and language assets to promote literacy development?
- What learning strategies are explicitly taught to promote the cognitive academic language skills CLD students need to understand grade-level text and academic concepts?

*Source:* Prism is from Herrera (2008). Used with permission of KCAT/TLC, Kansas State University.

The following list identifies the multiple sociocultural influences on CLD students' literacy development, as noted by Raphael et al. (2001):

- *Historical background of the family:* the values, beliefs, and goals within the family, as influenced by cultural traditions and experiences
- *Literacy resources:* types and uses of literacy resources, as well as the time spent on literacy activities
- *Perceptions:* the children's perceptions of both teachers and the nature and importance of reading

To promote deeper understanding of these sociocultural influences on literacy development, we will explore each in greater detail.

### Historical Background of the Family

The *historical background* of the CLD student's family reflects the values, beliefs, and goals of the family. The more insight educators have into the historical backgrounds of their CLD students, the better equipped they are to use this information to enhance their instructional practice.

Consider, for example, the historical differences between immigrant and native-born CLD students. CLD students who are recent immigrants to the United States may have more pressure placed on them by their families to excel academically so they can achieve the "American dream." As such, newly or recently arrived CLD students may struggle to balance the expectations of the family with those of the new culture in which they are immersed. This process of *acculturation,* or adjusting to a new culture, while maintaining the values, beliefs, and goals of the family can be very difficult for CLD students. For instance, parents of newly arrived immigrants often want their children to acquire the English language as quickly as possible; therefore, they do not want their children to receive special services, such as ESL. Research has shown, however, that such a complete and abrupt loss of the native language may actually hinder rather than promote the acquisition of English (Cummins, 2000; Escamilla, 2004; Krashen, 2002).

The process of acculturation also occurs for CLD students who were born in the United States. However, CLD students who are second generation (i.e., their parents were also born in the United States) or even third generation (i.e., their grandparents were born in the United States) may not experience the same demands as those of recently or newly arrived CLD students. For example, second- and third-generation CLD students may have become so acculturated to life in the United States that they have actually begun to lose their native language. This is particularly true among third-generation students, who may still speak the native language at home or with grandparents but who have not been taught to read or write in their native language. Educators who are aware of such family dynamics are better equipped to understand the sociocultural demands that might be placed on students and the implications of these demands.

Understanding the family's goals, beliefs, and values provides educators with valuable insight into the behaviors and learning patterns of their CLD students. Educators who want to learn more about the historical backgrounds of their CLD students can engage in numerous formal and informal activities. For example, teachers might do a class activity such as creating family brochures. Family brochures can be structured in multiple ways, but the key is to request information that will inform educators about the family dynamics and cultural backgrounds of CLD students in the classroom. Strategies in Practice 2.1 provides a glimpse of the valuable information one teacher gained by doing family brochures with his CLD students.

Teachers can also conduct home visits to learn about their students' historical backgrounds and the literacy opportunities available at home. Home visits can provide valuable insights as to the roles of extended family members in supporting a child's education, family perceptions of involvement in school, and a family's overall goals for their children. For example, if a teacher learns during a home visit that the student has no access to books or other text in the home, he or she will have a new understanding about the challenges this student might face in practicing reading skills outside the classroom. To address the needs of students who do not have access to books or other text in the home, the teacher can send home books that students can easily read and share with siblings or parents. If the parents are literate in their native language, sending books home in the native language is a wonderful way to actively involve parents in the student's literacy practice while simultaneously validating the native language and culture. Research has shown that modeling of literacy skills in the native language supports the development of foundational literacy skills that can then be readily transferred to English (Collier & Thomas, 1992; Cummins, 2000; Escamilla, 1987; Rodríguez, 1988).

Another more informal way to learn about families is to conduct student interviews, in which educators talk to students about their family and home lives. This information can also be gathered through informal discussions with parents before and after school or even during parent–teacher conferences. The more teachers can learn about CLD students' sociocultural backgrounds, the better prepared they will be to address each student's individual needs in and out of the classroom.

## Literacy Resources

CLD students approach literacy learning from the basis of their own exposure to and experiences with text, and often, these experiences are less formal than those traditionally valued in U.S. classrooms. For instance, consider that many monolingual English-speaking children are raised with extensive exposure to text. Whether in the form of books read by parents at bedtime or the simple availability of books, magazines, and other reading materials in the home, literacy experiences and ongoing text

### Family Biography

**Materials Needed**

- Large sheet of art paper for each student
- Pencils, crayons, and/or markers for each student

**Directions**

- Have each student fold the paper into a trifold, making the opening flap on the left-hand side.
- Have each student create a title page for the brochure.
- Determine five other guiding topics (one per page) for students to use on the remaining five sections.

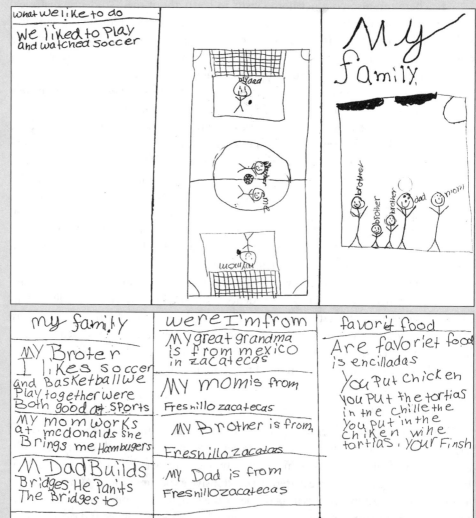

what we like to do

We liked to Play and watched soccer

My family

My Broter
I likes soccer
and Basketball We
Play together were
Both good at sports

My mom works
at mcdonalds she
Brings me Hambugers

M Dad Builds
Bridges, He Panits
The Bridges to

were I'm from

My great grandma
is from mexico
in zacatecas

My mom is from
Fresnillo zacatecas

My Brother is from
Fresnillo zacatas

My Dad is from
Fresnillo zacatecas

favorit food

Are favoriet food
is encilladas

You Put chicken
you Put the tortias
in the chille the
you put in the
chiken with
tortias, your Finsh

exposure are natural elements of these students' daily lives. By contrast, CLD students may not have such access to text in the home, let alone have formal interactions and repeated reading practice with a parent. Consequently, their experiential knowledge related to formal literacy instruction may not be as extensive as that of their peers. However, this lack of formality should not be interpreted as a lack of relevant knowledge or ability. Rather, the important point to consider is that different cultural groups encounter and develop literacy in different ways.

A study by Heath (1983) emphasizes varying modes of literacy development among diverse groups. Heath explored the literacy orientations of three culturally distinct sets of families and found marked differences in how they reinforced literacy development. For example, children from an African American mill community were socialized in the oral tradition, in which storytelling is the main form of literacy development. Caucasian children from the same mill community were expected to learn to read by memorizing the alphabet and doing drill and practice worksheets. The third group, however, came from upper-class Caucasian families, in which the children engaged with authentic text, created written and oral narratives, and encountered written materials and questioning routines geared toward higher-level thinking skills.

When a CLD student enters school with limited experiential knowledge of text or formal literacy practices, this lack of experience can have a profound impact on the rate and speed at which he or she learns to read. Therefore, those teachers who have the greatest success helping CLD students become literate in English do so by tapping into students' nontraditional literacy experiences. When literacy instruction builds on the background knowledge and experiences of CLD students, these students are able to make valuable connections to text as they construct meaning (Marzano, 2004).

One way teachers can gather information about these experiences is to create student literacy profiles, which paint a vivid picture of the experiential knowledge an individual CLD student brings to the reading process. A literacy profile can be created for each aspect of the CLD student's biography: sociocultural, linguistic, academic, and cognitive. Figure 2.2 presents a sampling of questions teachers can ask when developing a sociocultural literacy profile.

### Perceptions

When a CLD student enters school, he or she brings along the cultural identity of the home. Oftentimes, this home identity conflicts with the school culture, leading to discontinuity. The term *cultural discontinuity* describes the internal conflict a CLD student may experience when his or her cultural background or social values conflict with those taught in school or demonstrated by the teacher. This type of conflict can have a negative impact on how a CLD student approaches and learns about literacy in the classroom. As educators, it is important to recognize when and how cultural discontinuity occurs so it can be addressed proactively.

■ **figure 2.2**    Sociocultural Literacy Profile

| Sociocultural Profile | Completed Sociocultural Profile |
|---|---|
| Name:<br>Age: | Sahle<br>11 years old |
| Grade level:<br>Native language: | 6th Grade<br>Americ |
| Place of birth:<br>Country of origin: | Ethiopia<br>Ethiopia |
| 1. What language do you speak most at home? | English and Americ |
| 2. What language did you first learn to read? | Americ |
| 3. What do you read at home (e.g., letters, cookbooks, books in the native language, books in English, magazines, newspapers)? | The Bible. |
| 4. Who do you read with at home? | I read with no one at home. |
| 5. Do you like to read? What do you like or dislike about reading? | I don't like to read, but do it to get better. |
| 6. If you could choose anything to read about, what would it be and why? | I would read about Jesus, it changes my attitude and gives me strength. |
| 7. What kind of reader do you think you are?<br><br>A. A very good reader<br>B. A good reader<br>C. An average reader<br>D. A poor reader<br>E. A very poor reader | C—Average reader |

When CLD students first enter the classroom, they continually assess the environment to determine what perceptions the teacher and other students may have about them. For example, they may look to see if any aspects of their culture are acknowledged or represented through posters or native language books. Students may note whether the teacher seats them at the back of the room or toward the front. CLD students also consider whether they are allowed to sit next to a peer who speaks their native language or even whether the teacher allows use of their native language in the classroom. These are but a few examples of the perceptual filters that CLD students often use when they enter a new classroom. It is essential to consider how such filters influence CLD students along with their understanding and approach to learning. The more support these students have and the more welcome they feel, the more likely they are to be active members of the class.

Once accepted within the community of learners, CLD students eagerly approach the learning process. However, just as they use their perceptual filters to determine their place in the classroom, CLD students also use their perceptual filters to determine their role as learners. When it comes to literacy instruction, the more educators inspire CLD students to become readers, the more likely they are to become readers. One of the key ways for educators to do this is to immediately immerse CLD students in rich and authentic experiences with text. This approach not only helps CLD students see themselves as readers, but it also promotes increased English language development, as students are exposed to text in context-embedded and meaningful ways. To better understand how this exposure to text promotes CLD students' English language acquisition, the next section will explore the dynamics associated with the linguistic dimension of the CLD student biography.

## The Linguistic Dimension

Language is more than words and more than cognition. It contributes greatly to CLD students' sense of identity. It is through language that students comprehend the world around them. Language is also the vehicle through which students communicate and express themselves. For the CLD student learning to speak English as a second language, the native language is the medium through which he or she is socialized and through which his or her culture is transmitted. If educators fail to acknowledge the value of the CLD student's native language, they are in fact also devaluing the student's family and sense of self.

### *Transfer Theory*

Placing value on the native languages of students involves more than making a superficial effort at addressing cultural and linguistic diversity. It also requires teachers to embrace the value the native language has for English literacy development. Research by Cummins (1981, 2000) found that CLD students' acquisition of a first language (L1) and second language (L2) is developmentally intertwined. This *interdependence hypothesis* proposes that first language development directly impacts second language development. Cummins's (2000) *transfer theory* also suggests that "academic proficiency transfers across languages such that students who have developed literacy in their first language will tend to make stronger progress in acquiring literacy in their second language" (p. 173).

Additional research has also shown that the more proficient a CLD student is at reading in the native language, the faster he or she will acquire English, because existing native-language reading skills support second-language reading ability (Collier & Thomas, 1992; Escamilla, 1987; Rodriguez, 1988). Clay (1993) found that the least complicated starting point for literacy learning with CLD students is to use what the student already knows from the native language to boost English language acquisition.

Unfortunately, a common misconception is that use of the native language hinders English language development. Consider the following example (Escamilla, 1998):

> Two students finish kindergarten at the end of the school year. The first student, José, knows three colors in Spanish and three other colors in English. His teacher determines that he is limited in both Spanish and English and recommends that he be taught in English only as he enters the first grade. Bill is a monolingual English speaker. He knows five colors in English at the end of kindergarten and is labeled as an average student who has no problems. Who actually knows more, José or Bill?

José actually knows one more color than Bill, but because the teacher does not recognize the importance of knowledge in the native language, José is labeled as knowing less.

Educators who would like to learn about the native language literacy profiles of their CLD students can do a linguistic literacy profile. Figure 2.3 provides a sample of the types of questions an educator might ask in order to learn about a CLD student's native language literacy skills. These questions are only a starting point, from which educators can build to learn more about the linguistic profiles of their CLD students.

### *Stages of Second Language Acquisition and CLD Student Literacy Development*

Another important aspect of linguistic knowledge can be best understood in terms of the stages CLD students go through when developing second language proficiency and literacy skills. CLD students arrive in the classroom with varying levels of English language proficiency. Although most CLD students are conversationally proficient in English within two years, it takes five to seven years to acquire the academic language needed to perform at grade level with their native English-speaking peers (Collier & Thomas, 1999; Cummins, 1989). The more a teacher knows about a student's particular stage of second language acquisition, the better able the teacher is to plan literacy lessons that support the student's comprehension and engagement in academic tasks. Figure 2.4 summarizes the literacy development

■ **f i g u r e   2 . 3**   Linguistic Literacy Profile

| Linguistic Profile | Completed Linguistic Profile |
|---|---|
| Name:<br>Age: | Alicia<br>9 years old |
| Grade level:<br>Native language: | 5th Grade<br>Spanish |
| Place of birth:<br>Country of origin: | Mexico<br>Mexico |
| 1. What is your first language? | Spanish |
| 2. What language do you most often speak at home? | English |
| 3. What other languages do you speak at home and with whom? | I speak Spanish at home with my mother. |
| 4. Do you read in your native language? If yes, who taught you how to read and how well do you think you read in your native language? | I like to read in Spanish. I learned how to read in school, but I think my English reading is better. |
| 5. What types of things do you read in your native language (e.g., books, magazines, newspapers, letters from your native country)? | My mother has a book that she kept when I was little. She has me read it to my little brother. |
| 6. Do you write in your native language? If yes, who taught you how to write and how well do you think you write in your native language? | I learned to write in Spanish when I first went to school. I think I write pretty good in Spanish. |
| 7. What types of things do you write in your native language? | I like to write my mother cards in Spanish because she reads in Spanish. |
| 8. Does it help you to read in English when you see words that are written or sound almost the same as words in your native language? | It helps me to read in English when the words are written or sound almost the same as words in my native language cause they sound the same and are spelled almost alike. |

**■ figure 2.4** Continua of English Language Development

Name: _____

| | Preproduction | Early Production | Speech Emergence | Intermediate Fluency | Advanced Fluency |
|---|---|---|---|---|---|
| **LISTENING** Date | • Cannot yet understand simple expressions or statements in English. | • Understands previously learned expressions.<br>• Understands new vocabulary in context. | • Understands sentence-length speech.<br>• Participates in conversation about simple information.<br>• Understands a simple message.<br>• Understands basic directions and instructions. | • Understands academic content.<br>• Understands more complex directions and instructions.<br>• Comprehends main idea.<br>• Effectively participates in classroom discussions. | • Understands most of what is heard.<br>• Understands and retells main idea and most details from oral presentations and conversations. |
| **SPEAKING** Date | • Is not yet able to make any statements in English. | • Uses isolated words and learned phrases.<br>• Uses vocabulary for classroom situations.<br>• Expresses basic courtesies.<br>• Asks very simple questions.<br>• Makes statements using learned materials.<br>• Asks and answers questions about basic needs. | • Asks and answers simple questions about academic content.<br>• Talks about familiar topics.<br>• Responds to simple statements.<br>• Expresses self in simple situations (e.g., ordering a meal, introducing oneself, asking directions). | • Initiates, sustains, and closes a conversation.<br>• Effectively participates in classroom discussions.<br>• Gives reasons for agreeing or disagreeing.<br>• Retells a story or event.<br>• Compares and contrasts a variety of topics. | • Communicates facts and talks casually about topics of general interest using specific vocabulary.<br>• Participates in age-appropriate academic, technical, and social conversations using English correctly. |

Name: _____

**READING**

Date: | Preproduction | Early Production | Speech Emergence | Intermediate Fluency | Advanced Fluency |
|---|---|---|---|---|
| • Is not yet able to read any words in English.<br>• Is not yet able to identify the letters of the Roman alphabet.<br>• Is not yet able to decode sounds of written English. | • Reads common messages, phrases, and/or expressions.<br>• Identifies the letters of the Roman alphabet.<br>• Decodes most sounds of written English.<br>• Identifies learned words and phrases. | • Reads and comprehends main ideas and/or facts from simple materials. | • Understands main ideas and details from a variety of sources. | • Reads authentic text materials for comprehension.<br>• Understands most of what is read in authentic texts. |

**WRITING**

Date: | Preproduction | Early Production | Speech Emergence | Intermediate Fluency | Advanced Fluency |
|---|---|---|---|---|
| • Is not yet able to write any words in English.<br>• Is not yet able to write the letters of the Roman alphabet. | • Copies or transcribes familiar words or phrases.<br>• Writes the letters from memory and/or dictation.<br>• Writes simple expressions from memory.<br>• Writes simple autobiographical information as well as some short phrases and simple lists.<br>• Composes short sentences with guidance. | • Creates basic statements and questions.<br>• Writes simple letters and messages.<br>• Writes simple narratives. | • Writes more complex narratives.<br>• Composes age-appropriate original materials using present, past, and future tenses.<br>• Writes about a variety of topics for a variety of purposes. | • Write summaries.<br>• Takes notes.<br>• Compares and contrasts familiar topics.<br>• Uses vivid, specific language in writing. |

*Source:* Wichita Public Schools, Wichita, Kansas. Reprinted by permission.

demonstrated by CLD students according to Krashen and Terrell's (1983) five stages of second language acquisition: preproduction, early production, speech emergence, intermediate fluency, and advanced fluency. As demonstrated in the figure, there are multiple considerations for instructional practice based on a CLD student's stage of second language acquisition. It is important to note that these stages are not fixed, as students can move in and out of these stages at various rates. The transition from one stage to the next is highly influenced by the CLD student's native language literacy level. The more proficient the CLD student is in his or her own language, the faster he or she will transition from one stage to the next. To better understand how a CLD student's native language literacy supports this transition, educators can consider the academic dimension of the CLD student biography.

## The Academic Dimension

The *academic dimension* reflects the CLD student's prior academic experiences, as well as the curriculum and instruction that he or she is currently experiencing in school. Knowing the types of academic experiences a CLD student has had provides valuable information about the kind of access he or she has had to literacy development. Such insight into students' literacy experiences helps educators make sense of differences they may observe in students' levels of engagement and students' hopes that they can and will acquire the literacy skills they need.

According to Herrera and Murry (2005), also "critical to this dimension is an understanding of the differential academic challenges that CLD students encounter, especially those that relate to academic policy" (p. 45). This section, therefore, will explore each of these elements in greater depth, including their implications for literacy development and instruction.

### *Prior Schooling*

The academic dimension takes into consideration the CLD student's prior academic experiences in school. These include both experiences the CLD student has had within the United States and those in his or her native country (if applicable). The following three short case studies exemplify the importance of knowing CLD students' prior academic experiences.

> Juan Carlos arrived in the United States as an eighth-grader. He emigrated with his family from Colombia, where he had attended school since he was three years old. In Colombia, he was placed in advanced courses and was set to begin coursework that would prepare him for a college degree.

> Araseli immigrated to the United States as a fourth-grader from a rural community in Mexico. Given the rural area in which she lived, Araseli did not have access to a school in her community and had to take a bus for 30 minutes to get to the nearest

school. Because of the distance to school and the need to support her family at home, Araseli rarely attended school and could not read or write in Spanish when she arrived in the United States.

Uriem, a sixth-grade student, was born in the United States and attended kindergarten in a monolingual English-speaking classroom in California. In first grade, he stayed in the monolingual classroom but was pulled out for one hour of ESL instruction each day. At the beginning of third grade, Uriem moved to a different school, district, and state, where he was placed in a sheltered ESL classroom all day with other CLD students.

As these three case studies demonstrate, knowing a student's prior academic experience offers great insight into the literacy skills he or she brings to the classroom. If, for example, the CLD student is literate in his or her native language, like Juan Carlos, the teacher can use the student's native language skills and academic background to promote his or her literacy development in English (Cummins, 2000; Escamilla, 1987; Krashen, 1987; Skutnabb-Kangas, 1975). Among the most common literacy understandings that frequently transfer from the native language are the following:

- *Knowledge:* Once a CLD student has learned a concept, he or she does not need to relearn it.
- *Literacy is symbolic:* Regardless of how a language is spoken or written, words in any language symbolize underlying concepts, ideas, and concrete objects.
- *Literacy is communicative:* The purpose of text is for the reader to understand the message being sent by the author.
- *Phonological awareness:* Each CLD student develops phonological awareness based on the sound system of his or her native language.
- *Alphabetic and orthographic awareness:* All text is made up of a series of letters or symbols that are put together in a specific written format.
- *Concepts about print:* Each text has specific features that are learned by CLD students through exposure to print.
- *Habits and attitudes:* Study skills, task completion, persistence, and motivation are all factors that aid CLD students in literacy development.
- *Self-esteem:* The more CLD students believe they are readers and writers, the more likely they are to become successful readers and writers.

Other students, such as Araseli, may have fewer transferable literacy skills because they are not literate in their native languages. This is not to say that educators should discount the oral language proficiency in the native language that these students bring. Oral language proficiency provides students with foundational skills that will promote phonemic awareness development in English when specific links are made to the sound system of the native language. To learn more about the academic profiles of CLD students and the academic assets they bring to the classroom, teachers can complete an academic literacy profile (see Figure 2.5).

### Academic Policy

Regardless of the level of language proficiency or academic background knowledge that a CLD student brings to the classroom, he or she needs to be immersed in academically challenging tasks that promote grade-level literacy acquisition. Herrera and Murry (2005) highlight the reason this issue is so important for educators to note:

> From the standpoint of curriculum and instruction, one of the most contemporary, harmful, and emergent academic challenges for CLD students is the trend toward increasingly reductionistic curriculum driven by a strict focus on high-stakes assessments at the national, state, or local levels. Extra-educational and national reform agendas, such as the No Child Left Behind initiative, drive efforts to increase accountability, as measured by high-stakes assessments, often at the expense of low socioeconomic status (SES) and CLD students. (p. 47)

When under pressure to demonstrate student achievement, teachers of CLD students may feel excessive pressure to "teach to the test," which severely restricts CLD students' access to and interaction with text. In fact, research by McNeil (2000) found that in the area of reading, a reductionistic approach to literacy development actually limited students' ability to "read for meaning outside the test setting" (p. 3). As this example illustrates, a reductionistic approach to instruction actually inhibits CLD students' academic success. To understand the power of engaging CLD students in complex and cognitively challenging grade-level academic tasks, is it important to examine the cognitive assets that CLD students bring and to consider how educators can identify and build on these assets to support ongoing academic success.

## The Cognitive Dimension

The *cognitive dimension* is perhaps the most complex because it represents how students know, think about, and apply information. As such, it is closely related to the other dimensions of the CLD student biography. For example, the cognitive dimension explores the relationship between known language proficiency and applied literacy skills. Similarly, the cognitive dimension examines the cognitive and sociocultural connections that exist in the ways students think about what they are reading. There are numerous additional relationships between the cognitive and academic dimensions as well. However, for the purposes of this text, only the interrelationships just identified will be discussed.

■ **figure 2.5** Academic Literacy Profile

| Academic Profile | Completed Academic Profile |
|---|---|
| Name:<br>Age: | Miguel<br>7 years old |
| Grade level:<br>Native language: | 3rd Grade<br>Spanish |
| Place of birth:<br>Country of origin: | Peru<br>Peru |
| 1. Which schools have you attended? | I went to a different school for kindergarten and first grade. |
| 2. Did you participate in any type of ESL classes or get additional help in the classroom to learn English? | Some teachers worked with small groups of us kids who didn't speak English very well. |
| 3. What do you find hardest about reading in English? | I have trouble with words that sound the same, like wear and where. |
| 4. What have past teachers done that really helped you to understand books in English? | In kindergarten, we had centers where we got to look at books after the teacher read them to us. |
| 5. What helps you understand new words? | I make up my own sentence with the new word that I understand, and then I remember that sentence. |
| 6. What do you do when you get to a word you don't know in English? | I sound out the word and read the sentence without the word in it to figure out what the word means. |
| 7. What strategies do you use when reading to help you understand? | I try to picture it in my mind. Then I read it again and try to remember the sentence I had a question about to help me understand. |

### Cognition, Language, and Literacy Development

When it comes to understanding cognition, language, and literacy development among CLD students, it is important to first understand how these three elements are interrelated within the context of daily literacy instruction. As stated in Chapter 1, educators may approach literacy instruction with CLD students by focusing on identifying individual words and the sounds within them. This phonics-based approach to literacy instruction is founded primarily on the belief that CLD students in the early stages of acquiring English do not have the language skills they need to read or, more importantly, to comprehend text in English. However, CLD students are generally more successful at acquiring English vocabulary and content knowledge when learning is focused on identifying word meanings in context, rather than on isolated word parts that have no contextual ties (August & Hakuta, 1997; Herrera & Murry, 2005).

Educators of CLD students who identify and build on existing cognitive and language assets do much to promote literacy development. Such efforts might include teaching learning strategies that promote the cognitive academic language skills CLD students need to understand grade-level text and academic concepts. (Specific strategies for how educators can do this are explored in greater depth in subsequent chapters of this text.) Educators also can encourage parents to maintain and foster CLD students' native language skills to promote cognitive development, which is utilized in English literacy development processes. Students who do not have this ongoing support in the native language may experience more challenges in processing cognitively challenging tasks, as they will have to learn and apply concepts in a second language. Teachers can actively seek ways to make meaningful connections in their daily instructional practice to students' current knowledge and cognitive skills. Perhaps one of the most powerful ways educators do this is by incorporating culturally relevant texts into their existing curriculum.

### Culturally Relevant Texts: Making the Sociocultural Connection

A key way to build cognitive knowledge is to provide CLD students with culturally relevant texts. Traditionally, the materials used by teachers in grade-level classrooms are selected from a predetermined curriculum. For example, teachers who use basals or anthologies for literacy instruction teach the prepackaged stories from these texts. Historically, these curriculum materials have targeted a monolingual English-speaking student audience and therefore have reflected the experiences and backgrounds of this population. Consequently, CLD students often experience a cultural disconnect from many of the stories within such curricula. However, in the last decade, publishing companies have become more attuned to the need for stories that reflect the diverse backgrounds of CLD students and have

■ **f i g u r e   2 . 6**   Assessing the Cultural Relevance of Texts

- ☐ Does the text reflect the culture of the CLD student?
- ☐ Can the CLD student relate to the experiences of the characters in the story?
- ☐ Are the illustrations of the text ones the CLD student can identify with?
- ☐ Can the CLD student relate to the plot of the text?
- ☐ Is the native language of the CLD students used in the text?
- ☐ Is the language of the text culturally relevant for the CLD student?
- ☐ Does the CLD student have the linguistic proficiency necessary to read and comprehend the text?

worked to incorporate more multicultural stories into their series. Educators who want to assess the cultural relevance of the stories they teach can use the "Assessing the Cultural Relevance of Texts" checklist provided in Figure 2.6.

Research has found that reading culturally familiar texts enhances CLD students' literacy achievement (Abu-Rabia, 1995; Kenner, 2000; Schon, Hopkins, & Vojir, 1984). When CLD students can relate to the material presented, they are better able to make schematic and cognitive connections to it. These cognitive connections promote a deeper level of understanding and have been shown to increase comprehension. By making diligent efforts to include multicultural and multilingual texts in daily instruction, educators not only promote reading comprehension for CLD students but also validate their cultural identity.

## ■ Conclusion

In this chapter, we explored the CLD student biography and the implications of this biography on literacy development. At the heart of the CLD student biography is the sociocultural dimension, which represents the love, laughter, and life of the CLD student. This dimension provides valuable insights into the behavior and learning patterns of each student and reflects the goals, beliefs, and values of the CLD student and his or her family. The more teachers can learn about the sociocultural dimensions of CLD students, the better prepared they will be to address the individual needs of each student. Home visits are recommended as one of the most powerful ways of gathering information about this dimension.

The linguistic dimension encompasses the way CLD students comprehend, communicate, and express themselves in both their native languages and their second languages. Understanding that the language a CLD student first learns in the home is the medium through which he or she is socialized and through which cultural values are transmitted is central to this dimension. The more proficient a student is in his or her native language, the more easily he or she will acquire a second language. Identifying each student's stage of second language acquisition helps teachers plan literacy lessons that effectively support students' comprehension and engagement in academic tasks.

The academic dimension of the CLD student biography emphasizes the importance of knowing what type of access a student has had to schooling and literacy development. Access includes formal schooling a CLD student has received in his or her native language and in English, as well as the informal experiences the student has had in daily life. Students who have had more access to literacy development frequently have more strategies and skills to build on. To support the academic success of all CLD students, educators can immerse students in academically challenging tasks that promote engagement, hope, and grade-level literacy acquisition.

The final dimension of the CLD student biography is the cognitive dimension. Building on existing cognitive and language assets by explicitly teaching learning strategies promotes CLD students' literacy development. Using culturally relevant texts is another way to enhance students' cognitive connections and knowledge. Given the diversity of the CLD student population, teachers who understand and access the sociocultural, linguistic, academic, and cognitive assets of their CLD students' biographies are better equipped to provide instruction that meets these students' differential learning needs.

## ■ key theories and concepts

- academic dimension
- CLD student biography
- cognitive dimension
- cultural discontinuity
- home visit

- interdependence hypothesis
- linguistic dimension
- sociocultural dimension
- stages of second language acquisition

## ■ professional conversations on practice

1. The four dimensions of the CLD student biography are sociocultural, linguistic, academic, and cognitive. Discuss the ways you currently gather information about your CLD students within each of these dimensions.

2. The CLD student biography is presented as a prerequisite to effective literacy instruction for CLD students. Identify the components of the CLD student biography that you believe are central to supporting literacy instruction with CLD students.

3. Share two strategies you might use with your CLD students to learn more about their biographies, based on what you learned in this chapter. Be sure to articulate why you selected these strategies and how you think they will support your future literacy instruction.

## ■ questions for review and reflection

1. Why is it helpful for teachers to know the biographies of their CLD students before beginning literacy instruction?

2. CLD students read at varying levels of linguistic proficiency. How can a teacher identify a CLD student's proficiency level and then use this information to support his or her literacy development?

3. What kind of academic knowledge supports literacy development for CLD students, and how can teachers help students apply this knowledge?

4. In what ways can CLD students' existing cognitive assets be built on to promote literacy development?

**Where the Classroom Comes to Life**

Now go to the Herrera, Perez, and Escamilla MyEducationLab course at www.myeducationlab.com to:

- read and connect with the chapter Objectives;
- use the Study Plan questions to assess your comprehension of the chapter content;
- study chapter content with your Individualized Study Plan;
- engage in multimedia exercises to help you build a deeper and more applied understanding of chapter content.

## critical considerations

- What is the difference between phonological awareness and phonemic awareness?

- How can a CLD student's phonological awareness in the native language be applied to a second language?

- How does phonological awareness provide the catalyst for a CLD student's development of phonemic awareness?

- What are the key characteristics of the word recognition view of reading and the sociopsycholinguistic view of reading as they relate to phonemic awareness?

- What are the essential phonemic awareness tasks, and how can they be adapted and modified to meet the linguistic needs of CLD students?

# Rethinking Phonemic Awareness

## A Cross-Linguistic Transfer Perspective

*I have never thought about the effect of learning a native language and the results of pruning. The idea that there are certain sounds and pronunciations that people cannot pronounce in a second language is an eye opener. It makes more sense to me now when I hear individuals leave letters or sounds off or add them to certain words or statements that do not belong when he or she speaks English. I do not feel that I have had a realistic viewpoint toward those learning a new language. In fact, I believe that I have been judgmental of these individuals for not having patience and thinking that they are ignorant. I also have thought that the language difficulties were a result of laziness and not displaying the effort that it takes to learn a different language. I can see now that I was terribly wrong.*

—An elementary teacher

From the day children are born, they make their way in the world as auditory learners (Heilman, 2005). As children acquire speech, they develop *phonological awareness,* or the ability to manipulate the sounds they hear to distinguish the larger units of speech, such as words and syllables (Adams, 1991; Burns, Griffin, & Snow, 1999; Freeman & Freeman, 2004). Since children have been immersed in sound from birth, prevailing research conducted with monolingual English-speaking students proposes that literacy development should begin with sound and symbol relationships (Adams, 1990; Block & Israel, 2005; Rasinski & Padak, 2000).

Translated into classroom practice, literacy instruction begins with sound and symbol relationships by building on students' phonological awareness to develop phonemic awareness. *Phonological awareness* includes the ability to separate sentences into words and words into syllables (Cunningham, 2005). *Phonemic awareness* is the ability to hear, identify, and manipulate the individual sounds (*phonemes*) within spoken words (Block & Israel, 2005).

In this chapter, we draw from the literature base just identified and our experience with CLD students from multiple language groups to contextualize phonemic awareness in meaningful ways for CLD students. By building on Cummins's (1979) seminal research on the linguistic interdependence model, this chapter discusses specific transfer issues that promote and inhibit CLD students' phonological development in English. Strategies then are presented to support educators in the development of phonemic awareness skills for CLD students.

## ■ Phonological Awareness and Cross-Language Transfer

As previously discussed, CLD students naturally acquire the phonological system of their native language from the day they are born (Coelho, 2004). When acquiring a second language, CLD students build from the phonological patterns in their native language. In research on language transfer issues, Cummins (1979) concluded that the transfer of skills from one language to another is a result of the *linguistic interdependence* between two languages.

For example, a native Spanish speaker who knows the Spanish consonant sound "t" as in *tigre (tiger)* may more readily acquire the "t" sound in the English word *tiger,* as they are the same sound. However, this transfer of phonological sound systems from one language to the next is not done intrinsically. It is through the explicit identification and modeling of this linguistic interdependence that CLD students learn how to transfer these skills from one language to another. Yet CLD students are only able to transfer those phonological skills that they know in the native language.

More recent research builds on the linguistic interdependence model, further illuminating the effects of bilingualism on the development of preliteracy skills (Chiappe & Siegel, 1999; Cisero & Royer, 1995; Comeau, Cormier, Grandmaison, & Lacroix, 1999; Durgunoglu, Nagy, & Hancin-Bhatt, 1993; Durgunoglu & Oney, 1999; Durgunoglu & Verhoeven, 1998). This research shows that linguistic interdependence is greatest among languages that share similar alphabet systems. Consequently, English and Spanish are the most common languages studied for the impact of linguistic transfer.

A study conducted by Durgunoglu et al. (1993) specifically explored how the phonological awareness of native-Spanish-speaking children influenced their ability to recognize words in English. This research demonstrated a positive correlation between a Latino student's phonological awareness in Spanish and his or her ability to develop phonological awareness in English. Subsequent research by García and González (1995) confirmed and expanded the idea of linguistic interdependence, finding that a wide variety of phonological awareness skills can transfer between Spanish and English.

The cumulative weight of this research strongly supports the idea that a CLD student can explicitly learn to identify and manipulate the sounds of the second language by tapping into similar sounds he or she has already learned in the native language (Durgunoglu et al., 1993; García & González, 1995). As such, if a teacher is aware of the phonological skills a CLD student already has in the native language, he or she can tailor instruction to aid the transfer of these skills to English. An easy way for teachers to do this is to begin a *language file,* in which they collect basic information about the languages spoken by their CLD students and explicitly address the phonological differences between the native language and the English language during instruction.

Given a lack of bilingual proficiency and access to resources, monolingual English-speaking teachers may believe that they do not have the necessary skills or tools to determine which native language phonological skills CLD students possess, much less how these skills can be used to build phonological awareness in English. This chapter addresses this challenge by offering a series of activities and questions that can guide teachers as they engage CLD students in skill identification and transfer. However, before we can explore the practical aspects of building phonological awareness with CLD students, we must first understand how the broad concept of phonological awareness comprises a subset of skills known as *phonemic awareness.*

## ■ Phonemic Awareness and Cross-Language Transfer

While phonological awareness is the catalyst by which English-speaking students identify and manipulate the individual phonemes (basic units of sound) within words (Block & Israel, 2005), such awareness is also useful for CLD students. *Phonemes* are classified as either consonants (e.g., *b, c, d, f, g*) or vowels (i.e., *a, e, i, o, u*). As previously defined, *phonemic awareness* is based on the ability of students to move from hearing the larger clusters of sounds within a language to hearing, identifying, and manipulating individual letter sounds within words. Viewed in this context, phonological awareness provides the basis for phonemic skill development.

However, the process of isolating individual sounds within words is a difficult concept for many young children because they previously have only considered words as whole, meaning-carrying units (Burns, 1999). For CLD students who do not speak English as their first language, the process of isolating individual sounds is further complicated by the fact that their ability to isolate these sounds is directly linked to their ability to detect and identify the English letter sounds within each word. When we consider the fact that in normal speech, 10 to 20 phonemes are articulated per second, it is easy to see how challenging it can be for CLD students to detect and then identify these phonemes.

To develop phonemic awareness skills, educators engage students in phonemic awareness tasks (i.e., phoneme isolation, phoneme identity, phoneme categorization, phoneme blending, phoneme segmentation, phoneme deletion, phoneme addition, phoneme substitution, and rhyming). In these tasks, students are asked to manipulate in multiple ways the individual phonemes they hear within words. The purpose of this manipulation is to support students' understanding of the sound system within a language and to build the auditory building blocks for language development (Dahl, Scharer, Lawson, & Grogan, 2001). Specific descriptions of each of these tasks, as well as sample activities that promote English language development for CLD students, are discussed later in this chapter.

Each language uses a different inventory of sounds, some of which may be identical to those in English and some that may not be (Freeman & Freeman, 2004). The development of phonemic awareness in English is highly influenced by a student's native language proficiency and phonemic awareness of the letter sounds in his or her native language. August, Calderón, and Carlo (2002) found that Spanish phonemic awareness, letter identification, and word reading were reliable predictors of students' performance on parallel tasks in English at the end of the third and fourth grades. This lends further credibility to the idea that language and literacy skills, even at the level of phonemic awareness, are transferable between Spanish and English.

However, it is important to keep in mind that children can only transfer what they know. As such, teachers and parents who want to maximize cross-language skill transfer find ways to help their Spanish-speaking CLD students develop literacy in the first language. Neglecting a child's first-language literacy development only hinders literacy development in the second language. This cross-language transfer applies not only to Spanish speakers acquiring English but to other language speakers as well. The key is to research each language group, determine where similarities exist, and explicitly teach these similarities to CLD students.

Similarities between the English alphabet and the alphabets of multiple languages can promote the transfer of phonemic awareness skills; however, there are specific phonemes in English for which no counterparts exist in other languages. This is particularly true for CLD students who have a native language that employs a *logographic system* of symbols without sound correspondence, such as Chinese (Coelho, 2004). There are also differences among languages in how phonemes are combined. When teachers are aware of these differences, they can address them specifically in instruction.

Coelho (2004) has identified by language some of the most common cross-language transfer errors CLD students make:

- In Spanish, clusters beginning with [s] do not begin words. As a result, Spanish speakers often pronounce a word like *street* as /estriyt/.
- In Farsi, every consonant is paired with a vowel. As a result, Farsi speakers often try to add a lax or weak vowel either before or in the middle of an English consonant cluster. As a result, they may pronounce a word like *place* as /peleys/. In addition, Farsi students may have special difficulty with clusters of three consonants and often try to insert two additional vowels sounds, so that a word such as *street* may be pronounced /esteriyt/.
- Cantonese and Vietnamese speakers, by contrast, tend to eliminate one of the consonant sounds in a cluster, so *street* may be pronounced /sriyt/. At the end of a word, they may pronounce only the first sound in a cluster, so that a word like *fast* is pronounced as /faes/.

Table 3.1 identifies additional phonemic errors and cross-language transfer issues that CLD students face. The languages represented in this table are among the top three languages spoken by CLD students in the United States.

■ **table 3.1**   Cross-Language Transfer Issues

| Language | Letters/sounds that exist in the native language but not in English | Letters/sounds that do not exist in the native language or are hard to produce in English | Additional cross-language transfer issues | |
|---|---|---|---|---|
| | | | **Substitutions** | |
| | | | English | Native Language |
| Spanish | ñ, ll, rr | Only one vowel sound in Spanish but multiple vowel sounds in English | /sh/ | /ch/ |
| | | | /s/ | /es/ |
| | | | /y/ | /j/ |
| | | | /b/ | /v/ |
| Vietnamese | Five to six tones within the language | /l/ | /t/ | /th/ |
| | | /th/ | /p/ | /f/ |
| | | /ch/ | /b/ | /p/ |
| | | /sh/ | /g/ | /k/ |
| | | /d/ | /ch/ | /j/ |
| Chinese | Tonal language in nature | /l/ | /p/ | /b/ |
| | | No /ch/, /j/, /v/, /th/, /sh/, /z/ (vision), /r/, or /hw/ in Cantonese | /t/ | /d/ |
| | | | /k/ | /g/ |
| | | | /s/ | /z/ |
| | | | /l/ | /r/ |

Although teachers traditionally are not taught to consider the impact of the native language on phonemic awareness development in English, understanding critical differences among phonemic awareness and phonemes in CLD students' native languages can help promote the acquisition of phonemic awareness in English. This does not mean teachers must become linguistic experts on all the languages their CLD students speak. Rather, teachers can draw from myriad resources, such as those detailed in Figure 3.1, to better understand how various languages can support phonemic awareness in English. By tapping these resources, teachers of CLD students can more fully grasp those elements of the native language that support cross-language transfer and understand specific errors CLD students make when learning English.

Another consideration to bear in mind is that CLD students often do not distinguish all the sounds or phonemes within new English words. That is, a student may not hear or recognize distinctions between certain sounds the way native English speakers do because the student's native language does not rely on these distinctions. If specific phonemes are not used in the native language, they are "pruned" from the learner's repertoire of distinguishable sounds from birth to age ten (Jensen, 2000). Additionally, several sounds in English are almost impossible to produce without adding a vowel sound (e.g., /b/, /p/, /d/). This reality can make hearing individual phonemes extremely difficult for a CLD student.

■ **f i g u r e   3 . 1**     Resources to Support CLD Students' Phonemic Awareness

- Interview the parents to learn more about a student's native language.
- Interview older siblings who have developed a higher level of English language proficiency for information about the language.
- Talk to bilingual support staff or community members about the native language.
- Surf the Internet for immediate access to language guides and overviews about the native languages of your CLD students. Some initial websites you may want to look at include the ones in the following list. For most of these sites, type in the name of the language you want to learn more about:

  Yamada Language Center: http://babel.uoregon.edu/yamada/guides.html
  Wikipedia: http://en.wikipedia.org
  Google: www.google.com
  Yahoo: www.yahoo.com
  AskJeeves: www.ask.com
  Altavista: www.altavista.com (This site also offers a translating service. To access this service, click on Babel Fish Translation, below the search engine.)

# ■ Contextualizing Phonemic Awareness Instruction

The word recognition view and the sociopsycholinguistic view are two different perspectives on reading that guide the way educators approach teaching phonemic awareness. Educators who implement a *word recognition view* of reading believe that reading is primarily a process of identifying words. To teach students how to identify words, reading is broken down into the following five component parts, which are taught systematically (Freeman & Freeman, 2004, p. 78):

1. Phonemic awareness skills
2. Names and sounds of letters
3. Phonics rules
4. Sight words
5. Structural analysis skills

The first component of reading that is taught within the word recognition view is phonemic awareness skills. These skills are consciously developed via explicit instruction on phonemic awareness tasks. Because they are considered prerequisite skills, they must be mastered before moving on to the next component of reading.

Unlike the word recognition view of reading, the *sociopsycholinguistic view* of reading defines phonemic awareness as a component of the graphophonic cueing system, which is one of three language cueing systems readers use to make sense of text. (These systems are discussed in detail in Chapter 4.) Within this system, "readers use both visual and sound knowledge as well as the knowledge of correspondences between letters and sounds as they sample texts and make and confirm predictions to construct meaning from texts" (Freeman & Freeman, 2004, p. 80). Given the integrated nature of the sociopsycholinguistic view of reading, phonemic awareness is developed subconsciously through the process of reading, hearing, and talking about text.

Within this book, phonemic awareness instruction is approached from a sociopsycholinguistic view of reading. To contextualize this approach to phonemic awareness for educators who are using curricula based on a word recognition view of reading that requires explicit and direct instruction on phonemic awareness tasks, the remainder of this chapter will first introduce and define these tasks. Examples of how these tasks can be approached from the sociopsycholinguistic view of reading will then be provided to support CLD students' development of the graphophonic cueing system.

## Phonemic Awareness Tasks: Identifying the Subtleties of the English Language

Eight types of English phonemic awareness tasks are explicitly taught in schools (Adams, 1990; Freeman & Freeman, 2004; Rasinski & Padak, 2000):

- Phoneme isolation
- Phoneme identity
- Phoneme categorization
- Phoneme blending
- Phoneme segmentation
- Phoneme deletion
- Phoneme addition
- Phoneme substitution

These eight tasks provide students with the specific tools they need for identifying individual phonemes in English words, and they have been shown to support monolingual English speakers in developing essential preliteracy skills for reading. The sociopsycholinguistic view of reading and accompanying research have concluded that phonemic awareness instruction is most effective when children are taught to manipulate phonemes by using letters of the alphabet (Armbruster, Lehr, & Osborn, 2001). As such, we contextualize each of these via instructional examples using actual texts.

### Phoneme Isolation

*Phoneme isolation* tasks require students to isolate the individual phonemes (sounds) in a word (Block & Israel, 2005). One of the primary ways phoneme isolation tasks are taught is through teacher-directed questioning, in which students are asked to identify individual phonemes within a series of words. For example, the teacher might ask the students "What is the first sound in *map*?" The correct response from students is /m/.

To successfully complete this task, the student must be able to do the following:

1. Understand what the word means in English (as this supports the correct identification of the phoneme).
2. Hear the individual phonemes (consonants and vowels) within the word.
3. Correctly identify the phoneme.
4. Articulate the phoneme back for the teacher.

When working with CLD students, it is not safe to make these assumptions. First, if CLD students are not provided with a context that can be used to determine word meanings, they have no point of reference from which to draw. Additionally, this task assumes that CLD students can hear and identify the individual phoneme in English. However, as we have discussed, if a phoneme does not exist in the CLD student's native language or is articulated differently, he or she may struggle to hear and identify the target phoneme. Finally, asking a CLD student to articulate the phoneme back for the teacher may prove challenging, as the CLD student may not be familiar with producing this sound in English. On the other hand, some CLD students (particularly those whose native language is alphabetic in origin) can readily articulate the target phonemes in English. What is often missing for these students, however, is the comprehension associated with the individual words and their meanings.

The Me, Myself, and I activity described in Strategies in Practice 3.1 has proven an effective phoneme isolation task for CLD students because students are able to use one of the most meaningful words they know—their own names—as

## Strategies in Practice 3.1

### Phoneme Isolation Activity

#### Me, Myself, and I

Materials Needed
- Paper (one sheet per student)
- Markers (one per student)

Directions
- Write students' names on separate sheets of paper.
- Give each student the paper with his or her name.
- Have each student circle the first letter of his or her name with a marker and tell you the sound it makes.
- Go around the room and have each student say his or her name, holding the paper so only he or she can see it. (This scaffolds the activity for CLD students by providing a visual aid.)
- Have each student share with the group the letter sound at the beginning of his or her name (the sound that was isolated when he or she circled it).
- To extend the activity, you can have students find and form groups with all the other students in the class whose names begin with the same letter sound. Then, in their small groups, have students say their names again and identify the letter sound as a group.
- When each group has identified the letter sound, have them show their names to see if the sound they identified and the letter that begins their names are the same.

they learn how to isolate and identify initial phoneme sounds. Because students typically learn to read and write their own names as they begin developing literacy skills, they can usually sound out the phonemes in their names subconsciously as a natural part of their oral language development. Moreover, when CLD students use their own names to identify phonemes, they understand the meanings of their names as representations of who they are as individuals. Capitalizing on these examples in practice enables teachers to make explicit links between phonemes in a CLD student's native language and those in English. Such links help promote the student's level of phonemic awareness in English (Durgonoglu, Nagy, & Hancin-Bhatt, 1998; Snow, Burns, & Griffin, 1998).

According to Gonzalez-Bueno (2001), when CLD students use words that begin with corresponding phoneme sounds in Spanish and English, they more readily transfer understanding about the similarities in the letter sounds of these words. Additional studies by Kole (2003) and Herrera and Murry (2004) found that Spanish-speaking CLD students were more capable of isolating initial phonemes in English when links were explicitly made between the Spanish and English phonemes of *cognates*—that is, words that are spelled the same (or nearly the same) in both languages and have the same meaning. For example, when Spanish speakers are taught that the /r/ phoneme in the Spanish word *rosa* has the same initial phoneme sound in the English cognate *rose,* they can make the link between the /r/ phoneme in both languages and use this knowledge as they encounter /r/ phonemes in the future.

It is important to note, however, that after a foundation has been built on the commonalities of two languages, it is also necessary to systematically outline how the languages differ and to provide added support to address these differences (Helman, 2004). For instance, the vowel sounds in Spanish differ from those in English. In addition to having different sounds, each vowel in Spanish represents only one sound, whereas in English, the vowels represent multiple sounds. Unless these differences are explicitly taught to Spanish-speaking students, confusion over the vowel sounds in English can adversely affect CLD students' acquisition of English.

Connecting phoneme isolation tasks to text is the next step in promoting CLD students' ability to isolate phonemes in English. For example, teachers might read the story *Listen to the Desert/Oye al desierto,* by Pat Mora (1994). This bilingual children's book presents a story about the sounds of the desert. As each sound is introduced, it is first presented in English and then in Spanish, as demonstrated in the following excerpt:

> Listen to the snake hiss, tst-tst-tst, tst-tst-tst.
> Listen to the snake hiss, tst-tst-tst, tst-tst-tst.
>    Silbra la culebra, ssst, ssst, ssst.
>    Silbra la culebra, ssst, ssst, ssst. (p. 7)

The distinction between the sounds the snake makes in English and Spanish is a wonderful point of departure for exploring other differences in sounds between English and Spanish or between English and other languages represented in the classroom. The key is starting this discussion from a meaningful and rich context so that CLD students have a point of reference from which they can contextualize the task of phoneme isolation.

### *Phoneme Identity*

The task of *phoneme identity* requires students to recognize, identify, and match the same sound in a series of different words (Block & Israel, 2005; Burns, 1999). For example, the teacher might ask a student, "What sound is the same in *pat, put,* and *pin?*" The correct response from the student would, of course, be /p/.

This task assumes that CLD students are able to do the following:

1. Understand what the word means in English (as this supports the correct identification of the phoneme).
2. Hear and identify the phoneme in English.
3. Articulate back the phoneme sound in English.

One way to make phoneme identity tasks more meaningful, and thereby more comprehensible to CLD students, is to pull words for the activity from actual texts that students have read or been taught in class. Alphabet books are excellent texts for promoting phoneme identity, particularly alphabet books that incorporate CLD students' languages and/or cultures. Recommended bilingual alphabet texts include *A to Zen: A Book of Japanese Culture* (Wells & Yoshi, 1992), *ABeCedarios: Mexican Folk Art, ABCs in Spanish and English* (Weill, 2007), and *Gathering the Sun—An Alphabet in Spanish and English* (Ada, 2001). By using bilingual alphabet books, teachers immediately provide CLD students with a contextual base to draw on during phoneme identity tasks. Many of these bilingual alphabet books also incorporate cognates. When teachers explicitly point out cognates to CLD students, they help the students focus their attention on the phonemes that are similar as well as those that are different in their native languages and English.

Recommended cultural ABC books include *C is for China* (So, 2004), *India ABCs: A Book about the People and Places of India* (Aboff, 2006), *P Is for Passport: A World Alphabet* (Scillian, 2003), and *W Is for World: A Round-the-World ABC* (Cave, 2004). In the alphabet book *India ABCs,* teachers can use the bolded words from the following letter /s/ page to promote CLD students' engagement in phoneme identity tasks:

S is for saris.
**Saris** are the traditional clothing worn by Hindu women in India. Usually made of cotton or **silk,** saris come in thousands of colors and designs. Each area of the

country has its own designs. The most expensive saris are **sewn** with threads of real gold or silver. Women wear saris in different ways, depending on the region in which they live. (p. 22, emphasis added)

After having students identify the phoneme that is the same in the bolded words (/s/), the teacher should make sure that CLD students can articulate the meanings of the words within the context of the text. This additional focus on contextualizing the phoneme identity task by linking it to the culture of the student not only makes the activity more meaningful to him or her, but it also promotes vocabulary development and comprehension.

### Phoneme Categorization

*Phoneme categorization* tasks require students to recognize the one word in a series that sounds odd (Block & Israel, 2005). For example, the teacher might ask a student "Which word doesn't belong: *fit, fun, cat,* or *fan*?" The student's ability to identify *cat* as the dissimilar word demonstrates his or her mastery of phoneme categorization.

For CLD students to be successful at this task, they need to be able to do the following:

1. Create a context from which they can determine the meanings of the words (to support decoding and phoneme identification).
2. Identify the phonemes in a series of different words.
3. Contrast the phonemes in the series against one another to determine which one does not belong (a cognitively complex task).

When the words used for phoneme categorization tasks use initial phoneme sounds that are familiar to a student, the distinction between sounds is much easier to hear. When the initial phonemes are not a part of the student's native language, however, it is essential to provide explicit instruction and practice with the unfamiliar sounds. For example, in Spanish, the /j/ phoneme is articulated as the /h/ phoneme in English. Therefore, when using these types of words for phoneme categorization tasks, it is important to explicitly identify and teach such differences between letter sounds in the native language and those in English.

To actively engage CLD students in identifying which word does not fit, teachers might do an activity such as Boxing in the Odd Sound, as described in Strategies in Practice 3.2. The interactive nature of this activity supports CLD students' successful completion of phoneme categorization tasks in several ways:

1. CLD students are physically engaged in the activity through the use of kinesthetic movement.

## Phoneme Categorization Activity

### Boxing in the Odd Sound

Materials Needed
- Masking tape
- Visual picture cues (one per student)

Directions
- Before conducting the activity, use tape to create the shape of a large triangle (for four students) or square (for five students) on the floor.
- Organize students into groups of four or five.
- After taping off the area, give each student in the group a different picture cue card with the name of the picture written on the back of the card (see examples below). Each card should represent one word, and all but one of the words for each group should start with the same initial phoneme.
- Have each student in the group come to the area where the shape has been taped on the floor and stand around the shape.
- Ask each student to say the word naming the item on his or her cue card.
- After hearing all the words naming the items in the group, have the students discuss which word does not fit and why.
- Once the students decide which word does not fit, have them send the person with the corresponding card to stand inside the shape. The rest of the students should stand on a corner of the shape, effectively boxing in the word with the odd sound.
- To conclude the activity, have the group members share with the class why they boxed in the word they chose.

**Fronts of the Cards**

**Backs of the Cards**

| ANIMALS | CHAMELEON | CLIMBED | COLOR |
|---|---|---|---|

2. Students are given visual cues to promote comprehension of each word. The visual cues used for this activity can be commercially produced cue cards, teacher-made cards, pictures from the Internet, pictures from a text, or student illustrations.

3. Students can be strategically grouped so that more proficient peers can model the correct pronunciation of a word, if needed, as well as support group discussion about which word does not fit and why.

Additionally important is contextualizing the words that students are being asked to categorize by selecting words from a text that CLD students have previously read or are currently reading. For example, a story that might be read to first-graders is Leo Lionni's (1975) classic *A Color of His Own,* which is about a chameleon's quest to find a color that is his own. As children read this text, they are exposed to vibrant pictures and an array of vocabulary terms. When selecting words from the text that can be used for phoneme categorization activities, the teacher should choose key terms that summarize the main points of the story. Doing so will promote CLD students' comprehension of the lesson and facilitate phonemic awareness tasks. For example, the following terms from this story could be chosen for a phoneme categorization task: *animals, chameleon, climbed,* and *color.*

### Phoneme Blending

*Phoneme blending* tasks call on students to listen to a sequence of separately spoken phonemes and then combine them to form a word (Block & Israel, 2005). For example, the teacher might ask a student "What word would you have if you put these sounds together: /c/-/a/-/t/?" The correct response would be *cat.*

Research on phoneme blending tasks has concluded that the skills developed during these activities help students decode written words during phonics tasks (Rasinski & Padak, 2000). For CLD students who have a native language that is alphabetic in nature (e.g., French, Spanish), the act of blending phonemes to create words is a transferable skill. However, the ways that sounds are blended may not be the same across languages. In Spanish, for example, the word for *cat* is *gato,* and the teacher would identify the sounds to be blended as /ga/-/to/. Knowing that Spanish-speaking children learn to blend words by chunks of phonemes rather than individual phonemes is important, as it has direct implications for how students approach blending sounds in English. Students of other language groups may also have difficulty with phoneme blending. For instance, students who speak Chinese, which is based on a logographic system of symbols that do not correspond to specific sounds, often find phoneme blending particularly challenging (Tompkins, 2004).

To support CLD students in completing phoneme blending tasks, teachers can use the Sliding into Phoneme Blending activity described in Strategies in Practice 3.3. This activity helps CLD students understand how to blend the individual phonemes in English words in a concrete and hands-on manner. By first modeling how to blend sounds on an actual playground slide, students are able to visually see how the words come together in the completed picture. This activity also allows all students to be participants in the modeling process. In addition, the modeling of each individual phoneme as an isolated sound prior to blending provides CLD students with explicit examples they can then draw on.

When completing the second part of the activity using the individual slides and pictures, CLD students should be paired with peers for initial modeling before being released to do the activity on their own. As with other phonemic awareness tasks, the words selected for the individual application component of the activity should be words that CLD students have seen in text or had previous exposure to in a lesson. Nursery rhymes are a great source of words for this type of activity. Consider the following example:

Jack and Jill went up the hill to fetch a pail of water.
Jack fell down and broke his crown and Jill came tumbling after.

*Jack, Jill, hill, pail,* and *water* are just a few examples of the words that can be easily drawn by students, cut apart, and then blended.

## Phoneme Segmentation

*Phoneme segmentation* requires students to isolate individual phonemes within a word. For example, the teacher might ask a student to break a syllable or word like *hat* into its constituent phonemes, /h/ /a/ /t/ (Helman, 2005). To work with students on phoneme segmentation, teachers traditionally pass out a sheet of paper on which four or five Elkonin boxes are drawn (see example in Strategies in Practice 3.4) as well as a handful of markers (e.g., cubes, pennies, dots). As students listen to the word said by the teacher, they push markers into the Elkonin boxes, one marker for each sound.

This task assumes that CLD students can do the following:

1. Understand the words they are being asked to segment.
2. Segment words by their individual phonemes.
3. Hear each English phoneme.

As discussed with phoneme blending tasks, CLD students may not segment words by their individual phonemes in their native language. If this is the case, teachers need to explicitly model this skill with CLD students. In addition, using

### Phoneme Blending Activity

#### Sliding into Phoneme Blending

Materials Needed
- Sheets of $8\frac{1}{2}'' \times 11''$ paper (one per student)
- $3'' \times 5''$ cards (one per student)
- Crayons or markers
- Playground slide
- Visual cues of a playground slide (one per student)

Directions
- Tape together three sheets of paper, and have students draw a picture of a cat across the three pages. (Visually depicting the word helps to support CLD students' comprehension of it.)
- Once the picture has been completed, write the word *cat* across the back of it. Use large letters, and place one letter on each sheet.
- Separate the three sheets of paper, and pass them out to three different students.
- Repeat this process of creating picture/letter sheets using different words so that each student has a sheet.
- Have the class go outside to the playground slide.
- To model how the phonemes blend, have the students with the picture of the cat line up in order (c-a-t) and slide down the slide one by one.
- As each student comes down the slide, have him or her say the phoneme that represents the word *cat* (i.e., the first person down the slide says the /c/ phoneme, the second person says the /a/ phoneme, and the third person says the final phoneme, /t/).
- When all three students are at the bottom of the slide, have them hold up their cards and, as a group, blend the word together to say the word *cat*.
- Repeat this activity several times with different words so that every student has an opportunity to experience the process of going down the slide to model how the individual letter sounds blend with other sounds to form words.
- After modeling this strategy physically, have students return to the classroom. Pass out paper models of slides and repeat this activity with new words using pictures that students have drawn on $3'' \times 5''$ cards. (While students are creating their own cards, encourage them to draw the picture across the whole card.) Have students write the word across the back of the card; then fold the card according to the number of letters in the word to facilitate cutting it apart and practicing the letter sounds on the individual paper "slides."

**Front**

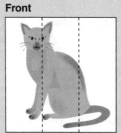

**Back**

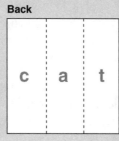

Elkonin boxes to segment words is a very abstract activity for CLD students. As such, it is important first to provide a more concrete model of the process of phoneme segmentation.

Stepping Stones, as described in Strategies in Practice 3.4, is a phoneme segmentation activity that does just this. By having students physically model the concept of Elkonin boxes, using visual cues, cooperative learning, and kinesthetic movement, CLD students are better able to understand the process of segmentation. After repeated modeling using Stepping Stones, CLD students can transfer this strategy to the task of completing Elkonin boxes. However, to provide CLD students with a scaffold when using Elkonin boxes, a template for a handout titled "Elkonin Boxes with a Twist" is included after the directions for the Stepping Stones activity. A place on this handout has been included for visual cues to support CLD students' comprehension of the individual words they are being asked to identify. These visual cues can be inserted before the lesson, or CLD students can draw in the cues themselves before the task.

Once again, nursery rhymes are a great source from which to select words for phoneme segmentation tasks. Nursery rhymes provide CLD students with a context for the words, and the chosen words can be used to promote comprehension

## Strategies in Practice 3.4

### Phoneme Segmentation Activity

#### Stepping Stones

**Materials Needed**
- Visual cues
- Masking tape
- Handouts (one per student)

**Directions**
- Using tape, create a large Elkonin box on the floor.

| | | | |
|---|---|---|---|
| | | | |

*continued*

- Have students line up in a row.
- As you say a word aloud, have one student per sound step into a box.
- At the end of the activity, ask CLD students to count the number of boxes that students are standing in. Then make this link to the number of sounds in the English word.
- Repeat the activity several times with different words.
- Hand out the "Elkonin Boxes with a Twist" sheet, one to each student. Have students use picture cues that are provided (or that they have drawn) to support their comprehension.
- To further scaffold the lesson, as you say the word you want the students to segment, have them write each letter sound they hear in a box. (Doing this allows you to see which sounds are and are not being identified.)

**Elkonin Boxes with a Twist**

| p | a | i | l | Picture Cue |
|---|---|---|---|---|
| | | | | Picture Cue |
| | | | | Picture Cue |
| | | | | Picture Cue |

of the rhymes themselves. For instance, in the "Jack and Jill" nursery rhyme, some CLD students may not know what a *crown* is; if this word is selected to be segmented, CLD students will have the opportunity to see a visual cue for the word. Teachers who have students draw their own visual cues on their individual Elkonin handouts can then provide students with the opportunity to discuss the meaning of the word with partners, in small groups, or even as a whole class.

## Phoneme Deletion

*Phoneme deletion* tasks require students to recognize the word that remains when a phoneme is removed from the larger original word (Block & Israel, 2005). For example, a teacher might ask what word is left when the initial /s/ phoneme is removed from the word *smile*. The correct response would be *mile*. Although on the surface, this task appears simple, it is actually quite complex. Phoneme deletion is especially difficult for CLD students, because they must identify the appropriate phoneme to delete to create the new word. It is also important to note, however, that mastery of this skill is a strong predictor of reading achievement in native-English-speaking students (Adams, 1990) and as such should not be immediately discounted as a tool for literacy development with CLD students.

The Eating Letters activity, as described in Strategies in Practice 3.5, is one example of how phoneme deletion activities can be scaffolded for CLD students. Building on the recommendation of Armburster, Lehr, and Osborn (2001), this task emphasizes the manipulation of phonemes by using the letters of the alphabet. This activity makes the process of deleting phonemes more concrete for CLD students because the students physically cover up letters to make new words. Moreover, this activity promotes comprehension by allowing CLD students first to visually see what the original word means. After the task has been completed, teachers can check CLD students' comprehension by verifying that their drawings for the new word are correct.

One first-grade teacher commented that, while carrying out this activity in the classroom, she used words from a story that she was reading aloud to her students, *Amelia's Road* (Altman, 1993). This story was one of the teacher's favorites stories to share with her CLD students because it is based on the experiences of a young migrant girl. The character in the story is one that many of the teacher's CLD students could relate to as they, too, came from migrant homes. The teacher selected the following words from the story for the phoneme deletion task: *star* (*tar*) or *clump* (*lump*). The teacher shared that, as an extension, she also used compound words from the story and asked students to delete larger sets of phonemes to make new words. For example, she used *sunstruck* (*sun* or *struck*), *shortcut* (*short* or *cut*), and *cartwheels* (*cart* or *wheels*).

## Strategies in Practice 3.5

### Phoneme Deletion Activity

#### Eating Letters

**Materials Needed**
- Visual cue of an alligator
- 3″ × 5″ cards with words written on them (one per student)

**Directions**
- Have each student select a card containing a word.
- Have each student draw a picture to represent his or her word on the left-hand side of the card.
- Using the alligator (or any other animal) as a visual cue, have students physically move the alligator so that it "eats" the initial phoneme of the word (see the example below).
- Have each student draw a picture on the right-hand side of the card to represent the new word he or she made.
- As an added reinforcement, have each student write the new word below the picture.

### *Phoneme Addition*

When engaged in *phoneme addition* tasks, students make a new word by adding a phoneme to an existing word (Block & Israel, 2005). For example, the teacher might ask students what word is formed when an /s/ is added to the front of the word *top*. The correct response would be *stop*. One of the most common techniques for developing this skill with students involves word families. For instance, the teacher might write the word family -*at* on the board and ask students come up with a list of words that fit into this word family (e.g., *fat, bat, sat, hat*). Like phoneme deletion, phoneme addition tasks are somewhat abstract for CLD students. Therefore, teachers can also contextualize this task by using letters of the alphabet to support CLD students as they complete the cognitively complex task of creating whole new words.

Letter Detective, as described in Strategies in Practice 3.6, helps CLD students complete phoneme addition tasks. The use of whole-group and partner configurations provides CLD students with support in forming new words and promotes their understanding of the words' meanings. One story that is great for this activity due to its cultural relevance for some Hispanic students is *El Cucuy! A Bogeyman Story in English and Spanish* (Hayes, 2001). This is the traditional story of a bogeyman that takes bad children away from home and is typically told by parents as a behavior management tool. Some of the words from this story that can be used for phoneme addition tasks include *arm* (*harm* or *charm*), *ear* (*hear* or *spear*), and *all* (*call, ball, fall*).

## Strategies in Practice 3.6

### Phoneme Addition Activity

#### Letter Detective

**Materials Needed**

- Whiteboard
- Sheets of $8^1/_2'' \times 11''$ paper (one per student)
- Pencils (one per student)

**Directions**

- Write a word family (e.g., *at*) on the whiteboard.
- As a whole group, identify new words based on the word family.
- Before writing each new word on the whiteboard, have students define the word and suggest a picture that represents it. (*Note:* In the example below, the word can have two distinct meanings, so this discussion is critical.)
- Write the word and draw the picture on the board (or have the students write the word and draw the picture).
- After this whole-group activity, have students work with partners to create cards with visual cues and sentences that use the words modeled (see the sample below).

**Word Family: at**

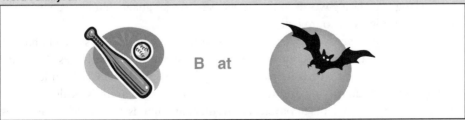

I got a new baseball <u>bat</u> for my birthday.

### *Phoneme Substitution*

The goal of *phoneme substitution* is to replace one phoneme for another in a word, thereby forming a new word (Block & Israel, 2005). For example, a teacher might ask students what word is formed when the /g/ in *bug* is changed to /n/. The correct response would be the word *bun*. As demonstrated in this example, phoneme substitution requires students to subtract from, add to, and substitute sounds within existing words to make new words (Rasinski & Padak, 2000). The ability to substitute phonemes is a highly advanced skill that monolingual English speakers continue to develop through high school (Adams, 1991).

The activity Picture Me a Word, as described in Strategies in Practice 3.7, provides CLD students with a contextual base for engaging in phoneme substitution tasks. As demonstrated in the activity, the act of physically substituting letters and drawing the new word transforms an abstract task into one that is more concrete.

Unless teachers consciously consider and actively support CLD students' comprehension of the words used in phonemic awareness tasks, little or no literacy development will take place. Given the complex nature of phoneme substitution tasks, using initial words that CLD students are familiar with is critical. Words for this type of activity can be selected from almost any text. However, we encourage educators to select texts that are bilingual or culturally relevant, to the extent possible, to provide more meaningful connections for CLD students.

## Instructional Guidelines for Phonemic Awareness

The activities shared for each of the phonemic awareness tasks discussed are but a few examples of the ways educators can contextualize these tasks. The key is to remember that when working with CLD students, there are several critical considerations:

- A CLD student who already demonstrates phonemic awareness skills in his or her native language is more successful at English phonemic awareness tasks when provided with explicit links to the native language. This explicit instruction should identify the phonemic elements that transfer from the native language to English, as well as those elements of English that have no counterparts in the native language. Using words in the student's native language that have cognates in English is highly encouraged.
- Phonemic awareness instruction is most effective when CLD students have a contextual frame of reference to draw from when doing activities. Utilizing culturally relevant words helps to actively involve both the CLD student and the family in identifying and transferring phonemic awareness skills.
- Involving CLD students in physical movement and hands-on activities reinforces comprehension of phonemic awareness tasks and promotes active engagement.
- Phonemic awareness tasks are more meaningful when they incorporate words CLD students have already learned.

## Strategies in Practice 3.7

### Phoneme Substitution Activity

#### Picture Me a Word

**Materials Needed**
- Cutouts of magnifying glasses, with a different letter(s) written on each cutout
- Words with visual cues written on 3" × 5" cards (one per student)

**Directions**
- Have each student select a word card and then write the word on a separate sheet of paper. (Make sure the student knows what the word means.)
- Have students use the magnifying glasses to put letters in front of their words to create new words.
- Once the students have created new words, have them draw pictures to represent their new words. Doing so helps verify that they know what their new words mean.

*Note:* Model this activity several times for students, and then have them work in pairs/small groups before asking CLD students to complete the activity on their own.

- Having CLD students work in small groups fosters language development and increases the transfer of phonemic awareness skills.
- Tasks that contextualize the manipulation of phonemes by using the letters of the alphabet support CLD students' phonemic awareness development.

The final and perhaps most important thing to remember is that CLD students need not master all of the eight phonemic awareness tasks before beginning to read authentic text. Rather, for students who may not have had extensive exposure to print or the opportunity to play with language, the chance to read authentic text bolsters the development and transfer of their phonemic awareness skills to English. As such, a balanced approach of phonemic awareness tasks, direct instruction on sound/symbol relationships, and opportunities to engage with authentic text holds particular promise for CLD students (Burns, 1999; Freeman & Freeman, 2002).

## ■ Conclusion

In this chapter, we focused on cross-language transfer and its role in the development of phonological awareness. *Phonological awareness* provides the catalyst for CLD students' ability to hear, identify, and manipulate the individual letter sounds in words. This ability to dissect the individual letter sounds in words is known as *phonemic awareness*. Phonological and phonemic awareness are central components for learning to read. When educators can build on CLD students' existing native language proficiency to maximize cross-language transfer skills, phonological and phonemic awareness in the second language will be greatly increased.

This chapter also identified eight types of phonemic awareness tasks that are explicitly taught in schools. Instruction in these tasks was rooted in the sociopsycholinguistic view of reading, which challenges conventional wisdom and mandated curricula by arguing that these skills are best taught within the context of reading and analyzing authentic text. We illustrated how each of these tasks can be taught using authentic text and meaningful activities to engage students in rich literacy experiences. Such connections to text are critical, as they provide CLD students with opportunities to make personal connections and apply their learning in meaningful ways.

## ■ key theories and concepts

- cognates
- cross-language transfer
- phoneme addition
- phoneme blending
- phoneme categorization
- phoneme deletion
- phoneme identity
- phoneme isolation

- phoneme segmentation
- phoneme substitution
- phonemic awareness
- phonological awareness
- sociopsycholinguistic view
- word recognition view

## ■ professional conversations on practice

1. Evaluate your current reading program's theoretical approach to phonemic awareness instruction. What are key elements of the program model, and how does it reflect the specific cultural and linguistic needs of your CLD students? If it does not reflect the specific cultural and linguistic needs of your CLD students, what adaptations would you now make, given what you have learned in this chapter?

2. This chapter identified a variety of phonemic awareness tasks that build foundational literacy skills. Discuss how you might incorporate these tasks into daily instruction and what tools you would need to do this successfully.

## ■ questions for review and reflection

1. What is the difference between phonological awareness and phonemic awareness?

2. What is the role of cross-language transfer in the acquisition of English phonological and phonemic awareness skills?

3. CLD students encounter multiple challenges in acquiring the phonemic system of the English language due to the pruning of specific English sounds. What can you do as an educator to support the regeneration of these sounds?

4. How do the word recognition view of reading and the sociopsycholinguistic view of reading define *phonemic awareness instruction*? Which perspective is more beneficial for CLD students? Why?

5. Why is it important to adapt phonemic awareness tasks (which were originally designed for monolingual English speakers) for CLD students? What are the consequences of not adapting these tasks?

**Where the Classroom Comes to Life**

Now go to the Herrera, Perez, and Escamilla MyEducationLab course at www.myeducationlab.com to:

- read and connect with the chapter Objectives;
- use the Study Plan questions to assess your comprehension of the chapter content;
- study chapter content with your Individualized Study Plan;
- engage in multimedia exercises to help you build a deeper and more applied understanding of chapter content.

- What are some of the key historical events that shaped the role of phonics in reading instruction?

- Which language transfer issues might affect CLD students learning phonics?

- What is the difference between how the word recognition view and the sociopsycholinguistic view define and approach phonics instruction?

- What are some of the key strategies that can be used to promote CLD students' acquisition of phonics skills?

# Phonics

## More Than the A, B, Cs of Reading

*I have learned that it is important during phonics instruction to use this
in context as part of reading and writing events, rather than as the traditional phonics program taught in isolation. Phonics instruction for the
CLD student needs to include how it is important to transfer skills from
L1 to L2 and address the stage of second language acquisition of the
CLD student. Knowing some basic facts of the student's native language
can also help with phonics instruction, such as sounds that don't occur
or are pronounced differently in the native language, as well as sentence
structure and word order.*

—An elementary teacher

*Phonics* is based on the idea of a predictable relationship between the sounds
(or *phonemes*) in spoken words and their corresponding letters (or *graphemes*)
in written words (Block & Israel, 2005; Fox, 2000). Students use what they
have learned about phoneme/grapheme correspondences, phonics generalizations, and spelling patterns to decode words when reading and to spell words
when writing (Tompkins, 2004). For CLD students who can read and write in
their native language, the acquisition of English *phonetics*, or sound systems,
may support their acquisition of phonics in English. However, in the case of
sound/symbol correspondences that do not correlate between languages, the
transfer of phonics skills is more complex.

In this chapter, we will examine the challenges associated with phonics instruction for CLD students in several ways. First, we will take a historical look
at the role of phonics in reading instruction. Second, we will discuss the various approaches to phonics instruction. Drawing on this literature base and our
experience with CLD students from multiple language groups, we will then introduce a student-centered approach to phonics instruction that supports and
builds on CLD students' existing phonics skills. These skills include those

learned in the native language and English. Finally, we will provide specific strategies that encourage the use of linguistic investigation as the starting point from which educators can promote the development of phonics skills for CLD students.

## ■ What Comes First: The Letters or the Words?

The role of phonics in reading instruction is one of the most hotly debated topics among educators and researchers. This ongoing debate has sometimes been referred to as "the reading wars" (Rycik & Rycik, 2007). Figure 4.1 presents a

**■ figure 4.1**     History of Phonics and Reading

**The Early Years** (1800s)

- *McGuffey Readers* were introduced in 1836 as a series of five books with graduated difficulty. These readers emphasized teaching decontextualized word families (e.g., *play, pray, bray,* and *gray*), articulation, and correct pronunciation.
- Horace Mann proposed teaching children to learn whole, meaningful words first and for teachers to stop the drill of isolated letter/sound correspondences emphasized in the mid-1800s (Burns, 1999).

**Dick and Jane** (1900s–1940s)

- The *Elson Basic Reader* preprimer first introduced the figures of Dick and Jane. These readers used sight words first and then featured simple stories with highly controlled vocabulary (Burns, 1999).

**The Great Debate** (1950s and 1960s)

- Rudolph Flesch's book *Why Johnny Can't Read* (1955) contended that U.S. students could not read because they were not taught phonics (Rycik & Rycik, 2007).
- The book *Learning to Read: The Great Debate* (Chall, 1967) proposed that a student's ability to recognize letters was a better predictor of success than high intelligence and good oral language but cautioned that phonics instruction should not be done at the expense of other instructional practices that focused more on meaning.

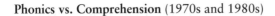

---

**Phonics vs. Comprehension** (1970s and 1980s)

- Research by Johnson and Baumann (1984) found that (1) programs that emphasized phonics resulted in superior word-calling ability but not necessarily comprehension and that (2) students taught in phonics programs placed more emphasis on decoding than meaning.
- Decoding skills were found to be a good predictor of a student's ability to comprehend text, but research studies did not prove that teaching phonics was the reason for students' good comprehension (Rycik & Rycik, 2007).

---

**Whole Language vs. Phonics** (1990s)

- Marilyn Adams's book *Beginning to Read: Thinking and Learning about Print* (1990) was published. This book emphasized the development of decoding and word recognition skills during authentic reading and writing tasks, which supported a whole-language view.
- The National Institute of Child Health and Human Development (NICHHD) supported direct instruction in phonemic awareness and phonics in spite of proponents of whole language, who argued that reading is a natural process (Lyon, 1998).
- The term *balanced literacy* was introduced to describe instruction in terms of a whole-part-whole framework, which balances direct skills instruction with authentic reading and writing (Rycik & Rycik, 2007).

---

timeline that documents the history of phonics and reading and illustrates how the pendulum has swung back and forth over the centuries from a pure phonics approach to a more holistic approach to reading instruction.

In 2000, the National Reading Panel (NRP) defined the role of phonics in reading instruction as follows:

> Phonics instruction is a way of teaching reading that stresses the acquisition of letter–sound correspondences and their use in reading and spelling. The primary focus of phonics instruction is to help beginning readers understand how letters are linked to sounds (phonemes) to form letter–sound correspondences and to help them learn how to apply this knowledge in their reading. (p. 13)

Based on this definition, phonics plays a role in current reading programs. Yet is important to note that the NRP stated that the *purpose* of providing phonics instruction is to teach students how to *apply* this knowledge in their reading. Thus, phonics instruction is clearly defined in terms of authentic usage, precluding approaches and programs that focus on isolated skill and drill (Garan, 2002). In this way, the NRP set the stage for a balanced reading program that uses literature to teach skills such as phonics. This more balanced definition of the role of phonics in instruction brings us to the middle of the pendulum, where phonics instruction is one component of a comprehensive reading program.

## ■ Phonics and Cross-Language Transfer

As noted in Chapter 3, *phonemic awareness* is the ability to hear, identify, and manipulate individual letter sounds within words. Phonemic awareness is considered one of the prerequisites to learning phonics, as students need to be able to identify individual sounds within words before they can link them to letters (Freeman & Freeman, 2007). This ability to transfer phonological knowledge to text is known as the *alphabetic principle*. According to Freeman and Freeman (2004), when children develop the alphabetic principle, they come to understand that there are relationships between the letters of written language and the individual sounds of oral language. Demonstrating how sound matches to print in students' native languages helps them develop the alphabetic principle and provides them with a more meaningful context for learning and practicing these skills (Escamilla, 1993).

One way to support the transfer of phonics between English and Spanish is to use a bilingual English/Spanish alphabet chart. According to Kole (2003, pp. 92–93), the following 19 phonic elements are the same in English and Spanish.

| | | |
|---|---|---|
| /b/ spelled *b* | /d/ spelled *d* | /f/ spelled *f* |
| /g/ spelled *g* in *ga, go, gu* | /g/ spelled *gu* in *gue, gui* | /l/ spelled *l* |
| /s/ spelled *s* and *c* in *ce, ci* | /t/ spelled *t* | /y/ spelled *y* |
| /ch/ spelled *ch* | *l*-blends (*bl, cl, fl, gl, pl*) | /o/ spelled *o* |
| /m/ spelled *m* | /n/ spelled *n* | /p/ spelled *p* |
| /oo/ spelled *u* | dipthong /oi/ spelled *oi, oy* | |

On a bilingual alphabet chart, the phonemes and letters that are the same in English as in the CLD student's native language are written on one side of the chart and can be illustrated on the opposite side of the chart. To help the student solidify the phonetic links between these elements, cognates are used whenever possible.

As discussed in Chapter 3, a *cognate* is a word that is spelled the same (or nearly the same) and has the same meaning in two languages. Some examples of Spanish/English cognates include the following:

*Bb = Bicycle, Bicicleta*

*Cc = Car, Carro*

*Dd = Dinosaur, Dinasuario*

For consonants (*j* and *q*) and vowels (*a, e, i, o, u*) that do not sound the same in both languages, the chart can have two words, one in English and one in Spanish, to identify the distinct sounds each consonant makes. For the letters *h* and *x*, which do not have the same letter sounds or roles in English and Spanish, the teacher can explicitly point out the phonetic differences. According to Herrera (2001), making connections between the phonic elements that are the same in English and Spanish through cognates on a bilingual alphabet chart can accelerate CLD students' learning related to letter identification, phonemic awareness, concepts about print, engagement in reading, and willingness to take risks in writing.

In addition to Spanish, many other languages use the Roman alphabet, including French, German, Haitian Creole, Italian, Latin, Polish, and Portuguese. Within these languages, similar phonetic connections can be made to promote the transfer of phonemic awareness to phonics. A few of these connections are illustrated in the example of an English/Polish alphabet chart in Figure 4.2. As depicted in this example, there are several letters in English that are not used in Polish; as such, these letters have been left blank on the students' English/Polish alphabet chart. Regardless of whether teachers speak the native language(s) of their CLD students, they can support students' phonetic connections by sending a blank bilingual alphabet chart home with students. A template and directions for the bilingual alphabet chart are included in Strategies in Practice 4.1.

For languages that are not based on the Roman alphabet (e.g., Arabic, Chinese, Hebrew, Korean, Japanese), the bilingual alphabet chart can be used to make links between the written representation of a letter sound in the CLD student's native language and the English letter that represents the same sound. Although the script is different in such languages, this link still supports the CLD student's transfer of phonetic skills from the native language to English. In cases where there is no direct link, that letter of the alphabet chart can be left blank.

To complete such a chart, the help of parents or community members can be enlisted. Figure 4.3 (page 75) illustrates how this chart can be completed in a script language, such as Korean. The written representation of the letter sound in Korean script gives students an immediate link to the sound the letter represents

■ **f i g u r e   4 . 2**     Polish Bilingual Alphabet Chart

| The Alphabet (English) Alfabet (Polish) | | Aa Absurd (the absurd) | Bb Brzoza (birch) | Cc Cenzura (censorship) |
|---|---|---|---|---|
| Dd Dentysta (dentist) | Ee Epidemia (epidemic) | Ff Fabryka (factory) | Gg Grupa (the group) | Hh Horyzont (horizon) |
| Ii Idealizm (idealism) | Jj Jowisz (Jupiter) | Kk Kot (cat) | Ll Lampa (lamp) | Mm Makijaz (makeup) |
| Nn Narracja (narrative) | Oo Obsesja (obsession) | Pp Patologia (pathology) | Qq | Rr Renesans (renaissance) |
| Ss Stres (stress) | Tt Trzy (three) | Uu Uniwersytet (university) | Vv | Ww Wakacje (vacation) |
| Xx | Yy | Zz Zebra (zebra) | | |

in English. Below this written representation is the phonetic translation of an English word using Korean sounds.

For CLD students whose native language is based on a logographic system of symbols without individual sound correspondence, such as Chinese (Coelho, 2004), phonics skills may be more difficult to acquire. In Chinese, words comprise characters that represent *morphemes,* or meaningful units that cannot be divided into component parts (García, 2003). Although some Chinese writing is now alphabet based, those aspects of Chinese that are still character based contain deep sound, pattern, and meaning layers that make the isolated transfer of individual letter sounds from the native language to English challenging.

Learning the phonetic system of English also may be difficult for CLD students because there is not a one-to-one correspondence between letters and sounds. There are 26 letters in English but 44 sounds (phonemes), because letters can represent more than one sound (Fox, 2005; Rycik & Rycik, 2007). For instance, the letter *a* sounds different in the following words: *cat, about, cave, draw, car,* and *call* (Rycik & Rycik, 2007). Adding further complication to learning the letter /a/ is the fact that this phoneme can be represented by different graphemes, such as the long

## Strategies in Practice 4.1

### Phoneme Isolation Activity

#### The Bilingual Alphabet Chart

**Materials Needed**
- Bilingual alphabet chart template (one per student)
- Pencils or pens

**Directions**
- Give each student a blank bilingual alphabet chart.
- Have students take the charts home and complete them with their parents (or guardians).
- Instruct students to work with their parents to identify cognates or words in their native languages that start with each of the letters on the chart.
- For students whose native language is not based on the Roman alphabet, have them write the symbol of the letter in the native language that corresponds with the English letter. If the letter does not exist in the native language, have them leave that letter blank.
- When students return their completed charts, have them share the information with the class. During this discussion, take note of the letter/sound correspondences that do and do not exist.
- Encourage students to keep the charts on their desks to use as a resource when engaged in reading or writing activities.

*continued*

| The Alphabet (English) | | Aa | Bb | Cc |
|---|---|---|---|---|
| Dd | Ee | Ff | Gg | Hh |
| Ii | Jj | Kk | Ll | Mm |
| Nn | Oo | Pp | Qq | Rr |
| Ss | Tt | Uu | Vv | Ww |
| Xx | Yy | Zz | | |

**■ figure 4.3** Korean Bilingual Alphabet Chart

| The Alphabet (English) 알파뱉 | Aa (아,애) apple 애플 | Bb (ㅂ) book 북 | Cc (ㅋ) car 칼 |
|---|---|---|---|
| Dd (ㄷ) dog 독 | Ee (애,이) egg 애ㄱ | Ff (ㅍ) fork 포크 | Gg (ㄱ,ㅈ) gag 개ㄱ | Hh (ㅎ) hug 허 |
| Ii (이,아이) ill 일 | Jj (ㅈ) joke 조크 | Kk (ㅋ) kite 카이트 | Ll (ㄹ) lemon 래몬 | Mm (ㅁ) mom 맘 |
| Nn (ㄴ) no 노 | Oo (오,아) oh 오 | Pp (ㅍ) puppy 퍼피 | Qq (ㅋ) quick 퀵 | Rr (ㄹ) room 룸 |
| Ss (ㅅ,ㅆ) sick 씩 | Tt (ㅌ) tick 틱 | Uu (우,어) urban 얼반 | Vv (ㅂ) vote 보트 | Ww (우) wood 우드 |
| Xx | Yy (이) yeast 이이스트 | Zz (ㅈ) zero 재로 | | |

/a/ sound, which may be written as *maid, stay, they, weigh,* or *late.* For CLD students whose native language has a more direct correspondence between letters and sounds, such as Spanish, the lack of letter/sound correspondence in English makes acquiring phonics skills more difficult.

According to Heilman (2002), CLD students face the following challenges in acquiring phonics skills in English:

1. A given letter or letters in English may represent different sounds in different words (e.g., *father, fan*).
2. Some words (homonyms) are pronounced the same yet spelled differently, and each is phonetically "lawful" (e.g., *son, sun*).
3. In hundreds of English words, a letter or letters represent no sound (e.g., *cape, psychology*).
4. A word may have one or more silent letters that differentiate it from another word pronounced exactly the same way (e.g., *knight, night*).
5. Long vowel sounds in English words may be represented by multiple letter combinations (e.g., *hope, throat, dough*).

One of the primary ways educators can support CLD students in acquiring the various phonics skills they need to read in English is to identify the linguistic knowledge in the native language that can be transferred to English. Educators can do this by engaging in Language Investigations, which involve learning about the sound system, orthography, and grammar of their students' native languages. To support teachers' engagement in such investigations, Appendix 4.1 identifies key aspects of the following seven languages: Hindi, Korean, Chinese, Japanese, Spanish, Vietnamese, and Hmong.

## ■ Contextualizing Phonics Instruction

As a teaching method, "phonics is described in terms of the kinds of lessons that teachers present, the sorts of assignments that they give, and sometimes the materials that they use" (Rycik & Rycik, 2007, p. 3). There are numerous approaches to teaching phonics. Some of the major approaches identified in the research (Freeman & Freeman, 2004; Rycik & Rycik, 2007; Stahl, Duffy-Hester, & Stahl, 1998) include these:

- *Synthetic phonics approach:* Students sound out (or segment) individual letter sounds and then blend the sounds to form words.
- *Analytical approach:* Students identify letter and sound correspondences by analyzing known words and breaking them into their component sounds.

- *Analogy-based approach:* Students use word families of known words to support the pronunciation of new words.
- *Spelling approach:* Students write words by segmenting them into phonemes and then writing words from these sounds.
- *Embedded approach:* Students learn letter/sound correspondences in context by reading authentic literature.
- *Onset-rime approach:* Students decode and spell words by dividing them into *onsets* (all the consonants before a vowel in a syllable) and *rimes* (the vowel and the rest of the syllable).

In this text, phonics instruction is contextualized within both the word recognition view of reading and the sociopsycholinguistic view of reading. Just as these two views guide the way educators approach teaching phonemic awareness, they also guide the way educators approach teaching phonics.

Within the word recognition view of reading, Freeman and Freeman (2004) suggest that phonics instruction fits into the following sequence of skills:

1. learning that words are made up of individual sounds (phonemic awareness)
2. learning the names of letters
3. learning the sounds associated with each letter
4. learning the correspondences between sounds and letters (phonics)

The part-to-whole nature of the word recognition view reflects a systematic and explicit approach to phonics instruction. In classrooms where such an approach is taken, students engage in a three-step process: learn the rule, practice the rule, and then take a test to demonstrate mastery of the rule. With this kind of instruction, the overall goal of phonics instruction is to help students understand the intricacies of the alphabetic principle.

However, there are many limitations to this approach to phonics instruction. First, although phonics generalizations attempt to summarize over 200 so-called rules of English that govern how letters, sounds, and syllables are placed together to create meaning (Block & Israel, 2005; Cunningham, 2005), these rules are of limited usefulness because of the numerous exceptions to them (Freeman & Freeman, 2007; Heilman, 2002). From a linguistic perspective, there are simply too many phonics rules and too many exceptions to make teaching them beneficial to students (Freeman & Freeman, 2007). For example, consider the rule "When two vowels go walking, the first one does the talking." It works less than half the time, so it is not particularly useful to know (Freeman & Freeman, 2007). In addition, research has found that readers need to see the whole word to decide how to pronounce the individual letters within it (Freeman & Freeman, 2004). Moreover, eye movement research has found that readers fixate on 60 percent to 80 percent of words in a text, not on every word (Paulson & Freeman, 2003).

In contrast to the word recognition view, the sociopsycholinguistic view proposes that readers acquire knowledge of *graphophonics* as they read. Graphophonics knowledge includes "subconscious knowledge of phonology, orthography, and the relationship between phonology and orthography" (Freeman & Freeman, 2004, p. 139). Rather than focus on rules and generalizations about sound/letter correspondences, the whole-to-part nature of the sociopsycholinguistic view of reading emphasizes immersing students in reading to support their development of phonics skills. Table 4.1 highlights the key differences between phonics and graphophonics.

As illustrated in Table 4.1, graphophonic knowledge is one of three cueing systems that help a reader construct meaning as he or she reads. The other two systems are the semantic cueing system and the syntactic cueing system.

The *semantic cueing system* involves the reader using his or her background knowledge and other context clues in the sentence to understand the meaning of a word (Rycik & Rycik, 2007). For example, to understand the meaning of the word *ball* in the following sentences, the reader must use context clues:

We had a *ball* at the game.
The baseball player hit the *ball* out of the park.

The *syntactic cueing system* reflects the *grammar* of the language, or the patterns or rules about the ways words can and cannot be put together in a sentence.

■ **t a b l e   4 . 1**    Phonics and Graphophonics

| Phonics | Graphophonics |
|---|---|
| *Conscious:* learned as a result of direct, systematic, explicit teaching. | *Subconscious:* acquired in the process of reading. |
| The primary source of information used in decoding. | One of three sources of information used in constructing meaning. |
| A prerequisite for reading that develops through practice with decodable texts. | A result of reading that develops through engagement with texts that have characteristics that support reading. |
| Can be tested independently of meaningful reading. | Can be assessed only in the context of meaningful reading. |

*Source:* Reprinted with permission from *Essential Linguistics: What You Need to Know to Teach Reading, ESL, Spelling, Phonics, and Grammar* by David E. Freeman and Yvonne S. Freeman, p. 139. Copyright © 2004 by David E. Freeman and Yvonne S. Freeman. Published by Heinemann, Portsmouth, NH. All rights reserved.

For speakers of other languages, the English syntactic cueing system might be very different from the system that reflects the grammatical rules of their native language. For example, in Spanish the noun precedes the adjective, as demonstrated in the sentence *La casa roja* (*The house red*).

Knowing that these syntactical differences occur across languages has important implications for how CLD students use their own syntactic cueing systems to support reading. Goodman (1982) found that some readers overuse graphophonic cues by trying to sound out every word. Therefore, it is important for educators to support students' use of all three cueing systems. Within the sociopsycholinguistic view, context is provided as CLD students engage in reading authentic text. Numerous studies support this emphasis and indicate that such context aids the reader in developing comprehension in addition to phonics skills (Burns, 1999; Dahl, Scharer, Lawson, & Grogan, 2001; Fox, 2005).

Strategies in Practice 4.2 provides a sample lesson plan that illustrates how teachers can engage CLD students in the use of all three cueing systems. Within this sample lesson, particular emphasis is placed on using contextually rich literature that reflects diverse culture and language backgrounds.

## ■ Writing Your Own Script: Creating an Integrated Approach to Phonics Instruction

Decontextualized skills taught in isolation, as prescribed by most phonics programs, do not transfer to authentic literacy activities (Freeman & Freeman, 2004; Garan, 2002; Meyer, 2002; Rycik & Rycik, 2007). Often, phonics skills are taught as a separate component within the reading block. In such programs, the materials used during phonics lessons do not necessarily reflect the content of the rest of the reading lesson. Strategies in Practice 4.3 (page 82) provides a sample of such a phonics-based activity. Although pictures are included, there is no scaffolding of the vocabulary beyond that. Moreover, for picture cues to be effective, CLD students need to know what they represent and how the words are pronounced.

Additional concerns with using scripted phonics programs when working with CLD students include the following:

- Commercial phonics programs are so structured that they do not account for individual student needs and language differences.
- Many phonics programs are delivered in a fixed sequence of lessons scheduled from the beginning of the year to the end of the year, which means that a student who comes in midyear will have missed half the content.
- Scripted programs often are so structured that they allow for little variety of voice (from the teacher or student), which can be unmotivating.

## Strategies in Practice 4.2

### Sociopsycholinguistic Lesson

#### Lesson with *Zinnia: How the Corn Was Saved*

**Materials Needed**
- *Zinnia: How the Corn Was Saved*, by Patricia Hruby Powell (2003)
- Pencils or pens

**Directions**
- If possible, copy the text from the first page of the story onto an overhead so it can be displayed (or display it using an alternative media source).
- Because this is a bilingual text, begin a discussion of phonics by asking students what they notice about the text written in Navajo. To guide this discussion, ask students the following types of questions:
  - What letters do you see?
  - In what ways does the Navajo writing look similar to the English writing?
  - In what ways does the Navajo writing look different than the English writing?
  - How do you think the words are read in Navajo? (If possible, ask a Navajo speaker to read the text to the students in Navajo so they can listen for similarities in the sounds/letters.)
- Turn students' attention to the English text. Read the passage on the first page aloud as a whole group:

  *The Diné, the Navajo people, were troubled. When the women planted corn, cutworms devoured the young stalks. When they planted beans, locusts ate the sprouts. When they planted squash and melons, caterpillars destroyed the vines.*

  *The women took corn and beans from their food jars. Again they planted, but the rain washed away the seedlings. They planted squash and melon in the sandy desert soil, but no rain fell and the sun robbed the vines of moisture. Vines crumbled like dry twigs.*

  *Again the women took seed from their food supply. They planted a third time. No rains came. The Diné prayed for rain, but no rain came. The crops perished in the drought.* (Powell, 2003, p. 1)

- After reading the passage together and noting where students struggled to read specific words, go back to these words and discuss them as a whole group:
  - Talk to students about what made each word hard to read.
  - Ask students to share *graphophonic cues* they could apply to each word to help them read it. For example, the word *devoured* might be difficult for some students to read. Ask students how they might break this word apart to read it (e.g., *de-vo-ur-ed*).
  - Talk about other strategies students might try as well. In this discussion, try to guide students to look at the *semantic cues* to help them figure out the meaning

of each word. For example, you might talk about what *cutworms* are and what they might have done to the corn.
- You can also have students look at the grammatical structures used within the sentences. For example, in the first paragraph, most of the sentences are structured to reflect an *action* (the women planted _____) and a *reaction* (_____ ate the sprouts). By exploring such *syntactic cues,* students can gain insight into the meaning of the words from the structure of the sentences.

- Scripted phonics programs take a one-size-fits-all approach that marginalizes students' cultural backgrounds by excluding them from the lesson.
- The use of commercial phonics programs can have a negative impact on students' comprehension and spelling (Garan, 2002).

Another drawback to commercial phonics programs is the emphasis on decodable books. *Decodable books* follow specific patterns and provide students with opportunities to practice specific letter/sound correspondences. These books reflect a word recognition view of phonics instruction that is based on providing students with structured reading practice that emphasizes specific phonics rules (Freeman & Freeman, 2007). The following story, titled "Cat and His Pals," is an example of a decodable text written by Bonnie Jill Lee (2001, pp. 61–68):

Three bees got in a cab.
Three bees wish to see Cat.
Three bees will give Cat a gift.
Duck and Pig see the three bees.
Three bees dash on Cat's path.
Cat sees his pals and is glad.
Cat and his pals sit and sip!

As illustrated by this example, decodable texts are decontextualized because the content is contrived and the sentence patterns are not very natural. For CLD students, reading stories such as this can provide them with targeted practice on phonics skills, but doing so may not help them make any real connections to the text.

Phonics instruction frequently is less effective when it is treated as an isolated component of a reading program that targets the development of individual phonics skills. CLD students need an integrated approach to phonics instruction that specifically builds on their existing background knowledge and expedites the process of learning to read and write in English (Vaughn & Linan-Thompson, 2004).

## Strategies in Practice 4.3

### Standard Phonics Program

#### Sample Phonics-Based Activity

**Materials Needed**
- The *It* word family handout (one per student)
- Pencils (one per student)

**Directions**
- Give each student a handout.
- Have students fill in the blanks to create words that match the picture cues.
- Score the worksheets and return them to the students.

---

Name: _____

Use the letters to fill in the blanks for the **it** word family.

| | | |
|---|---|---|
| | _____ it | **s** |
| | _____ it | **h** |
| | _____ it | **p** |
| | _____ it | **k** |
| | _____ it | **m** |

According to Dahl et al. (2001), six guiding principles can help teachers meaningfully integrate phonics instruction into a balanced literacy program:

1. *Phonics knowledge is developmental.* CLD students develop phonics knowledge from phonological and phonemic awareness skills in the native language. Depending on students' level of native language proficiency, the rate at which they acquire phonics skills in English will vary. The challenge for teachers is to utilize cross-language transfer as a tool for helping CLD students acquire English phonics skills, tapping into what they already know and teaching them the phonics skills they do not know.

2. *Phonics instruction is integrated into beginning reading and writing instruction.* Phonics instruction should not overshadow or supplant reading instruction. Although it was previously thought that CLD students needed to master basic phonics skills before engaging in actual reading tasks, current research demonstrates that reading authentic text can actually help students acquire phonics skills in English (Freeman & Freeman, 2004; García, 2002). By engaging CLD students in rich literacy experiences with authentic text, teachers provide a contextual frame of reference that enhances comprehension and meaningfully connects phonics-based activities to the reading and writing process.

3. *Phonics knowledge is important not for itself but in its application.* When CLD students are taught to use letter/sound knowledge in conjunction with their knowledge of semantics and syntax in actual reading and writing tasks, the *application* of phonics knowledge takes precedence over phonics instruction as an end in itself. According to Dahl et al. (2001), teachers can help students use phonics information to make sense of print and create their own written messages. When phonics instruction helps students communicate in meaningful ways, the instructional focus shifts from individual and isolated skill development to authentic, rich communication.

4. *Strategic knowledge is required to use phonics concepts and skills.* CLD students must have necessary strategic knowledge to apply phonics concepts and skills correctly. Dahl et al. (2001) note that the challenge of strategy instruction is to identify those strategies that explicitly support reading and writing. Students need to understand both the *what* and the *how* of reading and writing. The explicit identification and modeling of these strategies is vital for CLD students. One way to accomplish this is by providing whole-group and small-group practice with strategies before moving to independent application.

5. *Phonics instruction involves teacher decision making.* Given that CLD students use multiple languages and demonstrate varying levels of proficiency in their native languages, it is important to learn as much as possible about the cross-language transfer issues affecting individual students. Regularly assessing the phonics development of each student is crucial for making informed decisions about

which phonics information and strategies are most beneficial. Dahl et al. (2001) recommend that teachers connect phonics instruction to three kinds of knowledge:

1. the concepts that must be learned
2. the ongoing development of phonics skills to ensure each skill is applied in practice
3. the application of phonics skills to authentic text

6. *Peers teach each other phonics as they read and write side by side.* CLD students benefit greatly from phonics instruction that incorporates peer interaction. In particular, when a CLD student is paired with a more proficient peer who can support cross-language transfer through discussions in the native language, the CLD student is better able to internalize and transfer phonics skills from the native language to English.

These principles can serve as a guide for integrating phonics instruction. Throughout this chapter, we have emphasized the importance of such integration because it provides CLD students with the support they need to successfully learn and apply phonics skills in practice. However, for educators who are required to teach a district-mandated phonics program, such integration might not seem possible. Therefore, the subsequent sections in this chapter provide two examples of teachers who have worked within the parameters of their mandated phonics curriculum yet stretched the boundaries to ensure that their CLD students have had meaningful, authentic literacy experiences to support phonics skill development.

## Integrated Phonics in a Second-Grade Classroom

Ms. Wall is a second-grade teacher in an inner-city school district. Her classroom is culturally diverse, and more than half her students are English language learners (ELLs). The dominant language spoken by her ELL students is Spanish, although two of her students speak Korean and one student speaks Vietnamese.

As part of the district-mandated phonics program, Ms. Wall is required to teach students letter sounds using phonics worksheets. Lesson 20 of the phonics program requires students to match /ch/ words with pictures. After looking at the handout, Ms. Wall decides the pictures are very abstract and that a large portion of her students will not know the words they need to know in English to successfully complete this activity.

Still wanting to focus her phonics lesson on the /ch/ sound, Ms. Wall locates a poem entitled "Chocolate" on the Internet. Although the poem is in Spanish and Ms. Wall does not speak Spanish, she decides to use this poem because it is based on a cognate, *chocolate,* and it begins with the /ch/ sound. She also believes incorporating the native language of her Spanish-speaking students will help them see how this letter sound transfers from Spanish to English. Strategies in Practice 4.4 outlines the integrated phonics lesson that Ms. Wall carried out.

## Strategies in Practice 4.4

### Integrated Phonics in a Second-Grade Classroom

#### Chocolate

Materials Needed
- "Chocolate" poem (one copy per student)
- Pencils (one per student)

Directions
- Give each student a copy of the poem.
- Ask students to circle the words they know. (The majority of the students will circle *chocolate*, even if they do not speak Spanish.)
- After asking students what word(s) they have circled, write the word *chocolate* on the board and ask the students to read the word.
- Ask students how they know how to read the word when it is in Spanish. (The students will quickly responded that it looks like the word *chocolate* in English.)
- Asked the Spanish-speaking students how the word should be pronounced in Spanish. (The correct pronunciation is "cho-co-la-te.")
- Repeat the word several times as a class. Then focus students' attention on the /ch/ sound and ask them to identify what sound these two letters make.
- Have students talk with partners to determine if the /ch/ in *chocolate* makes the same sound in English as it does in Spanish.
- Bring the whole group back together to discuss this. The students will agree that the /ch/ makes the same sound in both languages.
- Ask a Spanish-speaking student to read the poem "Chocolate" aloud to the class.
- Have the whole class read the poem aloud in Spanish.
- Point out that the word *chocolate* is broken into syllables in the poem.
- Form student pairs, each having one Spanish and one English speaker. Together, students should practice reading the poem.
- Bring the whole class back together, and teach students actions to go along with the song.
- To end the lesson, have the whole class sing the song with the actions.

*Children in* Mexico *often drink chocolate with breakfast. They stir it with a special utensil called a* molinillo, *which is held between the palms and rotated back and forth. During the chorus of this rhyme, children rub their palms together and pretend to stir the chocolate with a* molinillo. *Children repeat the verse, going faster and faster each time.*

| Chocolate (Spanish) | Chocolate (English) |
|---|---|
| Bate, bate, chocolate, | Stir, stir, chocolate, |
| tu nariz de cacahuate. | your nose is a peanut. |
| Uno, dos, tres, CHO! | One, two, three, CHO! |
| Uno, dos, tres, CO! | One, two, three, CO! |

*continued*

| | |
|---|---|
| Uno, dos, tres, LA! | One, two, three, LA! |
| Uno, dos, tres, TE! | One, two, three, TE! |
| Chocolate, chocolate! | Chocolate, chocolate! |
| Bate, bate, chocolate! | Stir, stir, the chocolate! |
| Bate, bate, bate, bate, | Stir, stir, stir, stir, |
| Bate, bate, CHOCOLATE! | Stir, stir, CHOCOLATE! |

*Source:* This poem was taken from the following website: www.tsl.state.tx.us/ld/projects/ninos/songsrhymes.html. Additional songs, rhymes, finger plays, and games in Spanish and English can be found on this website.

As demonstrated in the lesson overview, Ms. Wall met the requirements of the phonics program by teaching the /ch/ sound. However, rather than present this sound via a phonics worksheet that used isolated and decontextualized words, she was able to actively engage her students in a meaningful, fun, and context-embedded lesson. By specifically pointing out that the word *chocolate* is a cognate, Ms. Wall helped her students make graphophonic connections between Spanish and English. In a reflection on this lesson, Ms. Wall stated:

*Many of our Spanish-speaking students do not have the opportunity to study the written Spanish language. By giving them the opportunity to see Spanish in writing and apply the same strategies to read that they use in English was a real thrill for them. They were able to make a connection between how they would pronounce it in English and how they would say it in Spanish. It also gave my native English speakers a chance to read in a foreign language. My Spanish-speaking students "came alive" during this activity. They had smiles on their faces and they were proud to teach their non-Spanish speaking peers what they could read in their native language. Literature and poems from other cultures is a great vehicle for teaching phonics!*

### Integrated Phonics in a Fourth-Grade Classroom

The role of phonics instruction in grades 3 through 6 is subject to debate. Most reading curricula at these grade levels do not have a separate phonics components; however, many programs include minilessons to review specific phonics skills. An example of a common minilesson is for the teacher to select a sentence from the basal story being read and write the sentence on the board, overhead, or chartpaper. Students are then directed to focus on one or two words in the sentence that illustrate a specific phonics skill. After discussing the phonics skill, the teacher might encourage students to do one of two things: (1) brainstorm a random list of words they know that reflect the same skill and write these on the board, or (2) look for and document other words in the text that illustrate the same skill. Although the text is used as the starting point of phonics instruction in these examples, this type of minilesson does not reflect the developmental nature of phonics.

CLD students in the upper-elementary grades who are just beginning to acquire the English sound system and letters need a much more integrated approach to phonics instruction that provides them with the strategic knowledge they need to apply phonics concepts and skills. To illustrate what this kind of approach might look like in practice, an integrated fourth-grade phonics lesson is outlined in Strategies in Practice 4.5.

As demonstrated in Strategies in Practice 4.5, an integrated lesson offers multiple levels of phonics support. For CLD students who are in upper-elementary grades, this integrated approach to phonics instruction helps them do the following:

- acquire phonics skills subconsciously while reading authentic literature
- draw on graphophonic, semantic, and syntactic cueing systems
- learn specific strategies to support their transfer of phonics knowledge and skills from the native language to English
- interact with peers to both learn and teach

One teacher who implements an integrated approach to phonics instruction in her fifth-grade classroom shared the following:

*In fifth grade, I support phonics development by using authentic text that is relevant to my CLD students' culture. For example, in our reading basal there is a story entitled "Carlos and the Skunks." This story is about a Hispanic boy who learns a valuable lesson. The story has pictures to help convey meaning. While reading this story we used semantic cues and context clues in addition to phonics skills. Stories like this take into account the student's cultural background, show I value the student's traditions and values, and allow the student to make connections to his prior experiences. There were a few words written in Spanish throughout the story that also helped promote the transfer of knowledge and phonics skills from the first to the second language.*

Phonics instruction in the upper-elementary grades is highly dependent on the teacher determining where his or her CLD students are in their development of

## Integrated Phonics in a Fourth-Grade Classroom

### Phonics Lesson with *Grandfather's Journey*

#### Materials Needed

- *Grandfather's Journey*, by Allen Say (1993)
- Sheets of paper (two per student pair)
- 3″ × 5″ note cards (one per student pair)
- Chartpaper
- Pencils (one per student pair)

#### Phonics Activities

The activities described in this lesson are tailored to CLD students who speak Spanish as their native language. However, similar activities can be used with students who speak other native languages.

#### Activity 1

- After introducing the text and previewing key vocabulary, read the first five pages of *Grandfather's Journey* aloud to your students (see the passage on p. 90).
- If you have access to the Spanish translation of the story, give your Spanish-speaking students a copy and ask one or more volunteers to read the first five pages of the story aloud in Spanish (see p. 90).
- Tell students that there are many cognates between English and Spanish. Explain that *cognates* are words that sound alike, are spelled alike (or nearly alike), and have the same meaning in both languages.
- Form student pairs, each having a native Spanish speaker and a native English speaker. Ask them to find as many cognates as they can in the first five pages of the story (i.e., *Japan/Japón, European/europea, Pacific Ocean/océano Pacífico, North America/América del Norte, train/tren, deserts/desiertos, rocks/rocas, sculptures/escultras, enormous/enormes, ocean/océano*). Have students record the cognates they find on a T-chart:

| English Word | Spanish Word |
|---|---|
| Japan | Japón |
| European | europea |

- After students have completed their T-charts, have each pair compare their chart with that of another pair to make sure that they have found all the cognates and that all the words they identified are actually cognates.
- Next, have students look at the initial letter of each word in the cognate set. Pointing out that each word starts with the same letter helps CLD students see the connections between how the words are written in each language.

*Note:* This activity taps into the graphophonic cueing system by helping CLD students understand and build from the phonological patterns in their native languages to support their transfer of skills to English.

## Activity 2

- Form student pairs, with each pair having a native Spanish speaker and a native English speaker.
- Give each set of partners a 3″ × 5″ note card on which the same sentence is written in English and Spanish:

  *He wore European clothes for the first time and began his journey on a steamship.*

  *Se puso ropa europea por primera vez y empezó su viaje en un barco de vapor.*

- Have the partners discuss the meaning of the word *journey/viaje*.
- Direct students to make links to their own backgrounds and experiences (i.e., Have they ever moved or immigrated to another country?).
- After sharing, have the partners choose one of their examples and illustrate it. Ask them to write three feelings associated with the experience on the back of their note card.
- Have each pair of students share their example with another pair.
- Bring the whole class back together. Write the word *journey* in the center of a large piece of chartpaper.
- Ask each pair of students to share one feeling they wrote on the back of their card. Write these feelings around the word *journey* on the chartpaper.
- As a group, predict how grandfather might have felt on his journey.

*Note:* This type of discussion promotes development of CLD students' semantic cueing system as students make personal links to their prior and background knowledge.

## Activity 3

- Write the same sentence on the board in English and Spanish, underlining the words as shown:

  *He wore <u>European clothes</u> for the first time and began his journey on a steamship.*

  *Se puso <u>ropa europea</u> por primera vez y empezó su viaje en un barco de vapor.*

- Ask students what they notice about the underlined words in each language. Most students will notice the two words are placed in the opposite order.
- Explain to students that syntactically, both examples are correct. Nouns and adjectives are placed in the opposite order in Spanish and English.
- Challenge students to find additional examples of noun/adjective pairs on the first five pages of *Grandfather's Journey* (see the passage on p. 90) (i.e., *Pacific Ocean/océano Pacífico, North America/América del Norte*). Some students may also pick up on the fact that the following sentence is split differently in English than in Spanish:

  *For three weeks he did not see land.*

  *No vio tierra durante tres semanas.*

*Note:* This activity promotes development of CLD students' syntactic cueing system by emphasizing grammatical differences in the way the two languages are written.

*continued*

**Text Passage from *Grandfather's Journey* (Say, 1993, pp. 4–9)**

*My grandfather was a young man when he left his home in Japan and went to see the world. He wore European clothes for the first time and began his journey on a steamship. The Pacific Ocean astonished him. For three weeks he did not see land. When land finally appeared it was the New World. He explored North America by train and riverboat, and often walked for days on end. Deserts with rocks like enormous sculptures amazed him. The endless farm fields reminded him of the ocean he had crossed.*

*Mi abuelo era muy joven cuando decidió marcharse de su casa en el Japón y recorrer el mundo. Se puso ropa europea por primera vez y empezó su viaje en un barco de vapor. El océano Pacífico lo dejó atónito. No vio tierra durante tres semanas. Y cuando, por fin, apareció la tierra, lo que vio era el Nuevo Mundo. Exploró América del Norte en tren y en barco; muy a menudo caminó durante días y días. Los desiertos con rocas que parecían esculturas enormes lo asombraron. Los campos de cultivo que no parecían tener fin le recordaron el océano que acababa de cruzar.*

phonics knowledge and skills. Using such insights, the teacher can then design integrated phonics lessons that support students' ongoing development and application of phonics skills in meaningful contexts.

## ■ Conclusion

This chapter discussed the historical role of phonics instruction in reading. Over the past 200 years, the emphasis given to phonics instruction has swung from one extreme to the other. At times, phonics has been viewed as the primary means of mastering the process of reading. At other times, phonics has been viewed as one small part of the overall skill set needed to develop reading skills. In this text, we propose an integrated approach to phonics instruction, in which phonics skills are developed by engaging CLD students in rich and authentic literacy experiences.

By focusing the CLD student's attention on how sound matches to print in his or her native language, the educator can help develop the alphabetic principle and provide a more meaningful context for learning. Promoting cross-language transfer among languages based on the Roman alphabet, as well as those that are not, helps CLD students make valuable links between their native languages and the English phonetic system. Given the lack of one-to-one correspondence between English letters and the sounds these letters make, such an emphasis supports CLD students' acquisition of English phonics.

We also emphasized the sociopsycholinguistic view of reading over the word recognition view, as phonics instruction in the sociopsycholinguistic view incorporates three cueing systems to support the learner: the graphophonic, semantic, and syntactic cueing systems. Using authentic literature, educators can build from their prescribed reading programs in a number of ways to provide integrated phonics lessons for CLD students.

## ◼ key theories and concepts

- alphabetic principle
- cognate
- decodable book
- grapheme
- graphophonic cueing system
- phoneme
- phonetics

- phonics
- Roman alphabet
- script language
- semantic cueing system
- sociopsycholinguistic view
- syntactic cueing system
- word recognition view

## ◼ professional conversations on practice

1. Identify your current reading program's approach to phonics instruction. What materials are used in the program? Do these materials reflect the specific cultural and linguistic needs of your CLD student population? If not, what adaptations would you now make, given what you learned in this chapter?

2. When learning phonics, CLD students draw from the phonetic knowledge of their native languages. How might educators facilitate the process of cross-language transfer for CLD students?

## ◼ questions for review and reflection

1. In what ways have the "reading wars" influenced the role of phonics in reading instruction?

2. What are three key issues associated with the cross-language transfer of phonics skills for CLD students?

3. How does the word recognition view of reading approach phonics instruction?

4. How does the sociopsycholinguistic view of reading approach phonics instruction? What

are the benefits of this approach for CLD students?

5. How do CLD students benefit from using three cueing systems (graphophonic, semantic, and syntactic) to learn phonics?

6. What points should teachers keep in mind when implementing integrated phonics instruction with CLD students?

**Where the Classroom Comes to Life**

Now go to the Herrera, Perez, and Escamilla MyEducationLab course at www.myeducationlab.com to:

- read and connect with the chapter Objectives;
- use the Study Plan questions to assess your comprehension of the chapter content;
- study chapter content with your Individualized Study Plan;
- engage in multimedia exercises to help you build a deeper and more applied understanding of chapter content.

## appendix 4.1

# Language Investigations

## HINDI

Hindi is a modern Indo-Aryan language spoken in South Asian countries (India, Pakistan, Nepal) and also in other countries outside Asia (e.g., Mauritius, Trinidad, Fiji, Surinam, Guyana, South Africa). It is ranked among the five most widely spoken languages of the world.

### Sound System and Orthography

Hindi is written in the Devanagari script, which is considered the most scientific writing system among the existing writing systems of the world. The script is phonetic in nature, and there is a fairly regular correspondence between the letters and their pronunciations. Unlike English, Hindi is pronounced as it is written. Therefore, it is easy to learn the characters of the script and the sounds of the language at the same time.

Devanagari is a form of alphabet called an *abugida*, as each consonant has an inherent vowel (*a*), that can be changed with the different vowel signs. Most consonants can be joined to one or two other consonants so that the inherent vowel is suppressed. The resulting form is called a *ligature*. Devanagari is written from left to right. It has no case distinction; in other words, there are no majuscule and minuscule letters. There is a distinction in pronunciation between aspirated and unaspirated consonants and between dental and alveolar (or retroflex) consonants.

### Grammar

Hindi uses a different word order than English. The main differences are that verbs are placed at the end of the sentence (like in German) and that postpositions are used instead of prepositions (like other Indian languages). A *postposition* is like a preposition except that it is written after the noun:

> *English:* Subject, Verb, Adjective, Object
>    Cats eat small mice.
> *Hindi:* Subject, Adjective, Object, Verb
>    Billi Chote Chuhe Khati Hai (*Cats small mice eat.*)
> Note that this is not the Devanagari script. Rather, it is a Hindi translation using
>    the Roman alphabet.

Hindi verbs are inflected with respect to gender of the subject (masculine, feminine), number of the subject (singular, plural), tense (present, past, future), action (perfect,

---

*Source:* The information in this appendix has been compiled from the websites listed on pages 100–101. Used with permission of KLAT/TLC, Kansas State University. From Herrera (2008).

imperfect, continuous), and degree of respect (intimate, familiar, respect). Verbs are referred to in the infinitive noun form which ends in *na:*

> *bolna:* to speak
> *likhna:* to write

Hindi has two genders, masculine (nouns ending in *a*) and feminine (nouns ending in *i*), but there are exceptions. The numbers are distinguished between singular and plural. There are also two cases in Hindi, direct and indirect. The indirect case is used when the noun is followed by a postposition, otherwise the direct case is used.

> Masculine nouns on *-a: larka* = boy
> Singular: *larka* (direct), *larke* (indirect)
> Plural: *larke* (direct), *larkon* (indirect)
> Feminine nouns on *-i: larki* = girl
> Singular: *larki* (direct), *larki* (indirect)
> Plural: *larkiyan* (direct), *larkiyon* (indirect)

## KOREAN

The Korean language is spoken by 49 million people in South Korea and 23 million people in North Korea. In addition, more than 5 million Korean immigrants and their descendants speak Korean; they live primarily in China, Japan, North America, and Russia.

Korean does not belong to the same language family as Chinese and also differs from the Chinese language in structural characteristics. In grammatical structure, Korean is closest to Japanese.

### Sound System and Orthography

Korean has 19 distinct consonants and 10 vowels. The Korean consonants, in alphabetic order as observed in South Korean dictionaries (represented here in Romanization), are *k, g, kk, n, d, b, j, t, tt, l, m, p, pp, s, ss, ng, ch, tch,* and *h.* The vowels are *a, ya, eo, yeo, o, yo, u, yu, eu,* and *i.*

Korean is the only language to have a true alphabet completely native to East Asia. In a true alphabet, each character corresponds to a *phoneme* (a basic sound unit that represents a vowel, a consonant, or a vowel-like consonant called a *glide*). In Japanese, each character corresponds to a syllable; in Chinese, each character corresponds to a word or a *morpheme* (the smallest language unit that carries an independent meaning).

### Grammar

Korean word order is Subject, Object, Verb:

> *English:* Subject, Verb, Adjective, Object
> Cats eat small mice.

*Korean:* Subject, Adjective, Object, Verb

## 고양이들은 작은 쥐들을 먹는다

(*Cats small mice eat.*)

Another example of Korean word order is "I (*Subject*) him (*Object*) see (*Verb*)." Subjects, especially *I* and *you,* are often omitted if they are clear from the context. There are no adjectives but verbs with the meanings of adjectives, which can be used as verbs or like adjectives.

There are no articles, genders, or declensions. Korean has extensive verb conjugations indicating tense and honorific level. There is a plural form, but it is very often omitted. The subjects and objects of Korean sentences are often marked with a postfix that is attached to the end of the noun.

Korean has postpositions instead of prepositions: *hanguk-e,* "Korea in" instead of "in Korea."

## CHINESE

The standardized form of spoken Chinese is Standard Mandarin based on the Beijing dialect. The number of Chinese-speaking people probably exceeds a billion! This makes Chinese the most common language of the world. While written Chinese is universal to the Chinese-speaking community, spoken Chinese features a number of variations and dialects, most of which are not mutually comprehensible.

### Sound System and Orthography

Chinese is written with characters known as *hànzi.* Each character represents a syllable of spoken Chinese and also has a meaning. The characters were originally pictures of people, animals, and other things, but over the centuries, they have become increasingly stylized and no longer resemble the things they represent. Many of the characters are actually compounds of two or more characters.

The fact that characters are associated with both *form* and *meaning* has a very important consequence. Where forms are pronounced the same but have different meanings, different characters are used. This happens in English to some extent, too. For example, *rain, rein,* and *reign* are all pronounced the same but have different meanings—hence, different spellings. This principle is much more strongly entrenched in Chinese. Characters are very useful for distinguishing among the large number of homonyms in Chinese. In representing foreign names, characters are used for their sound value only.

The Chinese writing system is an open-ended one, meaning that there is no upper limit to the number of characters. The largest Chinese dictionaries include about 56,000 characters, but most of them are archaic, obscure, or rare variant forms. Knowledge of about 3,000 characters enables one to read about 99 percent of the characters in Chinese newspapers and magazines. To read Chinese literature, technical writings or classical Chinese, though, one needs to be familiar with about 6,000 characters.

Chinese characters are written with 12 basic strokes. A character may consist of between 1 and 64 strokes. The strokes are always written in the same direction, and there is a set order to write the strokes of each character. In dictionaries, characters are ordered partly by the number of strokes they contain.

There are approximately 1,700 possible syllables in Mandarin, which compares with over 8,000 in English. As a result, there are many homophones—words that sound the same but mean different things. These are distinguished in written Chinese by using different characters for each one.

Chinese is a tonal language, so that the meaning of a word changes according to its tone. There are four tones in Mandarin Chinese: flat, rising, falling then rising, and falling. Other dialects feature up to nine different tones.

### Grammar

All Chinese words have only one grammatical form; there is no grammatical distinction between singular or plural and no declination of verbs according to tense, mood, or aspect.

The distinction between singular or plural is accomplished by sentence structure. Tenses are indicated by adverbs of time (*yesterday, later*) or particles.

The word order (mostly Subject, Verb, Object) remains unchanged:

*English:* Subject, Verb, Adjective, Object
   Cats eat small mice.
*Traditional Mandarin Chinese:* Subject, Verb, Adjective, Object

貓吃小老鼠

(*Cats eat small mice.*)

### Japanese

The Japanese language is spoken by the approximately 120 million inhabitants of Japan and by the Japanese living in Hawaii and on the North and South American mainland. It is also spoken as a second language by the Chinese and Korean people who lived under Japanese occupation.

### Sound System and Orthography

Japanese has an open-syllable sound pattern, so that most syllables end in a vowel; a syllable may be composed solely of a vowel. There are five vowels: /a/, /i/, /u/, /e/, and /o/. Vowel length often distinguishes words, as for *door* and also for *ten*. The basic consonants are /k/, /s/, /t/, /n/, /h/, /m/, /y/, /r/, /w/, and the syllabic nasal /N/.

Unlike English, which has stress accent, Japanese has pitch accent, which means that after an accented syllable, the pitch falls. The word for *chopsticks, hashi,* has the accent on the first syllable, so its pitch contour is *ha shi*. Without the accent on the first syllable, *hashi* may mean "bridge" or "edge." *Bridge* has accent on the second syllable, which can be seen if a grammatical particle such as the subject marker *ga* is attached to the word: *hashi ga. Edge* has no accent, so it would be pronounced without any fall in the pitch, even with a grammatical marker such as *ga*.

Japanese is traditionally written vertically, with the lines starting from the right side of the page. While this way of writing is still predominant, there is another way that is identical to English in starting from the top left-hand side, with each line written horizontally.

Japanese is written using two systems of orthography, Chinese characters and syllabaries. Chinese characters, or *kanji*, were brought in from China starting about 1,500 years ago. The Chinese character system is by far the most difficult because of the sheer number of characters and the complexity both in writing and reading each character. Each character is associated with a meaning. The second system of writing is syllabaries, or *kana*, which was developed by the Japanese from certain Chinese characters about 1,000 years ago. There are two types of syllabaries with the same sounds, *hiragana* and *katakana*.

### Grammar

The rule of thumb in Japanese is that in a sentence, the verb comes at the end. This is no accident. The core element in a sentence is the verb, because the verb expresses the action or event involving the referents of the other words. Such a core is often referred to as the *head* of a sentence or a clause, and Japanese always places the head at the end of its clause.

In Japanese, the sentence structure is Subject, Adjective, Object, Verb:

> *English:* Subject, Verb, Adjective, Object
>    Cats eat small mice.
> *Japanese:* Subject, Adjective, Object, Verb
>    猫は小さいネズミを食べる。
>    (*Cats small mice eat.*)

The Japanese verb does not indicate number or gender. The same form for the verb is used with singular and plural subjects, and no gender distinction is made. The verb inflects for tense, negation, aspect, and mood. In Japanese, despite the lack of number and gender inflection on the verb, it is possible to leave out not only the subject but also any other element in the sentence except the verb, so long as it is understood in the sentence.

### SPANISH

Spanish is the most widely spoken of all the Romance languages, in terms of number of speakers and number of countries that claim it as the official language. Approximately 275 million people in 19 countries, from Spain to Costa Rica, speak Spanish. The Spanish language is also spoken in the Balearic and Canary Islands, in many communities in the United States, and in parts of the west coast of Africa.

### Sound System and Orthography

Spanish is pronounced phonetically. However, Spanish pronunciation varies from country to country. This difference is especially prominent in the pronunciation of *z, s, c, ll,* and *y.* The Spanish pronunciations of certain letters can be difficult for those learning to speak Spanish. The most notable sound that is difficult for English speakers learning

Spanish is *rr,* which is trilled. The letters *b* and *v* are indistinguishable. The letter *h* is silent. The *ñ* is considered a letter in its own right, and so it appears in dictionaries after *n.* For example, in a Spanish dictionary, *piñata* comes after *pinza.*

Spanish is written using the Latin alphabet, along with a few special characters: the vowels with an acute accent (*á, é, í, ó, ú*), the vowel *u* with diaeresis (*ü*), and *ñ.* The letters *k* and *w* appear mostly in loan words, such as *karate, kilo,* and *Walkman.*

Spanish orthography is such that every speaker can guess the pronunciation (adapted for accent) from the written form. These rules are similar to but not the same as those of other peninsular languages, such as Portuguese, Catalan, and Galician.

### Grammar

The example below illustrates the difference in word order between Spanish and English:

> *English:* Subject, Verb, Adjective, Object
> Cats eat small mice.
> *Spanish:* Subject, Verb, Object, Adjective
> Los gatos comen ratones pequeños.
> (*Cats eat mice small.*)

While an English speaker learning Spanish may recognize some Spanish words, there are several things that can trick an English speaker trying to learn Spanish grammar. For example, unlike English words, Spanish nouns, adjectives, pronouns, and articles all have gender assigned to them. For instance, *casa* (*house*) is feminine and *libro* (*book*) is masculine; *bonita* (*pretty*) is feminine and *bonito* (*pretty*) is masculine. This concept can be difficult to get used to because it simply does not exist in English.

In the Spanish language, there are two verbs for *to be, ser* and *estar. Ser* is used for things that are permanent, such as identifying oneself or others and describing occupations. *Estar* is used to describe more temporary things and to indicate location. For example, *Elena es actriz* (*Elena is an actress*) and *¿Dónde está Elena?* (*Where is Elena?*) use *ser* and *estar,* respectively.

### VIETNAMESE

Vietnamese is an Austro-Asiatic language spoken by about 82 million people, mainly in Vietnam. There are also Vietnamese speakers in the United States, China, Cambodia, France, Australia, Laos, Canada, and a number of other countries. Vietnamese has been the official language of Vietnam since the country gained independence from France in 1954.

### Sound System and Orthography

Vietnamese is a vowel-rich language, with 10 simple vowels (monophthongs) plus a variety of simple vowel + /j/ or /w/ combinations (diphthongs and triphthongs). There is a good deal of dialectal variation in the vowel system. The correspondence between pronunciation and writing is quite complicated as far as vowels are concerned. The same letter can represent either of two different monophthongs or both a monophthong and a diphthong, or different letters can represent the same monophthong.

Vietnamese is a tonal language. In other words, the meanings of words are affected by the tone with which vowels are pronounced. Vietnamese tones are quite complex because vowels can be pronounced with variations in pitch, length, contour, intensity, and degree of vocal cord constriction. There are six tones in Vietnamese. Their pronunciations vary from dialect to dialect.

Modern Vietnamese is written with the Latin alphabet, known as *quoc ngu* (quốc ngữ) in Vietnamese. Quoc ngu consists of 29 letters:

- The 26 letters of the English alphabet minus *f, j, w,* and *z.*
- Seven modified letters using diacritics: đ, ă, â, ê, ô, ơ, and ư. These modified letters are all considered separate letters of the alphabet.

In addition, diacritics are used to indicate the tones of Vietnamese. Tone markings are a (no mark), à, á, ả, ã, and ạ. When letters are combined with tone markings, some complex diacritics can result, such as ắ, ở, ẫ, and ệ.

### Grammar

Here is an example of the Vietnamese word order:

*English:* Subject, Verb, Adjective, Object
   Cats eat small mice.
*Vietnamese:* Subject, Verb, Adjective, Object
   *Cats eat small mice.*

Like other languages of the Austro-Asiatic family, Vietnamese is an analytic language; it does not use prefixes and suffixes to express grammatical relations. Instead, it uses syntactic constructions to express what Indo-European languages express through prefixes and suffixes.

Vietnamese nouns are not marked for number, gender, or case. However, they make extensive use of classifiers, which are as common as articles are in English. *Classifiers* indicate what class a noun belongs to (e.g., animate objects, inanimate objects, books, sharp objects, buildings, flat objects).

Verbs are not marked for person, number, or tense. *Reduplication,* or repeating a word or a portion of a word, is a regular part of the language. It usually denotes intensity. Names of birds, insects, and plants are also often reduplicated.

### HMONG

Hmong is a Hmongic language belonging to the Hmong-Mien language family, a group consisting predominantly of minority languages spoken in southern China and Southeast Asia. For many centuries, the Hmong language was strictly an oral type of communication. There was no alphabet system, no written texts, and no cultural activation to need a literacy system. Cultural aspects and learning were passed on to the next generation from memory. Elders were the individuals who had the most knowledge and memories about the skills and abilities necessary for everyday living.

**Sound System and Orthography**

The Hmong language is complex and tonal, even though words in Hmong are generally monosyllabic. The last consonant in a word will determine the tone on which the preceding vowel is produced. This ending tone also often determines the meaning of the word.

Hmong words have some unique characteristics. Each word is a single syllable, featured by an initial consonant (or cluster), a vowel, and a tone. If a word is said at a higher pitch, it has a different meaning than if it is said at a lower pitch. Tones are as important as consonants and vowels. Each syllable has a basic tone. This is symbolized by one of several consonant letters written at the close of the syllable. Since no syllable requires a consonant symbol to represent a spoken consonant in final position, this lends no confusion.

The Hmong did not have a written language until missionaries in Laos introduced the Romanized Popular Alphabet (RPA) in 1953. In current practice, at least four writing systems are used to write Hmong. The principal and most widely used Hmong orthography is the RPA, which exclusively employs the symbols of the Roman alphabet and makes use of a small inventory of notational innovations. The consonant characters employed are largely influenced by the Vietnamese writing system. With the exception of the midtone, which is unmarked in the orthography, the six remaining surface tones in Hmong are represented by means of distinct letters written at the end of each syllable. For example, high tones are indicated by placing the letter *b* at the end of the syllable (e.g., [í] is written *ib*). The remaining three Hmong orthographies are Phahawh, the Pollard Script, and Chinese Romanized Hmong.

**Grammar**

In Hmong, words do not have any inflected forms, such as those used in English to indicate the plural and possessive forms of nouns (e.g., *boys, boy's*), the different genders and cases of pronouns (e.g., *he, his, him*), or the present, past, gerund, and participle of verbs (e.g., *take, takes, took, taking, taken*). Hmong words possess only one form.

Hmong words are made clear by the order of the words and by the combinations in which they are used. Nouns in Hmong are divided into a sizable number of different classes, similar to genders in some European languages, but they are based on categories other than sex. In most cases, a Hmong noun is preceded by a classifying word that makes clear its class membership. For example, *tsev* (house) goes with the classifier *lub*, as in *lub tsev*, to make *the house*. Sometimes a Hmong noun has different meanings depending on the classifier used.

A characteristic that Hmong shares with Chinese is its utilization of multiple verbs in sentences. Hmong sentences often use two main verbs in one clause without any connections, such as the English *and*, between them.

**INTERNET RESOURCES**

**Hindi**

www.omniglot.com/writing/hindi.htm
www.nvtc.gov/lotw/months/february/hindi.html

www.lingvozone.com/Hindi
www.hindilanguage.org/hindi/grammar.asp

**Korean**
www.101languages.net/korean/grammar.html
www.omniglot.com/writing/korean.htm
http://thinkzone.wlonk.com/Language/Korean.htm

**Chinese**
www.learn-chinese-language-software.com/overview.htm
www.learn-chinese-language-online.com/chinese-grammar.html

**Japanese**
www.jref.com/language/japanese_grammar.shtml
http://web.mit.edu/jpnet/articles/JapaneseLanguage.html
www.japanese-language.org/japanese/grammar.asp
www.japan-guide.com/e/e621.html

**Spanish**
www.spanishlanguageguide.com
www.enchantedlearning.com/themes/spanish.shtml
http://spanish.about.com/
http://en.wikipedia.org/wiki/Spanish_language
www.learn-spanish-language-software.com/overview.htm

**Vietnamese**
www.omniglot.com/writing/vietnamese.htm
http://en.wikipedia.org/wiki/Vietnamese_language
www.101languages.net/vietnamese/grammar.html

**Hmong**
http://en.wikipedia.org/wiki/Hmong_language
www.ncela.gwu.edu/resabout/culture/7_languages/hmong.html
www.omniglot.com/writing/hmong.htm

———

*Note:* From Herrera (2008), pp. 73–81. Used with permission.

- What are the paths to developing academic vocabulary with CLD students?

- How does the cultural biography of the CLD student impact his or her vocabulary development?

- What are the essential characteristics of effective vocabulary instruction for CLD students?

- What kinds of accommodations are necessary when working with CLD students?

- Why is important to access CLD students' prior and background knowledge before the lesson to support vocabulary development?

- How can interactive practice and application strategies during the lesson increase students' vocabulary retention?

- What is the role of assessment after the lesson?

# Vocabulary Development

## A Framework for Differentiated and Explicit Instruction

> *It is easy to think that since many of the students are limited in their English vocabulary that they will struggle with vocabulary and reading in general. When I first started my teaching career I was under the impression that I would have to start at ground zero and teach them every word in the English language because they were not being taught English at home. Boy, have I come a long way! I know now, many years later, that is not necessarily the case. Many of these children have a huge social and academic vocabulary. My job is to make those words that they already know in Spanish connect to the new English words and hopefully teach them new words along the way. I have learned that observation, trial and error, and explicit vocabulary instruction are essential for ELL students.*
> —An elementary teacher

Vocabulary development is clearly at the forefront of the educational agenda in classrooms across the United States. Research continues to provide limited conclusive information regarding the avenues of instruction that are most effective for students whose first language is not English. Furthermore, many educators struggle with following the program or model they are asked to implement while knowing the implications it may have for CLD students.

As identified through the work the authors of this text have done with teachers across the United States, the following are five central topics of concern to educators in teaching vocabulary across grade levels:

1. selecting appropriate vocabulary to teach CLD students
2. identifying the most appropriate strategies to support vocabulary development
3. knowing when to use the native language during vocabulary development
4. determining appropriate vocabulary assessments based on students' levels of language proficiency
5. navigating instruction within the sociopolitical climate of their current practice

Although many questions surround how vocabulary development can best be promoted with CLD students, little debate exists that effective vocabulary instruction is one of the untapped resources for increasing the motivation, engagement, and learning of these students.

Current research has established the importance of vocabulary development to reading comprehension for all students (Calderon et al., 2005; Davis, 1994; Leu & Kinzer, 2003; Stahl, 1999; Tompkins, 2004; Vaughn & Linan-Thompson, 2004). For CLD students, differentiated and explicit vocabulary instruction is essential. For these students, such instruction supports the motivation and engagement necessary for reading comprehension. This chapter will explore the issues of concern identified by teachers, as well as the complexities associated with vocabulary development and instruction with CLD students noted in current research.

## ■ Implications of Approaches to Vocabulary Development

Across the United States, one can find evidence of five types of vocabulary knowledge being developed during instruction. The International Reading Association (2002) has identified these types as listening vocabulary, speaking vocabulary, reading vocabulary, writing vocabulary, and sight vocabulary. Each has been said to greatly impact a student's ability to read and write. Various approaches have been taken to teach these types of vocabulary skills.

Currently, the three most common approaches to vocabulary instruction are based on three divergent beliefs about vocabulary acquisition. Each approach has its own philosophical and theoretical underpinnings and seeks to provide a framework for effective vocabulary development in classroom practice. The three approaches are (1) reader-based instruction, (2) interactive language learning, and (3) direct instruction. Each of these approaches will be discussed briefly in a following section, as they set the context for the integrated approach taken in this text to support the academic vocabulary development for CLD students in classroom practice.

### Reader-Based Instruction

Reader-based instruction emphasizes word parts (prefixes, roots, and suffixes) and activities that analyze how parts join together to form meaning (Tompkins, 2004). In this approach to instruction, the teacher also shows students how and when to use semantic and syntactic context clues and parts of speech to determine a word's meaning (Block & Israel, 2005). With this knowledge, students can identify the role that a vocabulary word plays in a sentence (e.g., it is a noun, verb, adjective). Teachers implementing this approach often use the dictionary in vocabulary lessons, as it aids in the decoding and structural analysis of new vocabulary (Tompkins, 2004).

For CLD students, this approach is beneficial when explicit links are made between the word parts in English and the word parts in the CLD students' native languages. Consider the following example:

> **Mrs. Brown:** Today, we are going to be talking about the following vocabulary words: *constitution, resolution,* and *liberation.* What do you notice about all these words?
>
> **Student 1:** They all end the same way: with *tion.*
>
> **Mrs. Brown:** You are right; they do all end the same way. This ending is called a *suffix.*
>
> **Student 2:** Mrs. Brown, I know what the first word is in Spanish: *constitución.*
>
> **Mrs. Brown:** That's great! I looked up all these words in Spanish, and I am going to write them under the English words. I want you to tell me what you notice. (Mrs. Brown writes the words *constitución, resolución,* and *liberación* on the board under the corresponding English words. Four of her five native-Spanish-speaking students immediately raise their hands.)
>
> **Student 3:** They all sound the same and they all end in the same four letters: *ción!*
>
> **Mrs. Brown:** Good observation! These Spanish words also have suffixes. The main difference between them is the way they are spelled and the accent mark over the letter *o* in each Spanish word. I wonder what the suffix *ción* means? Let's look at a sentence with the word *constitution* in it and see if we can figure out what this suffix might mean.

In this example, Mrs. Brown made explicit links between the English vocabulary words and their suffixes and the same words and suffixes in her CLD students' native language. When explicit links such as this are not made, this approach may prove less effective for CLD students.

## Interactive Language Learning

Educators who implement an interactive language learning approach "feel that reading consists of both expectations for upcoming word meaning and strong decoding and structural analysis skills, which combine to help students discover and learn word meanings" (Tompkins, 2004, p. 291). Building on the decoding and structural analysis skills identified in reader-based instruction, this approach to vocabulary instruction incorporates the active engagement of students in determining vocabulary meaning before the reading through meaningful discussion and context.

Teachers who use the interactive language learning approach view prior and background knowledge as "equally important as the other knowledge sources that readers use when reading" (Tompkins, 2004, p. 291). Therefore, teachers using this approach tend to spend time incorporating both interactive strategies in context and structural analysis in their vocabulary lessons. Vocabulary is pretaught to students before the lesson to help them anticipate what is to come during the lesson. This preteaching, contextualization, and structural analysis of key vocabulary during reading instruction is highly beneficial for CLD students.

## Direct Instruction

Put Reading First (2001) suggests that direct instruction for vocabulary development "helps students learn difficult words, such as words that represent complex concepts that are not part of the students' everyday experiences" (p. 36). The direct instruction approach to vocabulary development is based on the belief that the most straightforward way to enhance students' academic background knowledge is to provide them with academically enriching vocabulary experiences during classroom instruction.

Marzano (2004) states that the direct instruction approach is particularly useful for students whose home environments do not provide the necessary experiences for success in school. This lack of experience is often directly linked to a limited academic vocabulary. Direct instruction focuses on systematically teaching selected vocabulary and learning strategies that support students' vocabulary learning and retention of academic vocabulary. Research conducted on this type of direct instruction has found that it not only promotes the acquisition of new vocabulary but also increases reading comprehension (Beck, McKeown, & Kucan, 2002; McKeown & Beck, 1988; Snow, Burns, & Griffin, 1998).

Each of the three approaches to vocabulary instruction is rooted in a classroom context where English is the primary vehicle of instruction. With specific accommodations, each approach can be beneficial for CLD students.

In the following section, accommodations that reflect the linguistic and cultural backgrounds of CLD students will be explored. The accommodations reflect recent research that has consistently found that the best way to help CLD students acquire the vocabulary needed for academic success is to actively engage them in rich and authentic experiences with text (Durkin, 2004; Freeman & Freeman, 2000; García, 2003; Jesness, 2004; Searfoss, Readence, & Mallette, 2001; Tompkins, 2004).

## ■ Teaching Vocabulary within a Linguistic and Cultural Context

Marzano (2004) states that interacting dynamics are related to vocabulary acquisition and retention. Among these is the strength of the *memory trace,* or pathway to the information, and its role in learning vocabulary (p. 193).

Of critical importance to vocabulary retention is the learner's need for repeated practice with vocabulary terms. Marzano (2004) has found that a student's ability to remember vocabulary is enhanced when he or she has opportunities to practice and apply the vocabulary in multiple contexts. For CLD students, these opportunities for practice and application can be tied to the specific cultures and languages of their biographies. Teachers promote the development of a strong memory trace when they guide students to reflect and draw on their cultures, languages, and prior experiences. Similarly, Greenwood (2002) states that educators are better able to activate the vocabulary learning process when they connect new words to their students' lived experiences in and out of school.

Brock and Raphael (2005) conclude that teachers who are successful with CLD students consider students' prior experiences in school and in the community, as well as the cultural and ethnic identities they bring to the classroom setting. Understanding the full biography of the CLD student sets the stage for effective vocabulary planning and instruction.

## The Cultural Biography of the CLD Student

When CLD students enter school, they bring with them the rich and culturally based vocabularies they learned in the home through the many and varied life experiences they were exposed to prior to attending school. Although some of these experiences initially may appear to have limited value for academic vocabulary instruction, they often provide the springboard for making connections to new vocabulary in school. The student's cultural and experiential vocabulary can be used as the foundation for teaching the new language, introducing new vocabulary, and accelerating concept development in all academic areas.

Experiential or prior knowledge is culture bound and reflects the personal and linguistic experiences of the CLD student. According to Nagy (1988), it is imperative to vocabulary development that students make connections to their prior knowledge during lessons. The experiential knowledge that each CLD student brings to the classroom is as different as each family and community. When learning new vocabulary, CLD students need to be able make meaningful connections to new vocabulary by first reflecting on prior knowledge (known) and then linking it to new material (unknown). Guiding CLD students to make meaningful connections to both experiential and academic knowledge supports and enhances vocabulary development (Beck et al., 2002; Tompkins, 2004).

Current reading approaches do not provide teachers with explicit strategies for learning about and using CLD students' lived experiences and academic knowledge to add new information to their existing schemas. Texts often identify key vocabulary for instruction that addresses the needs of students in grade-level or content-area classrooms. When CLD students do not understand this target vocabulary, the assumption is frequently made that they do not have the necessary background to be successful in school. However, it is important to remember that all students have vocabulary knowledge; they simply may not have the *academic vocabulary* required in schools (Marzano, 2004). When CLD students are given the explicit support and learning strategies that guide them to associate what they currently are learning with what they previously have experienced or learned, they can successfully acquire and retain academic English vocabulary.

CLD students who enter school without the necessary background knowledge demanded by academic tasks require explicit vocabulary instruction and support that uses their existing prior knowledge (experiences) as a catalyst for acquiring academic vocabulary. Without explicit instruction and support in vocabulary development, CLD students are denied access to and limited in their ability to comprehend text. Teachers should consider questions such as the following to tap into CLD students' existing vocabulary knowledge:

- What prior knowledge does the CLD student have about the topic based on his or her life experiences and cultural background?
- What educational experiences related to this topic has the CLD student had that I can build on?
- How can I use the student's native language to support his or her understanding of the vocabulary term or concept?
- Which strategy will provide preinstructional information I can use to bridge from the known to the unknown?

By strategically selecting strategies that support answering these questions, teachers can maximize students' vocabulary learning and retention. This selection of appropriate strategies is achieved by first understanding the fundamental aspects of a CLD student's biography: the sociocultural dimension, the linguistic dimension, the academic dimension, and the cognitive dimension.

### Sociocultural Dimension

Teachers should reflect on questions like the following when considering the sociocultural dimension of a CLD student:

- Do I make connections in my instruction to what the student brings from his or her home and community experiences?
- Do I provide the student with opportunities for expressing ideas originating from his or her ethnic identity?
- What emotional aspects might I consider given the academic context in which I teach?
- What are the student's attitudes toward the topic or concept being taught?

Asking these types of questions helps educators learn about the knowledge and other assets their CLD students bring to the classroom. By building on these assets, educators can make critical links to support students' vocabulary development.

Equally important is for teachers to consider their own socialization and the impact it may have both on their beliefs about CLD students and the way they approach instruction. As one elementary teacher noted:

> *I grew up in a school system where there were no ESL students let alone a student of a different race. I know that because of never being exposed or having interaction with people from another country, I thought when I heard foreign-born individuals speak that they were less educated because of their funny accent and broken English. I have learned that this is definitely not the case and that just like them, I would struggle to know every vocabulary word and how to say the word. I understand how frustrating it must be to have to come up with the vocabulary necessary to try and communicate and convey their message or thoughts. But there is no reason as to why ESL students can't find meaning in vocabulary words. I have to be aware that concepts and subject matter rarely change or alter from one country to another. For what dissolves in the U.S. as Kool-Aid powder is sure to dissolve in Brazil. I now see the benefits of helping my students make meaningful connections to their own background knowledge that will help their understanding of new vocabulary.*

Honest reflection on personal attitudes, beliefs, and assumptions often illuminates the path educators can take to enhance their instructional practices in ways that promote greater vocabulary development among CLD students.

### Linguistic Dimension

CLD students who are learning English as an additional language arrive in the classroom with varying levels of language proficiency. Understanding the stages of second language acquisition (Krashen & Terrell, 1983) will facilitate educators' identification of key vocabulary that will promote students' comprehension and engagement in academic tasks. Understanding these stages will also help teachers select the most appropriate strategy to use and determine the kind of interactive group that will best support students as they learn new words. Following is a brief review of the five stages of second language acquisition, as well as considerations for planning instruction:

1. *Preproduction.* Students in the preproduction stage may know very few English words and have had limited exposure to the English language. Other students may have had some level of English language development; however, they may not be ready to risk language production in the classroom setting. Classroom instruction

that bathes students in all aspects of language familiarizes them with the new language and conceptual vocabulary. Moreover, non–English speaking students who are in the initial stages of acquiring vocabulary in English will be more motivated to participate if they are partnered with students who are bilingual and speak the same language. Teachers are encouraged to use bilingual students for introducing and elaborating on new conceptual vocabulary.

Vocabulary development with students at this level of proficiency increases when teachers do the following during instruction:

- introduce new vocabulary in context
- provide visual cues that CLD students can use to identify/understand the meaning of the new vocabulary terms
- link key vocabulary terms to cognates in the native language

2. *Early production.* During the early production stage, students begin to produce one-word English responses. Students in this phase continue to benefit from extensive modeling, peer work, and teacher strategies that provide access to the grade-level curriculum. Support systems that allow ample opportunities for talk using the vocabulary of the topic or story are helpful.

As teachers plan instruction, they should consider the following:

- implementing hands-on activities that enable CLD students to talk about, illustrate, and engage in meaningful practice of new vocabulary terms
- using peer discussions (in the native language, if possible) to articulate and define vocabulary terms
- having students act out vocabulary terms while peers try to guess the words

3. *Speech emergence.* Students entering the speech emergence stage begin to use grammar rules from the native language to make sense of the new language. Sentences begin to be part of the language used to respond to questions or during the practice and application phase of the lesson cycle. It is essential for teachers to avoid error correction. Instead, CLD students benefit from teachers "revoicing" their responses and modeling correct English use during instruction.

Students in this phase benefit from strategies during literacy development that guide them to do these things:

- use small-group activities to support their practice of vocabulary terms in meaningful contexts
- define vocabulary terms in their own words and share definitions with peers (with the teacher monitoring the accuracy of definitions)
- write short paragraphs using key vocabulary words

4. *Intermediate fluency.* Students in the intermediate fluency stage begin to mirror language use that approximates that of their native-English-speaking peers. Some level of error will continue to occur, although many of the errors of the

previous stage will have disappeared. During this stage, it is important for teachers to observe for fossilization of grammatical errors. Once identified, these errors can be corrected in the following ways:

- by modeling correct grammar through whole-group activities
- by having students act out plays in a readers' theater format to practice oral language production in meaningful contexts. (See Chapter 7 for a detailed description of readers' theater.)
- by having students work collaboratively to retell a detailed story about critical content-area concepts

*5. Advanced fluency.* During the advanced fluency stage, students have reached a level of oral language use that is similar to that of grade-level peers. Given this, teachers are often deceived into thinking that students will be able to independently navigate the linguistic demands of academic vocabulary in the grade-level classroom. Scripted literacy programs do not consider the multidimensional aspects of vocabulary acquisition and literacy development. To make literacy programs more effective for CLD students in this stage, educators can do these things:

- identify and build on the unique cultural and linguistic backgrounds of CLD students, which may be very different from those of monolingual English-speaking peers
- provide explicit instruction and modeling of academic vocabulary that may be new to CLD students
- offer linguistic support via the native language when possible

Knowledge of each of the stages outlined is important to instructional planning for the advancement of CLD students in area of literacy development. A further essential consideration is the BICS versus CALP distinction made by Cummins (2001). *BICS* (basic interpersonal communication skills) represents the language needed at the most fundamental level of communication. It is the language that is supported by sociocultural knowledge and nonverbal communication and tied to everyday situations and circumstances. On the other hand, *CALP* (cognitive academic language proficiency) refers to the ability to use language and think in more abstract ways about the vocabulary of a lesson. Without deep knowledge related to content-area vocabulary words, CLD students may experience difficulty with decontextualized language during instruction.

Academic vocabulary is best taught within the context of instruction (Wong-Fillmore, 2000). Keeping this language distinction at the forefront when planning instruction helps teachers guide CLD students toward increased academic achievement. Through explicit and extended vocabulary instruction, limited-English speakers can more fully acquire and subsequently transfer vocabulary knowledge.

### Academic Dimension

CLD students bring with them a rich vocabulary in the native language that often goes untapped in classroom practice. Use of the native language is beneficial, as it works from the known words in the native language and supports the acquisition of unknown words in English. When a student is unable to understand a word, making explicit connections to his or her native language and experiences typically helps him or her infer meaning (IRA, 2002). Building on the background knowledge and literacy skills a CLD student brings from his or her native language improves the student's literacy skills and reading comprehension in English (Cummins, 1996, 2000). For example, providing CLD students with links to key vocabulary in the native language supports their transfer of knowledge and subsequent understanding of new vocabulary terms in English.

One way to create these connections is through the use of cognates. As previously discussed in Chapters 3 and 4, *cognates* are words in two different languages that have common origins and mean the same thing. Cognates are spelled the same or nearly the same and sound similar (Fox, 2003). Identifying cognates is particularly beneficial for CLD students learning English. Because words may be thought of as labels for concepts, a student who knows a concept in the first language can more easily acquire the vocabulary word (label) for that concept in a second language (Freeman & Freeman, 2004). By teaching CLD students what cognates are and how to identify them in text, teachers help CLD students make meaningful connections to new vocabulary terms.

Cognates are common among French, German, Italian, Portuguese, Spanish, and English. Although these languages have the most cognates, other languages often share cognates in certain content areas, such as math and science. Table 5.1 shows some common academic cognates in English, Spanish, French, and German.

Fox (2003) found that for CLD students, the ability to recognize a cognate in the native language yields insights into the meaning of that same word in English.

■ **table  5.1**   Sample Academic Cognates in Different Languages

| English | Spanish | French | German |
|---|---|---|---|
| alphabet | el alfabeto | l'alphabet | das Alphabet |
| exam | el examen | l'examen | das Examen |
| globe | el globo | le globe | der Globus |
| medal | la medalla | la médaille | die Medaille |
| microscope | el microscopio | le microscope | das Mikroskop |
| paper | el papel | le papier | das Papier |
| school | la escuela | l'école | die Schule |
| science | ciencia | la science | |
| ruler | la regla | la régle | |

Given the sheer number of cognates that exist between English and Spanish, cognates have been called the "window" to teaching Spanish-speaking students how to read English (Freeman & Freeman, 2004; Rodríguez, 2001). If Spanish-speaking students are taught to focus their attention on cognates, they can make connections to new English vocabulary more readily.

However, not all words that look alike, are spelled the same or nearly the same, and sound similar are cognates. Such exceptions are called *false cognates*. Here are some examples of false cognates, as identified by Spinelli (1998):

| Spanish | English |
|---|---|
| actualmente (currently) | actually (in reality) |
| eventualmente (by chance) | eventually (in the end) |
| lectura (reading) | lecture (presentation) |
| dormitorio (bedroom) | dormitory (college housing) |
| largo (long) | large (big in size) |

By guiding CLD students to distinguish between true cognates and false cognates, teachers give them a tool they can use to supplement their use of context in determining the meanings of academic English words (García, 2003; Jesness, 2004). Strategies in Practice 5.1 supports students in accessing their conceptual knowledge by focusing their attention on identifying cognates in text.

## Cognitive Dimension

*Cognition* is the process that supports students in making sense of instruction. Drawing from the analytic procedures and operations used in both their experiential and academic backgrounds, students employ existing cognitive paths to learn new information. In addition, second language learners need comprehensible input during vocabulary instruction. *Comprehensible input*, which is what the teacher does to support students' understanding of the lesson, is critical to students' acquisition of new vocabulary. Using strategies to ignite cognitive pathways that may already exist with CLD students increases their chances of learning new vocabulary. Such strategies may include the following:

- providing ample scaffolding of instruction while students are acquiring the new vocabulary
- providing ample time for students to complete tasks
- configuring student groups to maximize vocabulary practice
- selecting strategies that lower the *affective filter,* or anxiety level, of students
- selecting strategies that provide students with opportunities for meaningful use of the vocabulary during the lesson

## Strategies in Practice 5.1

### Cognate Activity

#### Flagging for Cognates

**Materials Needed**

- Small sticky notes (enough for all students)
- One page of text written in English and Spanish (one copy per student)
- Paper (one piece per student)
- Pencils (one per student)

**Directions**

- Have students scan the English version of the text.
- Tell them that each time they see an English word that looks like a word they know in their native language, they are to put a sticky note next to it and to write the word they know on the note.
- After reading the English text, have students read the same text in Spanish.
- As they read the text, have them put a sticky note next to the Spanish version of each word they flagged in the English text and write the word in English on the note.
- After they have completed both readings, have students remove the notes and place them according to language on a T-chart:

| English Word | Spanish Word |
|:---:|:---:|
| animals | animales |
| tiger | tigre |
| elephant | elefante |

- Discuss which words are true cognates and which are not.
- Conclude the activity by pointing out to students how many words they already know from their native languages, and encourage them to watch for cognates when reading English texts.

Each of these strategies encourages CLD students to access their existing cognitive skills and processes, which often go untapped when classroom conditions do not promote active engagement in higher-order thinking. Once teachers have considered the sociocultural, linguistic, academic, and cognitive dimensions of their CLD students' biographies, they are ready to select vocabulary that is specific and necessary to the students' understanding of a given topic.

## Designing Instruction Based on the CLD Student Biography

There are multiple approaches to vocabulary development. Teachers may elect to teach the vocabulary selected by the textbook publisher, high-frequency words, or vocabulary words from grade-level word lists that are deemed important. However, it is important to note that publishers and curriculum development specialists have selected this vocabulary with monolingual English-speaking students in mind. These vocabulary words frequently do not reflect the cultural, linguistic, academic, and cognitive dimensions of the CLD student biography. Research findings indicate that the identification and instruction of key vocabulary that builds CLD students' backgrounds will increase vocabulary development (García & Nagy, 1993; Gersten & Baker, 2000; Nagy, García, Durgunoglu, & Hancin-Bhatt, 1993; Rousseau, Tam, & Ramnarain, 1993).

What follows is a brief discussion of the current frameworks for decision making on vocabulary selection and ways to contextualize vocabulary selection within these frameworks using students' biographies.

### *Vocabulary Selection*

The number and type of words a student brings to the classroom is highly dependent on his or her prior and background knowledge. Which words get taught and how these words are connected to the student's past experiences and knowledge has an impact on his or her academic achievement.

Beck, McKeown, and Kucan (2002) have developed a system for selecting vocabulary according to three tiers of vocabulary development. These tiers were designed to support mature, monolingual English-speaking students' development of a robust academic vocabulary. As defined by Beck et al., tier 1 words are those that rarely require instructional attention to their meanings in school. Sample tier 1 words for a meteorology lesson might include *sun, rain, clouds, cold, snow, night, warm,* and *daytime.* When identifying these basic words, teachers of CLD students consider words that are generic enough to cross cultural differences. For example, dogs and cats are animals that CLD students are likely to know from either having these animals as pets or seeing them in the community.

Beck et al. (2002) define tier 2 words as those that are of high frequency for mature language users and found across a variety of domains. According to their research, this is the most important tier. This finding is based on the assumption that readers at this level have the capacity to use more advanced language because they have a solid language base from which to work and transfer understanding. However, unless CLD students are explicitly taught these skills, the capacity Beck et al. are assuming CLD students have is not necessarily in place. Sample tier 2 words for a meteorology lesson include *temperature, front, moisture, gradient,* and *atmosphere.*

Tier 3 words are those whose frequency of use is quite low and often limited to specific domains (Beck et al., 2002). For many teachers, tier 3 words are specific words and terms related to individual content areas. Examples of tier 3 words from a lesson on meteorology might include *barometric, nimbus, isobar, adiabatic,* and *meteorology.* The fact that these words are not seen across multiple content areas makes them tier 3 words. According to Beck et al., these words are so infrequent that they should not be the focus of instruction. By contrast, Calderon et al. (2005) state that the low-frequency words in tier 3, although limited to specific domains (e.g., social studies, math, science), should still be explicitly taught to CLD students. The reason for this is that CLD students need to acquire specific content vocabulary to understand many lessons. Many of the academic terms classified as tier 3 words are cognates.

Beck et al. (2004) note that "beyond the words that play major roles, choices about what specific set of words to teach are quite arbitrary" (p. 20). Yet when working with CLD students, word selection is anything but arbitrary. Unless the linguistic, academic, cognitive, and sociocultural needs of CLD students are considered, vocabulary instruction will not be effective. For example, vocabulary words that are merely new labels for concepts that CLD students already know should be approached differently than words that represent new and potentially difficult concepts (García, 2003). If a vocabulary term is merely a new label for an existing concept, it can be a tier 1 word versus a tier 3 word. On the other hand, words that represent new and potentially difficult concepts become tier 2 or tier 3 words.

Selecting vocabulary should be a thoughtful and systematic process. Teachers should ask the following questions:

- What are the critical tier 3 words that must be taught to all students for understanding of key concepts?
- Are any of these tier 3 words cognates?
- Which tier 2 words are relevant to understanding the story or topic and might be misunderstood given their use in other areas?
- Which tier 1 words are essential and can be taught using words, visuals, or other concrete items?
- Have I considered the prior and background knowledge of my CLD students?

Words provided by textbook publishers provide an excellent place to start when selecting vocabulary words. However, teachers must keep in mind that publishers do not know the students in their classrooms. By selecting words that matter, given the biographies of CLD students in the classroom, educators improve the chance that they will provide these students with anchors to help motivate them as learners and increase their vocabulary retention.

### Before-the-Lesson Strategies

Before-the-lesson strategies are essential to the success of the rest of the lesson. Research has shown that vocabulary words are learned best when students can make connections with the words by linking them to prior experiences and background knowledge (Marzano, 2004). Without understanding what CLD students bring from the past, teachers will find it difficult to create a path toward new learning.

Engaging CLD students in a discussion of key vocabulary terms in the text before reading is one of the most common ways teachers can tap into what students bring to the topic or story. Although this is a quick strategy to get the conversation started, CLD students may not participate if their linguistic ability or emotional state has not reached a level where they are ready to risk sharing out loud. During this time, valuable information is lost from students who may need the most support in vocabulary development.

Before the lesson, teachers can ensure that all voices are heard by using strategies that ask for 100 percent of the class to participate in sharing what they know about a word or topic. Teachers can then extend this discussion by tapping into the cultural and linguistic experiences that CLD students bring to the classroom. This type of activity is discussed in Strategies in Practice 5.2. Consider how it meets the following criteria:

- taps into students' prior experience and background knowledge
- provides teachers with the preassessment information needed to link to target vocabulary
- allows 100 percent of the class to participate

## Strategies in Practice 5.2

### Linking Language Strategy

**Materials Needed**
- Chartpaper (three or four pieces)
- Pictures that illustrate the concepts being introduced
- Tape
- Different-colored pencils or markers (one per student)

**Directions**
- Before conducting the activity, select three or four pictures that illustrate the key concepts from the lesson. (Use pictures from the Internet, clip art, or magazines, or use the actual textbook pictures.) Tape each picture to the center of a large piece of chartpaper. (If using the textbook, place the textbook in the center of the chartpaper.)
- To begin the activity, give each student a different-colored marker or crayon. (This way, you can track each student's contributions.)
- Place one group of students (three to five students per group) at each piece of chartpaper.

*continued*

- Instruct students to write down on the chartpaper everything they think of or feel when they look at the picture. (Be sure to allow CLD students to write in the native language, if they prefer.)
- Allow only one to two minutes for students to write.
- Then have each group rotate to the next piece of chartpaper.
- Continue until all the groups have been to all the pieces of chartpaper.
- Once all the groups have returned to their original pictures, have them review all the information that was placed on the chartpaper and identify common ideas/vocabulary by circling them.
- Have each group share with the class the circled information from the chart, as well as other information they believe is important.
- As a class, highlight and discuss words that are similar.
- Give special emphasis to words that are part of the key vocabulary from the lesson. Also validate words that link to the overall concept of the lesson.

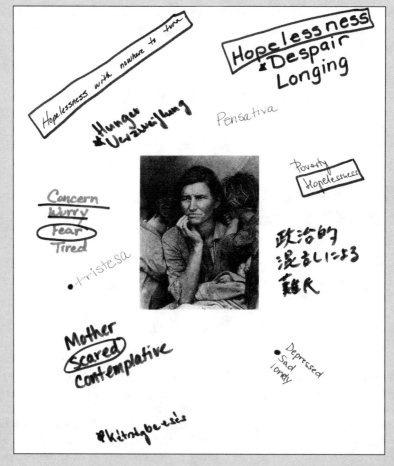

*Source:* Directions from Herrera (2007a), p. 32; illustration from Herrera (2007b); both used with permission of KCAT/TLC, Kansas State University.

The Linking Language strategy (Herrera, 2007a) is a wonderful way to generate student discussion and to identify the knowledge and vocabulary that CLD students already have in relationship to the story. This strategy provides avenues that allow students to demonstrate knowledge using the native language, use linguistic and nonlinguistic representations, and share with peers their links in language.

A Linking Language chart can be posted at the beginning of the lesson. During the lesson, students can be asked to go to the chart and confirm or disconfirm the vocabulary or drawings based on what they are learning. Opportunities for CLD students to share with a group the thoughts they have related to pictures from the text become a powerful tool for their development of both experiential and academic associations. Students begin to negotiate the text from multiple perspectives.

Educators who create opportunities to extend what each student brings and to draw attention to relationships between students' existing knowledge and the target vocabulary of the lesson help to promote vocabulary development by creating sensory connections. The activation of sensory memory (Marzano, 2004) through visuals helps CLD students connect to their background knowledge in meaningful ways. Visual links provide CLD students with visual representations of vocabulary terms or cues them into what vocabulary terms might mean. Visual links can be concrete examples or pictorial. For instance, in a lesson on fossils, students would have actual fossils to look at and touch. If fossils were not available, the teacher could provide pictures of what fossils look like for students to examine.

Additional visual strategies that can be used to support CLD students' sensory connections to vocabulary terms are described in Figure 5.1. Before using any of these strategies, teachers should give specific attention to their CLD students' language proficiency levels, prior knowledge, and academic skills to ensure the strategy will be meaningful to them.

Visual strategies such as those identified in Figure 5.1 best help CLD students understand the relationships between words within a content-area text when explicit connections are made to the students' culture and background knowledge. This level of discussion does not occur naturally. Rather, it takes specific, deliberate coaching and guidance from the teacher. To support deep discussion among CLD students, monolingual English-speaking peers, and the teacher, cultural differences need to be identified, acknowledged, and celebrated.

For example, when discussing the concept of independence, teachers can ask CLD students about events in their culture that celebrate or represent this concept. For instance, in the United States, the Statue of Liberty represents independence. In Mexico, the Angel de Independencia represents independence. In India, the Red Fort represents independence. By helping CLD students to make these sensory connections to visual and concrete symbols of independence from their own cultures, the overall concept of independence gains significance.

■ **f i g u r e   5 . 1**    Visual Strategies for Vocabulary Development

- *Graphic Organizers:* Key vocabulary terms are arranged in a simple chart or diagram to show the relationships among them (Blachowicz & Fisher, 1996; Searfoss, Readence, & Mallette, 2001). This strategy can be adapted for CLD students by placing them in small groups, providing a visual cue, giving ongoing feedback, and using native language support when possible.
- *Word Splash:* A word is written on a piece of paper, and students add all the words they know or think of when they read the word (Burns, 1999) (see the example below). Encouraging CLD students to write in their native language or to draw what they think of when they see or hear the word increases their engagement and success. This activity can also be adapted for CLD students by having more advanced English-speaking peers write the words in English.

- *Webbing:* This is a method of graphically illustrating meaningful associations among words. Creating webs helps students make connections between what they know about words and how words are related (IRA, 2002, p. 119). This strategy can be adapted for CLD students by making specific links to cultural backgrounds, cognates, and prior academic content.

- *Semantic Mapping:* In this strategy, key words are identified and associated words are listed with them. According to Heilman, Blair, and Rupley (1998), the following procedures should be used when creating a semantic map for the vocabulary in a story:

   1. Choose a word from the story, and write it on the chalkboard or a chart.
   2. Brainstorm with students and write related words on the board or chart.
   3. Categorize the words and add the related words essential to the story to the appropriate categories.

Semantic mapping is a wonderful way to generate links between new vocabulary terms and past knowledge. When working with CLD students, the use of semantic maps fosters vocabulary development and connections when the teacher makes explicit links to past lessons and background knowledge. Without these links, CLD students will struggle to make meaning from the list of related words and comprehend how these words help define the vocabulary term. Having elaborated discussions and making explicit links makes this activity meaningful for CLD students.

## Practicing and Applying Academic Vocabulary

Educators often introduce words and then forget about them as they forge ahead with a story or lesson. This approach to vocabulary development is called *fast mapping* and is based on the belief that students can acquire a word's meaning with a single exposure to it. CLD students will not internalize new terms as part of their permanent vocabulary, however, unless the terms are used throughout the lesson and in a variety of ways. Thus, the need for multiple exposures to new vocabulary words is critical in developing CLD students' vocabulary knowledge.

*Extended mapping* of vocabulary terms promotes vocabulary development by giving CLD students repeated opportunities to work with words. To promote repeated practice with a vocabulary term, the term should become part of a word-rich environment. A *word-rich environment*, as defined by Blachowicz and Fisher (1996), is one in which students are immersed in words for incidental and intentional learning and the development of word awareness. This means that the term is not only one that CLD students see in text but also one that becomes part of the daily environmental print that they experience.

As CLD students begin to process a new vocabulary term, they reach greater understanding by making links between the vocabulary term and their culture. To help students reach this depth of processing, teachers can emphasize explicit cultural connections. To guide students in reaching an academic depth of processing, teachers can highlight links between students' past learning and the new word. By making links to vocabulary knowledge at both of these levels, CLD students are able to share their connections in greater detail.

Elaboration of vocabulary knowledge can also be targeted during the practice and application phase of working with academic vocabulary. To support CLD students' elaboration of vocabulary knowledge, Marzano (2004) suggests that a variety of associations need to be made. Associations can be made in any number of ways. For example, the teacher can elaborate on the vocabulary term *feline* by relating the word to a tier 1 word such as *cat*. After discussing visuals and the word *cat*, the teacher might share examples of multiple types of cats (e.g., household pet, tiger, lion). From these examples, the teacher would reintroduce the term *feline*. Thus, the teacher has elaborated on students' vocabulary knowledge by making new or varied connections (Bradshaw & Anderson, 1982). Teachers' control over the elaboration of vocabulary is then gradually released to students, who make links of their own as they interact with the text.

When CLD students use their prior and background knowledge to personally define vocabulary and then use their definitions to locate or generate answers to questions related to the text, they move to a new level of reading comprehension. Guiding CLD students to access and build on their existing knowledge has been proven effective in increasing their level of reading comprehension (Anderson, 1999; Cummins, 1991a, 1996; Freeman & Freeman, 1998). Vocabulary strategies that support CLD students in extended mapping activities that enhance vocabulary comprehension and the development of student-generated definitions can range from simple to complex.

Examples of such vocabulary strategies are included in Strategies in Practice 5.3. The common underlying element in vocabulary cueing strategies is that they actively engage CLD students in constructing a deeper definition of the vocabulary term by making meaningful links to their existing knowledge. By allowing CLD students to be in charge of selecting the vocabulary terms they want to write down, as well as the language they use to write these terms, teachers encourage students to take ownership of their vocabulary learning. Research has found that developing learners who are active, who personalize their learning, who look for multiple sources of information to build meaning, and who make connections to background knowledge understand critical concepts and vocabulary at a deeper level (Blachowicz & Fisher, 1996).

### *Creating Interactive Learning Environments*

According to Harris and Hodges (1995), vocabulary development is the growth of a person's knowledge of word meanings and is built on existing meanings. When CLD students are placed in interactive learning situations (i.e., student/teacher and student/student), they are encouraged to share and elaborate on their existing experiential and academic vocabulary knowledge to support development of deeper understanding about new vocabulary terms. Through this sharing of knowledge,

## Strategies in Practice 5.3

### Vocabulary Cueing Strategies

#### Bilingual Picture Dictionaries

Bilingual picture dictionaries help non- or limited-English-speaking students to acquire key vocabulary through the use of student-generated picture cues and written words. To promote the transfer of vocabulary from the first language to the second language, bilingual picture dictionaries document the word in both languages.

**Materials Needed**
- Colored paper (at least one sheet per student)
- Markers or pencils
- Hole punch (optional)
- Brads or yarn (optional)

**Directions**
- Give each student a colored sheet of paper or construction paper that is folded in half.
- Have students write any of the following headings at the top of the paper: Picture Dictionary, My Picture Dictionary, or the native language translation of one of these titles.
- Have students copy the word from the board or a text that has the word in it and then draw a picture that represents the word. If you have bilingual support, provide help to the CLD student in writing the word in his or her native language, or send the project home so that the parents can help the student write the word.

**Kindergarten Samples**

*continued*

- Students can add additional pages by inserting folded sheets of paper and then binding the pages with brads or yarn after using a hole punch.

### Vocabulary Cue Cards

Vocabulary cue cards work well for non- or limited-English-speaking students, as they require providing a pictorial response or simple word/phrase responses.

**Materials Needed**
- 3″ × 5″ note cards (one per student)
- Markers or pencils

**Directions**
- Give each student a card. In the center on the front of the card, have him or her write the key vocabulary word.
- Around the key vocabulary word, have each student write key words/phrases or draw images describing the word.
- On the back of the card, have each student write a sentence from the text in which the key vocabulary word is used.

travels Place to Place            Someone travel

tourist

take picture

**Fifth-Grade Samples**

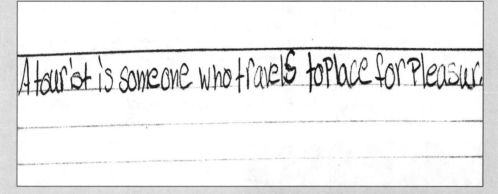

A tourist is someone who travels to place for Pleasur.

## Cultural Vocabulary Logs

A cultural vocabulary log is a student-generated vocabulary log. Each student is given a blank vocabulary log in which he or she can record vocabulary words encountered in the text or during a lesson. What makes cultural vocabulary logs unique is that each CLD student is in charge of selecting the specific vocabulary terms to record in the log. Given the different cultural backgrounds and experiences of CLD students, certain words are going to be more relevant to some students than to others.

## Vocabulary Flip Books

Vocabulary flip books engage students in more cognitively challenging definitions of vocabulary terms by having them identify key descriptors of each vocabulary term in addition to visuals to represent each term. Vocabulary flip books help students verbalize their understanding as they articulate the definitions of content vocabulary. The process, as detailed below, can be adapted based on the needs and language proficiency levels of CLD students.

### Materials Needed

- $8^{1}/_{2}'' \times 11''$ sheets of paper (two per student)
- Stapler
- Scissors
- Markers or pencils

### Directions

- Have each student put two sheets of paper together and fold them in half vertically. Staple them together at the seam to make a book.
- Ask students to fold their books together to form three rectangles and then open their books again. Have each student use scissors to cut along the folds on the first three pages (leaving the last page uncut).

*continued*

- On the front of the book, have each student write down in English and his or her native language (optional) one vocabulary term per section that represents the overarching content topic (e.g., when teaching the branches of government, each student would write the following three vocabulary terms: executive, legislative, and judicial).
- To define the term, have the student open each section and write his or her own definitions or examples on the left-hand tabs.
- Finally, have the student use the right-hand tabs to illustrate the meaning of each of his or her definitions or examples.

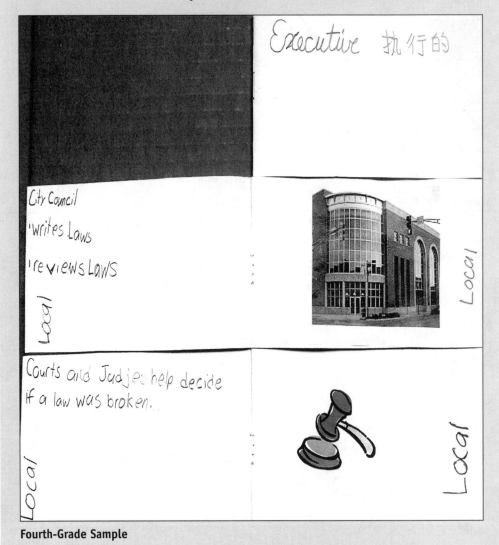

**Fourth-Grade Sample**

CLD students not only make powerful connections to their existing knowledge but also extend that knowledge by drawing from more linguistically capable peers.

Such collaboration and interaction with peers and teachers enables CLD students to reach their *zone of proximal development (ZPD)* regarding academic vocabulary. The ZPD, as defined by Vygotsky (1962, 1978), describes how having the support of another more proficient peer or the teacher allows a student to do more than he or she could do independently. During interactive learning situations, bilingual students also move beyond serving the role of interpreter to become peer mentors. This synergistic sharing of knowledge among students to define key vocabulary terms increases CLD students' academic vocabulary base.

Interactive learning activities provide CLD students with opportunities to stretch and learn vocabulary in meaningful ways. Here are a few suggestions for teachers implementing interactive learning activities:

- Use linguistic and nonlinguistic representations before and during the lesson to access CLD students' prior and background knowledge.
- Pair bilingual students to participate in structured activities designed to introduce or clarify vocabulary terms in a language they both understand.
- Select strategies that allow students to define vocabulary terms with peers in their own words and in the native language, whenever possible.
- Engage CLD students in discussions of words, and encourage them to share personal and cultural experiences that support comprehension of the vocabulary.

Multiple and varied interactive learning activities in the classroom are limited only by the teacher's imagination and situational context.

Interactive learning is an essential component of the strategies used before the lesson to preassess CLD students' knowledge and to introduce targeted academic vocabulary. Likewise, interactive during-the-lesson strategies are implemented that encourage student discussions to clarify vocabulary and make connections to past learning. When planning interactive learning opportunities, teachers should consider all previously mentioned aspects of the CLD student's biography as well as the purpose of the task. Ultimately, the information gathered from student participation leads to more authentic postinstructional assessment of vocabulary learning.

### *Assessing CLD Students' Acquisition of English Academic Vocabulary*

As teachers come to the end of every lesson, chapter, or unit, they should ask questions like these:

- Were students involved in an activity that encouraged them to use their new academic words in meaningful and engaging ways?

- Did students have opportunities to excel toward the end of the lesson using small communities and discussing what was learned?
- Were students allowed to independently work at their level, given their linguistic abilities, or were all students asked to fill in the blanks, write an essay, or write sentences using the words?

In short, teachers who find themselves using the workbook end-of-lesson materials may not be getting the most out of their efforts to assess students' vocabulary development.

Authentic assessment of vocabulary acquisition is tied to the baseline set at the beginning of the lesson: Where was the point of departure for each child? Insights regarding the beginning point for each student assist teachers in determining how far the student has gone in learning new academic vocabulary. Strategies in Practice 5.4 offers a few suggestions for engaging and challenging students and providing avenues for them to use vocabulary after the lesson in ways that both inform teachers about the effectiveness of instruction and demonstrate what they have learned.

## ■ Conclusion

This chapter presented an overview of the traditional approaches to vocabulary instruction and explored considerations specific to vocabulary instruction for CLD students. It emphasized that effective vocabulary instruction for CLD students builds on the sociocultural, linguistic, academic, and cognitive dimensions of the student biography. Designing vocabulary instruction to reflect these dimensions helps promote CLD students' meaningful acquisition of grade-level content vocabulary.

When implementing vocabulary instruction in the classroom, educators are urged to do the following: (1) "frontload" by preassessing students' prior and background knowledge; (2) capitalize on the information gained by accommodating students' needs during the lesson; (3) strategically select vocabulary words that capture the essence of the concepts or material being taught; (4) select and implement strategies to teach both skills and academic vocabulary during all phases of the lesson; (5) use CLD students' biographies to plan for group configurations; and (6) use postinstructional assessment to document multiple levels of linguistic and academic growth for CLD students.

Regardless of the approach or program a school or classroom is currently using, rethinking vocabulary instruction within the context of today's very diverse classrooms will only benefit CLD students. Adhering to an instructional program does not preclude teachers' ability to provide instruction that resonates with the lives of their students.

## Strategies in Practice 5.4

### Structural Vocabulary Indexing

Structural vocabulary indexing is a postreading activity that ties together the main concepts of the lesson and allows the teacher to check for students' deeper understanding. In this book, structural indexing is recommended for use toward the end of a lesson or unit prior to a test or as an assessment.

**Materials Needed**
- 3″ × 5″ note cards (one set per student group or one set for the class)
- Pens or pencils

**Directions**
- Before the activity, select nine words that are tied to the concepts taught. Write the nine words on separate note cards; create one set of cards for each student group or put the words on an overhead for the whole class to see. (Students can also help select the words and create the cards, as desired.)

| | | |
|---|---|---|
| retorted | investigate | alibi |
| sculptor | life-like | muttered |
| strengthening | guilty | straightaway |

- Form students into small groups. Each group should arbitrarily arrange the cards into a grid that resembles a tic-tac-toe game, or a three-word by three-word grid. (Give alternate directions if students are working from an overhead.)
- The task of each group is to come up with three sentences that use three consecutive words (in the manner of playing tic-tac-toe) in each sentence. The connections among words can be made in any direction, but the words cannot be selected out of line.
- Have each group disclose their sentences to the class. As a class, decide if the sentences are accurate or need modification.

*continued*

*guilty   +   life-like   +   investigate*

*The guilty men make a life-like statue to investigate the crime.*

### Tips for Extending Structural Indexing

- *Student writing:* CLD students can also demonstrate their vocabulary knowledge by using vocabulary terms in writing. The process of writing down the vocabulary words fosters their transfer to permanent memory by engaging CLD students in a higher level of interaction. Having to determine how and when to use the vocabulary term in a correct manner also bolsters CLD students' understanding of the word.

- *Student demonstrations:* Among the more powerful ways for CLD students to demonstrate (and for teachers to assess) vocabulary learning are vocabulary games, simulations in which students act out vocabulary terms, and student-generated definitions of vocabulary terms that are read aloud and discussed as a group. The key is to provide CLD students with opportunities to manipulate the vocabulary words in context through reading, discussing, and writing (Burns, 1999). Doing so allows CLD students to take ownership of the vocabulary terms and thus remember them beyond taking a vocabulary test.

## ■ key theories and concepts

- advanced fluency stage
- basic interpersonal communication skills (BICS)
- cognates
- cognitive academic language proficiency (CALP)
- comprehensible input
- direct instruction
- early production stage
- interactive language learning
- intermediate fluency stage
- preproduction stage
- reader-based instruction
- speech emergence stage
- tier 1 words
- tier 2 words
- tier 3 words

# ■ professional conversations on practice

1. Take a look at the way your current reading program approaches vocabulary instruction. Is vocabulary taught in isolation, or does it build on the specific cultural and linguistic backgrounds of your CLD student population? If it does not reflect the specific cultural and linguistic backgrounds of CLD students, what adaptations would you now make, given what you have learned in this chapter?

2. This chapter discussed the importance of teaching vocabulary within a linguistic and cultural context. Discuss how you might approach vocabulary instruction from this perspective by incorporating the sociocultural, linguistic, academic, and cognitive backgrounds of your CLD students.

3. Multiple strategies were introduced in this chapter to teach vocabulary to CLD students. Discuss the one strategy you most connected with and how you might use it in your own instructional practice to support CLD students' vocabulary development.

# ■ questions for review and reflection

1. What are the differences among the following approaches to vocabulary instruction: reader-based instruction, interactive language learning, and direct instruction?

2. Why is it important to consider the cultural biography of the CLD student when teaching vocabulary?

3. How does understanding a CLD student's stage of language proficiency aid the teacher in selecting the most appropriate vocabulary strategy?

4. What are cognates, and how can they be used to support CLD students' acquisition of academic, content-based vocabulary?

5. Why is it so important to preassess CLD students' vocabulary knowledge before the lesson?

6. How might you use the tier 1, tier 2, and tier 3 words, as identified by Beck et al., to support vocabulary instruction with CLD students?

7. How can you revisit key vocabulary during the lesson to support CLD students' acquisition of it and to adapt instruction, if needed?

8. How might you assess students' acquisition of key vocabulary at the end of the lesson to document their linguistic and academic growth?

**PEARSON**
**myeducationlab**
**Where the Classroom Comes to Life**

Now go to the Herrera, Perez, and Escamilla MyEducationLab course at www.myeducationlab.com to:

- read and connect with the chapter Objectives;
- use the Study Plan questions to assess your comprehension of the chapter content;
- study chapter content with your Individualized Study Plan;
- engage in multimedia exercises to help you build a deeper and more applied understanding of chapter content.

- What does it mean to *comprehend* text?

- How can CLD students move beyond decoding text to comprehending text?

- What role does schema play in a CLD student's comprehension of text, and how can teachers support a student's schematic connections to text?

- What role do metacognitive strategies play in reading comprehension?

- What cognitive strategies can CLD students use to maximize reading comprehension?

- How do grouping configurations promote the use of social/affective reading comprehension strategies?

# Strategies-Based Comprehension Instruction

## Linking the Known to the Unknown

*In order to understand the meaning of a text, students must have reading comprehension skills. For native English speakers and CLD students, the strategies are the same but the approach is very different. Many CLD students have developed certain comprehension skills in their native language and need guidance to transfer those to English. By making cultural connections utilizing their individual knowledge and experiences, teaching and modeling reading comprehension strategies, and consistently checking for understanding, I am able to increase the level of comprehension for my CLD students.*

—A high school social studies teacher

When teaching students to read, comprehension is the intended outcome. However, what does it mean to *comprehend* text? For many teachers, the response would be "to understand what was read." Researchers would readily agree with this definition, but they would add that, to understand what was read, the reader must be able to *construct meaning* from text (Harvey & Goudvis, 2000; Hoyt, 2005; Leu & Kinzer, 2003; Zwiers, 2004).

To better understand the process of constructing meaning from text, consider the following passage. As you read, focus on the strategies you are using to comprehend the text:

The multicolored *picadillos* waved happily in the breeze. The rhythmic beat of the *rancheros* vibrated deep in the soul and echoed throughout the yard. The fresh smell of *carne asada* wafted through the air, making mouths water. However, the focal point of all was on the brightly colored *piñata* that was being pulled up and down by Tío Jorge. The *rios* of the adults could be heard by all as the blindfolded *niña* swung once, twice, three times with the bat. With a loud "whack" on the fourth swing, the *piñata* shattered and *dulces* flew in every direction as the children swarmed the area!

Having read the passage, how would you respond to the following questions?

1. What are *picadillos*?
2. What is a *ranchero*?
3. What is *carne asada*?
4. What is a *piñata,* and why is it being hit with a bat?
5. What event is taking place?
6. What clues did you use to help you identify the event?

If you are familiar with Mexican culture, you may have surmised that the event described is a traditional birthday party for a child. The *picadillos* are decorations cut from brightly colored paper and hung from trees or clotheslines. A *ranchero* is a type of Mexican music, and *carne asada* is barbecued meat. If you are not very familiar with the Mexican culture, you may still have been able to respond to question 4, as you may have learned about *piñatas* in past experiences. Even so, you may not have known that the traditional use of the *piñata* is at a birthday party.

What strategies did you use to figure out what you were reading? You likely drew on past experiences and contextual clues to understand the text. For example, you may have used the contextual clue "waving happily in the breeze" to guess that *picadillos* are some sort of decoration. Another contextual clue that may have helped you figure out that *ranchero* is some sort of music is the phrase "rhythmic beat." The sentence about *carne asada* may have provoked a personal memory about a food that smelled good, and this connection may have helped you determine that *carne asada* has something to do with food. In sum, even though you may not have known all the words and details associated with a traditional birthday party for a Mexican child, you were able to draw on your own background knowledge and experiences to construct meaning from this culture-specific text. Although this was a brief example, it illustrates the complexity of constructing meaning from text.

The process of constructing meaning is similar for CLD students. Like you, CLD students draw on their background knowledge and experiences to make meaning from text. However, the critical distinction for these students is that their background knowledge and experiences are largely determined by their sociocultural backgrounds (socioeconomic status and cultural background), which are often very different than those of the students for which the curriculum traditionally has been designed. Additional factors that influence CLD students' reading comprehension include their academic and cognitive skills and their proficiency in both their native language and English. Finally, CLD students' construction of meaning

**■ figure 6.1**    Interactive Nature of Reading Comprehension for CLD Students

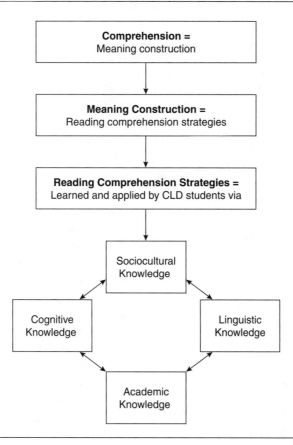

is also linked to their identification and application of reading comprehension strategies. This chapter will explore how these dimensions works together to promote CLD students' reading comprehension, as illustrated in Figure 6.1.

## ■ Comprehension: Constructing Meaning from Text

At the most basic level, a student's proficiency in reading is often measured by his or her ability to decode text. However, research has shown that simply decoding the words on the page does not equal comprehension (La Berge & Samuels, 1974). Rather, the act of reading requires the student to interact with the text and connect the information being read to the personal background knowledge he or she brings to the text (Perez, 1998; Pressley & Block, 2002). When the text does not reflect the sociocultural perspective of a CLD student, it is critical that he or she receives direct instruction that expands understanding of the perspective expressed in the text.

## Building from the Known to the Unknown

Great emphasis has been placed on the importance of promoting students' reading comprehension by fostering schematic connections to text (Anderson, 1999; Cushenberry, 1985; Gregory, 1996; Irwin, 1986; Maria, 1990; Narvaez, 2002; Nunan, 1999; Rumelhart, 1980). As mentioned in Chapter 1, *schema theory* was developed by Rumelhart (1980) to describe how knowledge of objects, events, and situations is categorized and retained in a person's memory. Imagine, for a moment, that *schemas* are a filing cabinet inside the reader's brain. The reader draws on schemas by opening up different files of information to understand what is being read. Each person's schemas are directly impacted by his or her background knowledge and experiences. For example, the schematic files in a CLD student's head might look something like the ones highlighted in Figure 6.2.

According to Maria (1990), schemas aid reading comprehension by enabling the reader to connect existing knowledge with new information presented in the text. The depth with which these connections are made varies by student based on the nature of individual schemas. CLD students' schematic connections to text are largely influenced by the sociocultural, linguistic, academic, and cognitive knowledge they bring to the reading process. Table 6.1 highlights schematic considerations related to each of these four domains. In addition, tips have been included to promote schematic connections in each area to enhance reading comprehension for CLD students.

■ **figure 6.2** Schema Theory

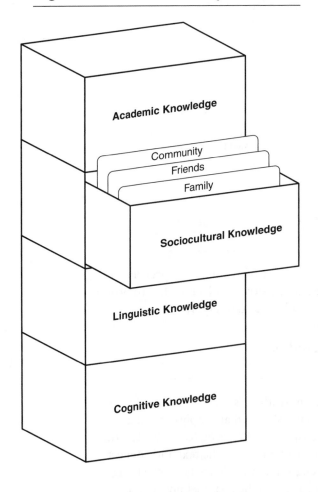

Academic Knowledge

Community

Friends

Family

Sociocultural Knowledge

Linguistic Knowledge

Cognitive Knowledge

**■ table 6.1**    Tapping into Schemas to Promote CLD Students' Reading Comprehension

| | CLD Considerations | Teaching Tips |
|---|---|---|
| **Sociocultural Knowledge**<br><br>*Text-to-Self Connections* | The life experiences of CLD students reflect the culture, family, and community in which they are raised. | • Engage CLD students in discussions about their own lives and experiences to promote schematic connections to text.<br>• Use interactive grouping configurations among students to promote the sharing of multiple points of view and personal experiences.<br>• Highlight and make links across cultural experiences whenever possible. |
| **Linguistic Knowledge** | Variations in the level of linguistic skills CLD students have for decoding text in English can positively or negatively affect their reading comprehension. | • Identify CLD students' English language proficiency level to provide appropriate texts for independent reading.<br>• Explicitly preteach key vocabulary from text.<br>• Make links between the native language and English (e.g., use cognates to highlight key vocabulary terms).<br>• Allow discussion in the native language to support understanding and promote higher-order thinking and questioning for students who have strong CALP skills in their native language. |
| **Academic Knowledge**<br><br>*Text-to-Text Connections* | The academic knowledge that CLD students bring to the classroom is based on past learning in the United States and/or in the native country. | • Encourage CLD students to discuss their prior academic experiences.<br>• Help CLD students make explicit links between past learning and new learning.<br>• Talk with each student about the types of strategies he or she has learned to promote the application of these strategies in practice.<br>• Engage in frequent authentic assessments of students' understanding. |
| **Cognitive Knowledge**<br><br>*Text-to-World Connections* | CLD students may or may not have a large repertoire of strategies to use when reading. | • Explicitly identify and teach cognitive learning strategies to CLD students to promote reading comprehension.<br>• Provide repeated and extended modeling and practice with each strategy to ensure comprehension and transfer of the skill.<br>• Encourage CLD students to question the text from multiple perspectives (e.g., author, reader).<br>• Identify the genre of the text to guide CLD students' orientation and approach to the text as they read with a specific purpose in mind. |

## Schematic Connections in Practice

One instructional strategy often used to promote students' schematic connections to text is to teach text-to-self connections. According to research by Harvey and Goudvis (2000), *text-to-self connections* help "readers make connections between the text and their past experiences or background knowledge" (p. 21). For CLD students, these past experiences and background knowledge often are rooted in the sociocultural and linguistic knowledge they bring to the text.

Consider the following example: A teacher assigns the book *Sadako and the Thousand Paper Cranes* (Coerr, 1999) to the class. This book is the true story about Sadako, a girl who lived in Japan toward the end of World War II. As a result of the atomic bomb being dropped on Hiroshima, Sadako develops leukemia and dies. To guide students in making text-to-self connections, the teacher might have them think about the impact war or violence has had on their own lives.

Strategies in Practice 6.1 presents MINE, a student-friendly graphic organizer that can support CLD students in making increasingly complex schematic

## Strategies in Practice 6.1

### MINE (My Experience + Ignite & Nurture + Exploration)

**Materials Needed**
- Copies of the "MINE" handout (one per student)
- Copies of the text (one per student)
- Pencils (one per student)

**Directions**
- In the M column of the handout, have the students make individual connections to the text based on their personal experiences. Then have the students share their connections with the teacher, a peer, or a small group of students.
- For the IN portion of the "MINE" handout, encourage students to identify ways they can "Ignite and Nurture" connections between past learnings/texts and new learnings/texts. Have students share these connections with the teacher, a peer, or a small group.
- To complete the E column, engage students in an "Exploration" of text-related issues in the context of society or the world. This connection is the most abstract for CLD students, as it requires the application of higher-order thinking skills and cognitively complex connections. Therefore, extensive modeling with students in whole- and small-group settings is highly encouraged.

Name: _____ Date: _____

Text: _____

| **M**<br>**My Connections**<br>**(Text-to-Self)** | **IN**<br>**Ignite and Nurture**<br>**(Text-to-Text)** | **E**<br>**Exploration**<br>**(Text-to-World)** |
|---|---|---|
| | | |

connections to text. Building on the importance of first making text-to-self connections, the first column of the graphic organizer is the M. The M represents a student's individual connections ("My Connections") to text based on his or her personal experiences. After students have completed this section of the graphic organizer, they should discuss with the teacher, a peer, or even a small group of students the personal connections they made to the text. These discussions help CLD students understand that everyone brings something different to the reading process based on his or her own schema. In addition, this sharing among students provides educators with important information about the connections students are making and where students might need to be redirected. In the case of a culturally bound text, in which the values and belief systems of the dominant population drive the text, it is particularly critical to make more explicit connections for CLD students. When the differences between a CLD student's schema and those of his or her monolingual English-speaking peers are ignored, large gaps in reading comprehension can occur (Anderson, 1999; Cushenberry, 1985; Gregory, 1996; Irwin, 1986; Navarez, 2002; Nunan, 1999).

As reading comprehension instruction evolves, teachers transition readers from making text-to-self connections to making text-to-text connections. *Text-to-text connections* are the "connections that readers make between the text they are reading and another text, including books, poems, scripts, songs, or anything that is written" (Harvey & Goudvis, 2000, p. 17). To make these connections, students continue to draw on their schemas. For CLD students, their success at making these text-to-text connections is rooted in their prior academic experiences. The more academic experiences the student has to draw on, whether from the United States or the native country, the higher his or her level of text-to-text connections.

The IN portion of the MINE graphic organizer helps CLD students make these connections by encouraging them to identify ways they can "Ignite and Nurture" connections between past learnings/texts and new learnings/texts. Using the example of *Sadako and the Thousand Paper Cranes* (Coerr, 1999) to make text-to-text connections, the teacher would have students "Ignite" their connections by talking about other books they have read on war or children dying and then "Nurture" these connections to the new text.

The highest level of schematic connections for CLD students is *text-to-world connections*. According to Harvey and Goudvis (2000), these are the "connections that readers make between text and the bigger issues, events, or concerns of society and the world at large" (p. 20). These types of text connections represent the highest level for CLD students because they require the application of higher-order thinking skills and cognitively complex connections. The final column of the MINE organizer, E, encourages these complex links by engaging students in an "Exploration" of text-related issues in the context of society or the world. For example, after reading *Sadako and the Thousand Paper Cranes* (Coerr, 1999), the teacher might ask students to make text-to-world connections about war and the implications it has on people today.

Supporting CLD students' connections to text via schematic connections is one of the first ways teachers can approach reading comprehension instruction. To further enhance CLD students' reading comprehension, explicit instruction and modeling of reading comprehension strategies is highly beneficial. The remainder of this chapter will explore the ways educators can explicitly teach CLD students how to develop and apply metacognitive, cognitive, and social/affective learning strategies in practice.

# ■ Putting Reading Comprehension Strategies into Practice

A study by the National Reading Panel (NRP, 2000) found a direct correlation between reading comprehension and CLD students' ability to identify and apply reading comprehension strategies in practice. Herrera and Murry (2005, p. 301) note that when it comes to the application of learning strategies, less successful language learners tend to do the following:

1. They are more likely to use phonetic decoding.
2. They tend to focus on cognitive strategies when they use strategies.
3. They are more likely to use strategies that are ineffective for a task and are less flexible in strategy use.
4. They tend to use only one strategy to resolve a situation.
5. They view comprehension discretely; if they get stuck on a word, comprehension is lost in the details.
6. They tend to focus more on form or structure than comprehension.

The remainder of this chapter will introduce and provide specific strategies for teaching metacognitive, cognitive, and social/affective reading comprehension strategies. According to Herrera and Murry (2005, p. 301), this type of strategy instruction helps create more successful language learners, who tend to do the following:

1. They are more likely to rely on background knowledge (inferences, predictions, elaborations).
2. They tend to focus more on metacognitive strategies.
3. They are more flexible at adapting strategy use to fit with a particular task and are more flexible in strategy use.
4. They tend to use multiple strategies to resolve situations.
5. They tend to view comprehension holistically; coming to an unknown word does not hinder comprehension.

6. They often use more complex strategies more appropriately.
7. They usually focus on meaning.

## Metacognitive Strategies

Irvin (1998) points out that explicit instruction on reading comprehension strategies helps students develop *metacognition,* or the ability to think about their own thinking. Good readers know how to monitor their thinking and assess their understanding, and when comprehension is not taking place, they know how to use the appropriate strategies to build comprehension. When the goals of reading are not being achieved and a CLD student is unable to comprehend a text, using metacognitive reading strategies can help him or her take corrective action and more effectively engage with the text.

One way teachers can provide students with guided practice in effective reading is to model how they use reading comprehension strategies in practice by doing think-alouds. According to Harris and Hodges (1995), a *think-aloud* is a "metacognitive strategy in which a teacher verbalizes thoughts aloud while reading a selection orally, thus modeling the process of comprehension" (p. 256). By explicitly modeling for students what to do while reading aloud, the teacher demonstrates how to check comprehension during reading. This empowers students to monitor their own comprehension by checking their understanding as they process the information (Chamot & O'Malley, 1994).

Mrs. Barr, a first-grade teacher, describes how she uses think-alouds with her CLD students:

> *I always model a think-aloud before asking anything from students. This means . . . using the strategy [myself] and [making sure] my expectations are made clear without asking students to take the risk of making a mistake in front of their peers. Then when I do ask students to participate, it is first with partners so that, again, students can share comfortably with a partner before taking the risk of sharing with the whole group. Then, finally, I ask students to write their thinking so that I can assess how they are using the strategy independently.*

The scaffolded approach Mrs. Barr takes to modeling her think-alouds greatly benefits CLD students. The modeling of the strategy in practice helps students understand the process so they can then more effectively apply the strategy in other contexts.

### *In My Head*

To support CLD students in the independent application of the think-aloud strategy, students can first document their thoughts on the "In My Head" handout. As demonstrated in Strategies in Practice 6.2, this is a simple, concrete tool that CLD students can use to record what they are thinking before articulating the information aloud. Students with limited speaking skills can use this tool to document their thoughts in several ways:

1. Students can draw a picture of what they are thinking.
2. Students can write down their thoughts in the native language. Then a more proficient peer or bilingual paraprofessional can help translate this information into English.
3. Students can tell a more proficient peer, paraprofessional, or even the teacher what they are thinking and have the other person record this information on the handout for them.

The power of this strategy is that CLD students are able to document what is happening inside their heads based on their individual understanding. Given the wide range of cultures and background experiences that CLD students often bring to the process, individuals' perspectives might be quite distinct. Knowing students' initial thoughts provides a teacher with a valuable foundation on which new learning can be built.

## Strategies in Practice 6.2

### In My Head

**Materials Needed**
- Copies of the "In My Head" handout (one per student)
- Copies of the text (one per student)
- Pencils (one per student)

**Directions**
- After students read the text, ask them to record what they are thinking about on the "In My Head" handout.
- Allow students with limited speaking skills to document their thoughts in multiple ways:
  1. by drawing a picture
  2. by writing down their thoughts in the native language
  3. by working with a more proficient peer or bilingual paraprofessional to help translate their thoughts into English
  4. by allowing them to tell a more proficient peer, paraprofessional, or the teacher what they are thinking orally while it is recorded on paper by this other person

- Use the information gained to support instruction.

*continued*

# In My Head

Name: _____

What are you thinking about as you read _____(*name of book*)?

**I think . . .**

## *True or False?*

"True or False?" is a metacognitive tool that supports advanced organization. CLD students can use this tool to preview the main ideas/concepts presented in the text. When using this strategy, the teacher poses a series of true or false statements, to which students respond before reading. Building on *anticipation reaction guides* (Readence, Bean, & Baldwin, 2004), the True or False? strategy activates students' background knowledge on a topic and sets the stage for reading by exploring critical concepts from the text. However, unlike anticipation reaction guides, this strategy not only enables teachers to preassess CLD students' content knowledge but also helps students tap into their prior sociocultural knowledge.

Strategies in Practice 6.3 provides a guide for implementing this strategy as well as a sample handout. Note that the guide asks educators to focus first on the lesson's standards before selecting a text and identifying the critical concepts. When students later discuss their responses, using strategic grouping can enable explanations or discussions in the native language that can be used to enhance comprehension and extend students' thinking.

## Strategies in Practice 6.3

### Steps to Create a "True or False?" Handout

**Materials Needed**
- Copies of teacher-generated "True or False?" handout (one per student)
- Copies of the text (one per student)
- Sticky notes (10 per student)
- Pencils (one per student)

**Directions**
- Review the standards you are trying to meet with the lesson, and select a text that addresses key elements of the identified standards.
- Using information from the text, create a handout that includes both true and false statements that students can respond to before reading the text. When developing these statements for CLD students, remember to create items that access their sociocultural knowledge and experiences, preexisting academic knowledge about the concept, and new information that needs to be learned.
- Distribute the "True or False?" handouts, and have students individually respond to the true or false statements before reading the text.
- As a whole group, discuss students' responses. Do not correct students at this point; rather, encourage them to elaborate on their individual rationales for their responses.

*continued*

- As students read the text, have them use sticky notes to flag the pages that prove their responses correct or incorrect. Then have them add the text quotes and page numbers to the handout.
- Allow students to work in small groups or teams to verify and rationalize their responses.
- Throughout the lesson, revisit the questions to support students' comprehension and engagement.

**My Name Is Maria Isabel**

| Read each of the following statements, and write down your prediction (True or False) before reading the text. | BEFORE: T or F | As you read the text, write down your reaction (True or False) to each of the statements. Also, write down a text quote and page number to support your response. Did your prediction change after reading the text? | DURING: T or F |
|---|---|---|---|
| 1. Maria is happy she is going to a new school. | | | |
| 2. It bothers Maria that the teacher does not pronounce her name correctly. | | | |
| 3. It is easy for Maria to make friends at her school. | | | |
| 4. The students are nice when Maria starts school. | | | |
| 5. Maria's parents can help her learn English. | | | |
| 6. It is easy for Maria to understand the teacher when she is teaching. | | | |
| 7. Students never make fun of someone who is different. | | | |

**Sample "True or False?" Handout for My Name Is Maria Isabel (Ada, 1993)**

### Sticking to the Main Idea

Sticking to the Main Idea is a metacognitive strategy that supports CLD students' monitoring of their individual learning before, during, and after reading. According to research by Chamot and O'Malley (1994), using *selective attention* helps CLD students read by looking for specific information in the text. Sticking to the Main Idea promotes CLD students' reading comprehension by providing them with nonlinguistic support at the beginning of the activity, a tool to monitor their understanding during the lesson, and a way to check their understanding at the end of the lesson. In addition, by focusing CLD students' attention on specific words/ concepts, the teacher is able to keep the affective filter low, so students are not overwhelmed by the amount of text they have to read. Strategies in Practice 6.4 describes the steps for carrying out this strategy with CLD students.

## Strategies in Practice 6.4

### Sticking to the Main Idea

**Materials Needed**
- List of vocabulary words representing four to six key concepts
- Sticky notes (four to six per student)
- Copies of the text (one per student)
- Pencils (one per student)

**Directions**
- Before the reading, give each student a set of sticky notes (four to six).
- Display the vocabulary list on the board or using an overhead projector.
- Have each student write down one word from the list at the top of each sticky note (one word per note).
- As each word is introduced, discuss as a group what the word could mean as it relates to the text.
- After the group discussion, have each student draw a picture of the word below where it's written on the sticky note. During this time, travel around the room to verify that the students' individual pictures accurately represent the words/concepts.
- Once all the sticky notes have been completed, have the students begin to read the text individually.
- Using their sticky notes as a guide, students should use their selective attention to focus on identifying the specific words on the notes.
- When students identify a word/concept in the text, have them write down the sentence from the text that contains the word on the back of the corresponding sticky note.
- After copying the sentence from the text, students should place the sticky note in the margin of the text to mark where the sentence was found.
- After students have placed all their sticky notes in the text, have them work in pairs or small groups to retell what they learned by sharing the information from their sticky notes.

### Question Bookmark

A more individualized tool, the Question Bookmark, helps students monitor their comprehension while reading by posing questions about the information. This ongoing process of readers posing questions they are interested in having answered helps CLD students monitor their own comprehension. Strategies in Practice 6.5 illustrates one student's use of a Question Bookmark to pose relevant questions about a text.

To extend student learning and language development, students can be paired to collaboratively answer the questions posed on their Question Bookmarks. All the students in the class extend their learning when the answers to the questions are not found in the text and require additional research. Thus, this strategy tends to enhance students' understanding by stretching their learning beyond the text. By having the CLD student record the page number that prompted the question, a teacher can later assess his or her thinking and learn more about the connections being made to the text.

Because students may need to use higher-order thinking to answer the questions, this process of responding to student-generated questions is a wonderful way to build cognitive skills. Before moving to this step, however, it is important to assess the quality and answerability of the students' questions.

## Cognitive Strategies

*Cognitive strategies* are those a reader uses to manipulate the material being read mentally (as in making images when elaborating) or physically (as in grouping items to be

---

## Strategies in Practice 6.5

### Question Bookmark

**Materials Needed**
- Question Bookmarks (one per student)
- Copies of the two- or three-page text (one per student)
- Pencils (one per student)

**Directions**
- Have students work individually to complete their Question Bookmarks as they read a short passage of text. Encourage students to stop after every paragraph to see if they can pose a question about the text.
- When students are done with the passage, have them partner with a peer to share their questions. Challenge students to try to answer one another's questions.
- Meet as a whole group, and have volunteers share their questions and answers.

| Question Bookmark | Question Bookmark |
|---|---|
| Name: | Name , |
| Title: | Title Farms, Ranches, Citie |
| Date: | Date 3/12/08 |
| Page_____ | Page 272 Where are the trails? |
| Page_____ | Page 274 how many resources are in ohio? |
| Page_____ | Page 273 When did nat love died? |
| Page_____ | Page 272 Why did the farmes tak cattle to mexico |
| Page_____ | Page 273 What is the most famous trails |

learned or taking notes) (Chamot & O'Malley, 1994). Cognitive strategies support reading comprehension for CLD students by providing them with specific, concrete tools they can manipulate and use. In this section, the cognitive strategies presented emphasize the following: (1) elaborating on prior knowledge, (2) using imagery/ visualizing, (3) making inferences/predicting, (4) notetaking, and (5) summarizing.

### SEA Box

The SEA Box strategy helps CLD students make schematic connections to text before the lesson by elaborating on their prior knowledge through the use of visual cues. The SEA acronym reminds teachers to consider the *Schemas: Experiential* and *Academic* (*SEA*) that CLD students bring to the text. The effectiveness of the SEA Box strategy lies in the support teachers give CLD students as they make text-to-self and text-to-text connections using visual cues. The steps for using the SEA box are outlined in Strategies in Practice 6.6.

This strategy is particularly beneficial for non-English speakers, as they can make connections to the artifacts visually and kinesthetically. If native language support is available, educators should write the names of the objects in the students' native languages and post them next to the English names of the artifacts. Referring back to the objects in the SEA box throughout the lesson also increases CLD students' ability to understand and apply the information they are learning in concrete ways (Cooper, 1986; Cunningham et al., 1995; Peregoy & Boyle, 2001; Rasinski & Padak, 2000; Vacca et al., 2000). As an informal review and assessment of students' comprehension, teachers can also revisit the SEA box at the end of the lesson and ask students to state how each object was critical to the information learned.

### Visualize-Interact-Predict (VIP)

According to Keene and Zimmerman (1997), *visualizing* is a comprehension strategy that enables readers to make the words on a page real and concrete. Benefits of visualization, as identified by Harvey and Goudvis (2000), include the following:

- enhancing meaning
- linking past experience to the words and ideas in the text
- enabling readers to place themselves in the story
- strengthening the reader's relationship to the text
- stimulating imaginative thinking
- bringing joy to reading

In addition to these benefits, the nonlinguistic nature of visual representations helps CLD students comprehend text by providing concrete connections to content. According to Zwiers (2004), visuals "extend students' mental endurance and better communicate what the words truly mean in order to improve overall comprehension" (p. 8).

However, to help students visualize effectively, it is important to consider which visual cues will be of greatest benefit. The following are important guidelines to keep in mind when selecting visual cues for CLD students:

## Strategies in Practice 6.6

### Creating a <u>S</u>EA Box (<u>S</u>chemas: <u>E</u>xperiential and <u>A</u>cademic)

**Materials Needed**
- Copies of the text (one per student)
- Visual cues to support the text
- Box or other storage container

**Directions**
- Identify the key elements from the text that are most important for CLD students to understand.
- Locate visual cues that will support students' understanding of the key elements. These visual cues can come directly from the text, from past texts that relate to the topic, or from various other sources (e.g., Internet, posters, maps, realia, videos).
- Label the objects you have gathered, and put them in a box or storage container. Place the box or container in a central location that students can easily access at the beginning of the lesson.
- To introduce the lesson, pull out the SEA box and share each item, one at a time, with students.
- As each item is shared, explicitly ask students if they know what the object is and how they know it. (That is, are they making a connection to the self or to another text?) This guided discussion supports the comprehension of key content and fosters schematic connections at both the experiential and academic levels.
- Leave the SEA box in a central location, where students can refer to it throughout the lesson. In this way, they can continually link to key concepts through the objects in the box.
- Encourage CLD students to bring in additional materials to add to the SEA box. By continuing to add items, CLD students can reinforce and extend their learning.

**Sample Materials for a SEA Box on *The Great Kapok Tree* (Cherry, 1990)**
- a map of the rainforest
- a globe to show where rainforests are located
- pictures of the rainforest printed from the Internet
- pictures of the various types of animals that can be found in the rainforest
- pictures of the tools used to chop down trees
- stories already introduced in class that deal with conservation and the environment
- a video about the rainforest
- pictures from *The Great Kapok Tree*

1. Select visuals from a variety of cultures so that all students can relate to them. For example, do not show only the visual of a traditional U.S. holiday celebration, such as the Fourth of July. Rather, also include important holidays that students in the classroom might celebrate in their home cultures. In this way, more students can connect to the visuals, and rich conversations about the celebrations can occur.
2. Have students bring visuals from home that illustrate the content or concept being presented. For example, if the class is doing a unit on American Indians and discussing traditional clothing, have students bring examples or pictures of traditional clothing from their native cultures.
3. Refer back to visuals and extend students' knowledge through discussions and activities associated with the visuals.
4. Link key vocabulary to visuals. This supports CLD students' comprehension and use of key vocabulary in meaningful contexts.

The Visualize-Interact-Predict (VIP) strategy, as described in Strategies in Practice 6.7, provides a detailed means of supporting CLD students' comprehension through visualization. VIP is a prediction strategy in which students individually visualize what they think about when they are first introduced to a text. After each student has individually created his or her own mental picture about the information to be learned, he or she is paired with a peer to share the mental images. Hearing how another student interpreted the information either helps the CLD student understand the concept in a different way or reinforces his or her own understanding. Finally, students make a joint prediction that incorporates both their viewpoints.

The key to the VIP strategy is pairing students in a way that supports their sociocultural, linguistic, and/or academic needs. For example, a student with very limited English proficiency can be paired with a more proficient student who speaks the same native language, so they can make predictions in the native language and then have them translated for the whole class by the more proficient English speaker. The teacher can also support the English language development of a CLD student by pairing him or her with a peer who is less proficient in English; in this way, the student has an opportunity to model the English language. Depending on the text, the teacher may also want to pair students with different cultural backgrounds, as students can then share diverse experiences that enhance their schematic connections to the text. The rule of thumb for the VIP strategy is to pair students in ways that support the best possible use of their knowledge.

### 1, 2, 3 Imagery

Building on the work of Neelands and Goode (2001), 1, 2, 3 Imagery is a strategy that focuses on having students create a visual context for a story. In this strategy,

## Strategies in Practice 6.7

### V-I-P (Visualize-Interact-Predict)

**Materials Needed**
- A text for the teacher to read aloud
- Whiteboards and markers or paper and pencils (one per student)

**Directions**
- *Visualize:* Engage students in a discussion of the text before reading it. As the discussion unfolds, ask each student to visualize what he or she is thinking about. Emphasize that each student's schematic connections will be different, since these connections are based on the student's own life. To increase accountability, ask each student to quickly draw what he or she visualized on a piece of paper or a whiteboard and then to share it with a partner. Not only does drawing increase individual accountability, but it also provides CLD students with a nonlinguistic way to document their thoughts.
- *Interact:* Pair students so they can share what they visualized with a partner. When possible, pair each student with a peer who speaks his or her native language to support this sharing in the native language.
- *Predict:* Still working in pairs, have students predict what the text is going to be about, based on their discussion. Make sure they use the information learned during the Interact step of VIP to support their predictions.
  - Have student pairs share their predictions with the rest of the class by relaying their discussion as well as drawing their predictions.
  - To assess the accuracy of students' predictions, begin reading the text. Stop at strategic points to check students' predictions against the information presented.

the teacher divides students into groups of three, paying close attention to group dynamics. The most effective groupings are those in which CLD students have access to a peer who can linguistically support their comprehension by restating directions or translating information into the native language. Each group should also include at least one student who can read at grade level.

Strategies in Practice 6.8 details the steps of 1, 2, 3 Imagery. With this strategy, teachers can gauge students' comprehension while supporting the sociocultural, linguistic, and academic background knowledge they bring to the text. Adding the written dimension to the student-created book also supports CLD students' cognitive development, as students have to work together to summarize the information they illustrated.

## Strategies in Practice 6.8

### 1,2,3 Imagery

**Materials Needed**
- Copies of the text (one per student group)
- Paper and pencils (one per student plus one per group)

**Directions**
- Form students into groups of three or four.
- Have the most proficient reader in each group read aloud a short passage from a story to the other group members.
- After the passage has been read, have each student sketch the images that came to mind as he or she listened to the passage. Give students a two- to three-minute time limit for sketching to make sure this is a quick sketch.
- Have students describe their sketches to their group and encourage them to provide as much detail as possible.
- Have the group choose the most important elements from each student's visualization and redraw them on a blank sheet of paper.
- Have each group share their completed drawing with the class.
- As the groups share, encourage them to explain why they included certain elements and why the elements are significant to the story. (This strategy can be used throughout reading the story by strategically dividing up the text to cover the critical concepts.)
- At the conclusion of the activity, collect the students' drawings and bind them to make a book students can use to retell the story visually.
- As a further extension, have students rewrite the story by summarizing each drawing in writing at the bottom of the page.

### *Signature Lines*

Signature Lines is a cognitive strategy that CLD students can use to document what they consider important lines within a story or text. The selection of important lines is a highly subjective and cognitively advanced task. Depending on the academic and cognitive skills that the CLD student brings to the reading process, this strategy can be relatively easy or highly complex.

To ensure CLD students' success in implementing this strategy, repeated modeling is critical. In addition, CLD students can be paired to practice identifying signature lines together before being doing this strategy individually. The peer collaboration offers CLD students a scaffold for the strategy, and the resulting discussion supports their understanding of what is and is not important in the text.

Strategies in Practice 6.9 provides a "Signature Lines" handout teachers can use with students as they identify important lines of text. The handout not only includes a place for the line and the page number but also prompts the student to state why he or she selected the line. By asking CLD students to justify their selections, teachers can guide them to an even higher level of cognitive understanding. For the student who needs additional scaffolding to apply this strategy, the teacher can have him or her focus on one character or concept in the text and identify only the signature lines for that character or concept.

### Story Retelling

Story retelling provides a wonderful way for CLD students to articulate what they have understood from a reading. This strategy also provides the teacher with a comprehensive look at what the students have understood. According to Cooper and Kiger (2001), additional purposes for story retelling include these:

- assessing a student's ability to discuss specific story elements of a narrative
- determining a student's ability to discuss important ideas and significant details of expository text as well as factors related to text structure, such as sequence, comparison and contrast of ideas, and fact versus opinion

## Strategies in Practice 6.9

### Signature Lines

Materials Needed
- Copies of the "Signature Lines" handout (one per student)
- Copies of the text (one per student)
- Pencils (one per student)

Directions
- Give each student a copy of the "Signature Lines" handout.
- Explain to students that *signature lines* are important sentences or statements made in the story or text.
- In the first column of the handout, have students identify signature lines and write them word for word from the text.
- In the second column, have students record the page number on which they found the line in the text.
- In the final column, have students explain why they selected each signature line.
- At the end of the activity, have students discuss their choices of signature lines with a partner, a small group, or the teacher.

  *Note:* When students are first learning how to identify signature lines, have them work with partners to promote discussion, collaboration, and understanding.

*continued*

## Signature Lines

Name(s): _____

Name of Text: _____

| Signature Line | Text Page # | This is a signature line because . . . |
|---|---|---|
| | | |
| | | |
| | | |
| | | |
| | | |
| | | |
| | | |
| | | |

- providing the teacher with information needed to make appropriate instructional decisions and plans

Story retelling can be done in two ways: orally or in writing (Cooper & Pikulski, 1997; Leslie & Caldwell, 1995). A variety of questions can serve as prompts for CLD students who are retelling stories orally (Perez, 2003). For example, the teacher might inquire of the student, "Please tell me everything you can remember about the story." If the student forgets to include information from the text or offers a minimal response, the teacher can prompt him or her by asking questions such as "What else do you remember about the story?" or "What more can you tell me about the story?" After the student has relayed everything he or she can, the teacher can have the student look at the book, turn to each picture, and describe what he or she sees.

Research by Perez (2003) found that using a story retelling matrix, such as the one depicted in Strategies in Practice 6.10, can guide both the teacher and the CLD student in effectively implementing this strategy. The matrix scaffolds the task of story retelling as the CLD student moves from demonstrating comprehension of very basic facts to generating more inferential responses. This retelling structure also helps the teacher assess which comprehension strategies the CLD student used during reading to enhance comprehension.

When using story retelling with CLD students, it is essential to consider both their level of English proficiency and their level of native language proficiency. Story retelling is meant to provide insights about a student's ability to comprehend text. If a CLD student is in the beginning stages of acquiring English, asking him or her to retell the story in English is likely to reveal more about his or her ability

## Strategies in Practice 6.10

### Story Retelling Matrix

**Materials Needed**
- Copies of "Story Retelling Matrix" (one per student)
- Copy of the text
- Pencil

**Directions**
- After each student has read the text, complete the "Story Retelling Matrix" one on one with him or her.
- If the student is in the initial stages of second language acquisition, you may want to conduct the story retelling in his or her native language to gain a more complete picture of what he or she does and does not understand.

*continued*

**Story Retelling Matrix**

Student Name: _____

Name of Book: _____

| Retelling the Story | Yes | No | Partially | Comments |
|---|---|---|---|---|
| Can identify setting | | | | |
| Can identify main characters | | | | |
| Can list main events in the story | | | | |
| Can list events from the story in order in which they occurred | | | | |
| Uses a storytelling voice to tell the story | | | | |
| Uses body language and gestures when retelling the story | | | | |
| **Can respond to the following questions:** | | | | |
| 1. What do you think would have happened if the main character had done something differently? | | | | |
| 2. How do you think the main character felt? Why? | | | | |
| 3. How would you have felt if you were the main character? Why? | | | | |
| **Comprehension Strategies in Practice** | | | | |
| 1. What helped you remember the story? | | | | |
| 2. What specific strategies did you use to help you understand the story? | | | | |
| 3. What did the teacher do to help you understand the story? | | | | |

to understand and produce the English language than his or her ability to comprehend and retell stories. To accommodate for this, educators might provide CLD students with the option to retell the story in the native language via a more proficient peer or paraprofessional.

## Social/Affective Strategies

*Social/affective strategies* engage CLD students in interactions with other people to enhance comprehension via questioning for clarification or cooperative learning (Chamot & O'Malley, 1994). Contextualizing student learning in this manner also lowers CLD students' affective filter by providing them with the support of small-group interaction. In this way, students can verify their learning before reporting to the whole group. This section will explore two social/affective strategies educators can use to help students build their comprehension skills.

### Critical Questions

Proficient readers increase their comprehension by asking questions before, during, and after reading. This questioning occurs at multiple levels, and for CLD students, some of the most important questions are constructed at the level of their own prior experience and academic background knowledge. It is at this level that students ask themselves questions like these: What have I experienced and what do I know that will help me understand this? What is this text saying to me personally? The next level of questioning involves a more critical approach, as students inquire about the author's purpose. At this level, students ask themselves, What message is the author trying to send? For example, a student might examine what was left unstated in the reading.

The Critical Questions strategy provides a two-step process in which CLD students first ask questions of themselves to monitor their own understanding and then of their peers to verify and elaborate on their learning. The prompts found on the "Critical Questions" card in Strategies in Practice 6.11 offer a valuable guide that students can use for posing critical questions when reading.

When used before, during, and after reading, the "Critical Questions" card explicitly guides students to make experiential, academic, and textual connections. By focusing students' attention on key questions, this tool also highlights the specific purpose for reading a given text. In essence, use of the questioning card helps CLD students be active thinkers and offers them a social/affective strategy for monitoring comprehension.

### Through My Eyes

Through My Eyes is an interactive comprehension strategy that can be done in pairs or small groups. By working together, CLD students have the opportunity to

## Strategies in Practice 6.11

### CLD Questioning for Clarification

#### Critical Questions

**Materials Needed**

- Copies of the "Critical Questions" handout (one per student)
- Copies of the text (one per student)

**Directions**

- After students have read the text, distribute the handouts.
- First, have students ask the "What Do I Know?" questions of themselves to monitor their own understanding. Encourage CLD students to record their responses in writing. (Allow for written responses to be in the native language or English.)
- Have students orally complete the "Elaborate and Verify" section with a partner or small group so they can discuss and confirm their learning.

*Note:* Individual questions from the "Critical Questions" handout can also be written on 3″ × 5″ cards to make them more user friendly.

---

### Critical Questions

*What Do I Know?*

1. What do I already know about the topic?

2. What experiences have I had that can help me understand the story?

3. What have I learned in the past that can help me understand the information in this story?

4. What vocabulary do I already know from the story?

5. Are there cognates I can use to understand new vocabulary in the story?

*Elaborate and Verify*

1. I think the story is about . . .
   What did you think the story was about?

2. I think the most important part of the story was . . .
   What did you think was the most important part of the story?

3. Some other things I thought about the story were . . .
   What else did you think about?

4. I didn't understand this part of the story.
   Can you tell me what you thought this part was about?

extend their own understanding, work collaboratively to understand the main point of the text, and get immediate feedback in an individualized setting.

To implement this strategy, the teacher first poses a prompt for students to think about in relation to a key concept that will be explored in the text. For example, if students will be studying *Charlotte's Web* (White, 1952), the teacher might ask if they have ever lived on or visited a farm. After posing the question, the teacher gives students time to individually respond in writing or with visual cues to the following prompts:

- What I know about [*topic of text*]: _____.
- How I learned about [*topic of text*]: _____ (*text-to-self or text-to-text connections*).
- A link I can make to my own life is _____.

After students have responded to the prompts, they meet in their pairs or small groups to share what they have written. This strategy not only provides CLD students with an immediate personal connection to the information presented in the text, but it also encourages elaboration of students' knowledge through experiences shared by peers.

## ■ Conclusion

This chapter explored a variety of concepts and strategies that educators can use to build the reading comprehension skills of CLD students. However, encouraging students to read better and comprehend more requires more than the simple application of concepts and strategies. Teaching reading comprehension is as much an art as a science, and as such, it requires the teacher's artistic vision as an instructional leader. Teachers are forever thinking and rethinking the strategies they use, applying them as specific situations and students warrant and constantly monitoring and evaluating the progress students are making. This process is ongoing and requires teachers to be proactive. Strategies in Practice 6.12 provides guidelines to structure the process and monitor progress.

As this chapter closes, we would like to reiterate that when working with CLD students, teachers must be ever cognizant of the goal of *reading for meaning*. If teachers fail to teach CLD students to construct meaning based on their own schemas, then reading is reduced to a process of simply decoding words on a page. The goal instead is to watch the text come to life for CLD students, as the words on the page speak to them, connecting to and richly informing their lives and experiences.

## Strategies in Practice 6.12

### Guidelines for Teaching Reading Comprehension

The following guidelines provide suggestions for monitoring instruction of reading comprehension strategies. The guidelines highlight the linguistic, cognitive, academic, and sociocultural considerations essential for teaching such strategies to CLD students.

1. Select the reading comprehension strategy that best aligns with the text you are teaching.
2. Determine how you will introduce the reading comprehension strategy to the whole group. Specifically, focus on the following considerations:
   - *Linguistic:* How will you post the steps for carrying out the strategy so students can implement it in pairs or small groups?
   - *Cognitive:* How can you visually demonstrate or model the strategy so CLD students will have a concrete understanding of the steps for implementing it?
   - *Academic:* How will you link the strategy to the text?
   - *Sociocultural:* How can you use interactive grouping and peer discussions to support CLD students' connections to the text?
3. Model the reading comprehension strategy for the whole group. For CLD students, the use of concrete materials and visual cues is an important aspect of modeling and helps them make meaningful schematic connections.
4. Provide guided practice with the whole group. Guided practice of reading comprehension strategies helps CLD students internalize and independently apply these strategies.
5. Have students work in pairs to practice the reading comprehension strategy. When placing CLD students in pairs, make sure to consider these points:
   - *Language proficiency levels:* Less proficient English speakers will need extended support.
   - *Native language support:* Students can be strategically grouped to provide native language support and clarification on strategy implementation.
   - *Cognitive/academic knowledge:* More advanced peers can help less proficient students comprehend and apply the strategy in practice.
   - *Sociocultural knowledge:* Students from diverse backgrounds can be purposefully grouped to ensure extended discussion and elaboration on key concepts.
6. Have students work in small groups to practice and apply the reading comprehension strategy. Determine a concrete outcome for assessing students' application of the strategy. Again, consider language proficiency levels, native language support, cognitive/academic knowledge, and sociocultural knowledge when configuring groups.
7. Provide opportunities for students to independently practice and apply the reading comprehension strategy, and determine a concrete outcome that will demonstrate how effectively students implemented the strategy.

## ■ key theories and concepts

- cognitive comprehension strategies
- comprehension
- metacognition
- metacognitive comprehension strategies

- schema theory
- schematic connection
- social/affective comprehension strategies

## ■ professional conversations on practice

1. This chapter explores in depth multiple facets of reading comprehension. Discuss specific points teachers should keep in mind when approaching reading comprehension instruction with CLD students.

2. Elaborate on how you can access and foster CLD students' schematic connections to text to promote their higher-order thinking and deep connections to the material being read.

3. This chapter discusses multiple strategies for teaching reading comprehension. Identify two or three sample strategies and discuss how each has been adapted to reflect the specific sociocultural, linguistic, academic, and/or cognitive needs of CLD students.

## ■ questions for review and reflection

1. What are the dimensions teachers should consider when approaching reading comprehension instruction with CLD students?

2. How do CLD students use schemas to support comprehension?

3. What are metacognitive comprehension strategies, and how do they enhance CLD students' reading comprehension?

4. What role do cognitive comprehension strategies play in the development of reading comprehension?

5. How does the use of social/affective comprehension strategies help to lower CLD students' affective filter?

---

**Where the Classroom Comes to Life**

Now go to the Herrera, Perez, and Escamilla MyEducationLab course at www.myeducationlab.com to:

- read and connect with the chapter Objectives;
- use the Study Plan questions to assess your comprehension of the chapter content;
- study chapter content with your Individualized Study Plan;
- engage in multimedia exercises to help you build a deeper and more applied understanding of chapter content.

- What are the key components of surface and deep constructs of fluency?

- How do cross-language transfer issues affect how CLD students fluently decode text?

- How does the orthography of a language impact CLD students' fluency development?

- What are the prosodic elements of language, and how do they influence the ability of CLD students to read text fluently in English?

- How does the stress used on words within a text affect CLD students' reading fluency in English?

- What is the role of intonation in reading fluency?

- What is the role of rhythm in reading, and how can CLD students best learn rhythm skills?

- What role does vocabulary knowledge have on CLD students' development of fluency?

- What role does automaticity play in fluency development, and how best can CLD students acquire automaticity?

- How can interactive group strategies support the development of fluency among CLD students?

# Fluency in Practice

## More Than Reading the Text

*Fluency instruction is based on comprehension. Children may read well and pronounce perfectly, but if they do not understand what they have read, they have gained nothing. I am constantly checking for understanding with my students. I read aloud to my students every week from a children's book selected for their developmental level. As we read together, I stop often and ask questions directly about the parts just read. I model fluent reading and ask questions like, Why did my voice go up there? Why did the stress of my voice fall on that particular part of the word? I can know immediately if they are "getting it."*

—An elementary teacher

Today, more than ever, fluency instruction is on teachers' minds. Driven by national initiatives and research findings indicating the importance of fluency development, teachers across the United States have come to recognize fluency as an important component of literacy instruction (Chard, Vaughn, & Tyler, 2002; Kuhn & Stahl, 2000; NICHD, 2000). In response to this push for fluency, schools across the nation are adopting programs that define fluent reading according to three *surface constructs:* accuracy, speed, and prosody (Rasinski, 2003).

Mastery of these surface constructs is assessed in multiple ways. *Accuracy* is traditionally measured by listening to a student read aloud and counting the number of errors per 100 words in a running record. *Speed* is measured by using tests of sight word knowledge and timed readings. Finally, *prosody* is measured using a checklist of reading expression while listening to a student read aloud. For CLD students, the results of these types of assessments often are not an accurate representation of their fluency skills.

This chapter will identify critical considerations related to the development and assessment of CLD students' fluency development. In addition, this chapter will propose that fluency instruction must go beyond these surface constructs of fluency to include a focus on *deep constructs* of fluency. Deep constructs of fluency suggest that the ultimate goal of fluency instruction is comprehension.

## Deep Constructs of Fluency

Although many fluency programs have been implemented, there has been minimal conclusive research on the implications of these programs for CLD students (August, Carlo, Dresser, & Snow, 2005). Rather, fluency instruction for CLD students has largely focused on the surface constructs of fluency, in which accuracy, speed, and prosody are the emphasis (Pikuiski & Chard, 2005). What follows is a discussion of the critical considerations for CLD students' development of the surface constructs of fluency.

### The Multiple Dimensions of Phonemic Awareness and Phonics

The foundation of many of the surface constructs of fluency rests on mastery of phonemic awareness and phonics skills in English. However, when working with CLD students, there are multiple dimensions of phonemic awareness and phonics skills, including decoding, orthographic cues, and prosodic elements of language.

#### Decoding through Cross-Language Transfer

The first dimension of phonemic awareness and phonics instruction that impacts CLD students' fluency is the ability to decode the words on the page. *Decoding* is the ability of the reader to accurately read the words within a text (Rasinski, 2004). In fluency instruction, accuracy in decoding the words on the page is one of the first measures of reading fluency. Although this skill is highly based on surface constructs of fluency, it is an important aspect of fluency development for CLD students to master.

To support CLD students' mastery of this skill, the decoding of words in text can be supported through the explicit transfer of phonological awareness skills in the native language to those in English. According to research by Pikulski and Chard (2005), however, this transfer of phonological awareness from a student's native language to English will not happen unless the English word can be connected to the student's three cueing systems, involving the student's phonological memory for the word (graphophonics) as well as the semantic and syntactic cues that help him or her understand the word in English:

- *Graphophonic connections* help CLD students make connections to the sounds of the native language and recognize the similarities between these sounds and the larger units of speech sounds, such as words and syllables, in the English language.

- *Semantic/syntactic cues* help CLD students understand the meaning base of the English words as they are found in the sentence.

To support CLD students' graphophonic connections and highlight semantic and syntactic cues, teachers should have explicit discussions of cross-language transfer issues with students who have learned how to read and write in the native language. CLD students can be taught how to identify and manipulate the sounds of the second language by tapping into sounds they have already learned how to read and write in their native language (Durgunoglu, Nagy, & Hancin-Bhatt, 1993; García & González, 1995). If, however, the CLD student has not learned how to read and write in the native language, this connection between the first and second language will not have as great an impact on his or her ability to quickly decode words in English.

Skills that promote CLD students' transfer of skills from the native language to English include the following:

1. the identification of initial letter sounds that are the same in the native language and in English
2. the articulation of phonemic elements of words
3. the isolation of word parts in both languages
4. the identification of context clues

Moreover, CLD students benefit most when decoding strategies are tied directly to the text. Research has shown that isolated word training may not transfer to the text, particularly for CLD students, because words presented in isolation are seen as independent identities rather than as part of a larger context (NRP, 2000). Providing a context via text also supports CLD students in making meaningful connections to background knowledge. When a CLD student can connect the concepts being presented in the text to his or her background knowledge, understanding of the text is greatly enhanced and the message the author is trying to convey is more readily understood.

### Articulation of Orthographic Cues

*Orthography* is a general term used to refer to all aspects of writing, including spelling, punctuation, spacing, fonts, and so forth (Freeman & Freeman, 2004). The ability to read a text, the second dimension of phonemic awareness and phonics, is highly influenced by a CLD student's ability to identify and articulate various dimensions of orthography present in the text.

Spelling frequently is one of the first stumbling blocks to fluent reading. For CLD students whose native language is based on an alphabetic system, knowledge of the letter sounds and patterns in writing is more readily acquired. However, for CLD students who have a native language that is character (Japanese) or script based (Kanji), the acquisition of English spelling may take more time. Compounding the acquisition of spelling in English are the multiple phonemes, rules, and exceptions to these rules. To help CLD students overcome these challenges, Freeman and Freeman (2004) recommend providing multiple encounters with comprehensible written language to increase spelling skills. Engaging CLD students in multiple opportunities to write also is helpful.

The many markers and symbols of orthography also affect how a text is meant to be read. When CLD students are skilled at reading and writing in the native language, they can use knowledge of orthographic markers in the native language to better understand those found in English. For example, Spanish-speaking students know when to raise their voice for a question because the punctuation mark is found both at the beginning and the end of a Spanish language sentence. Exclamation marks also are found at both places in Spanish sentences. Although these markers are only found at the ends of sentences in English, they are helpful to CLD students who have learned to read in Spanish. Because these punctuation markers do not appear at the beginnings of English sentences, it is important for teachers to model for CLD students where these markers appear in English and how to anticipate them when reading.

Being aware that the English system of punctuation is not necessarily the same as that of the native language of CLD students can help educators identify areas of confusion and better understand why CLD students might read text in a monotone voice. To address these issues, teachers can provide explicit instruction on punctuation markers in English. Through such instruction, CLD students begin to learn the intricacies of the English language and how they can use orthographic markers in English text to ensure correct inflection. When CLD students recognize and use orthographic cues when reading, they can better understand and interpret the text.

### Prosodic Elements of the English Language in Practice

*Prosody* is a linguistic term that "describes the rhythmic and tonal aspects of speech: the 'music' of oral language" (Samuels & Farstrup, 2006, p. 134). Prosody plays an important role in communicating the meaning of the written word and is a powerful part of fluency development among CLD students. Prosody implies the ability to read a text with expression and involves using appropriate stress, intonation, and phrasing (Griffith & Rasinski, 2004; IRA, 2002).

To help CLD students develop prosodic skills in English, teachers should make explicit connections between the written and oral aspects of English. Three suggestions for making those connections are as follow:

1. *Stressing the important sounds in words.* In English, multiple-syllable words have one syllable that is spoken with a stronger emphasis than the others. This emphasis is known as *stress,* and it refers to the degree of force with which a syllable is uttered (Coelho, 2004). Unless CLD students are specifically taught the broad stress patterns of English words, they may erroneously apply the stress patterns of the native language. This type of cross-language transfer issue can impede fluency development.

Depending on the native language of the CLD student, stress markers can be very distinct. In French, for example, the final syllable of a word is usually stressed (Coelho, 2004). This pattern is not found in English, so a French-speaking CLD student may struggle to understand or even hear the stress patterns of individual English words. When this happens, the student may substitute a pattern from the native language for the English stress pattern. In contrast, Korean is a fairly monotone language, in which the placement of stress within words does not often change their meanings. Consequently, when learning English, Korean speakers may struggle to pronounce English words with the proper stress. As previously noted, explicit instruction on the stress patterns in English can help CLD students know when and how to apply these patterns when learning to read and speak in English.

2. *Understanding high tones and low tones. Intonation* refers to a language's characteristic patterns of pitch (Coelho, 2004). Two main intonation patterns of the English language are rising and falling. For example, a final rising pitch can be found in a standard *yes/no* question, such as "Are you going to the party?" A final falling pitch is commonly found in *Wh*-questions, such as "What are you going to wear to the party?" A student who speaks a native language in which statements and questions are intoned differently than in English may use a falling pitch when speaking English whereas a native-English speaker will use a rising pitch (Coelho, 2004). As a result, a sentence the CLD student wants to come out as a question may end up sounding like a statement. Explicit instruction and modeling of correct English intonation is crucial for minimizing these sorts of errors.

Proficient English-speaking peers make excellent models for the intonation of English words. As demonstrated in Strategies in Practice 7.1, this type of modeling provides a powerful example of how peers can demonstrate correct intonation for CLD students. This example provides a short script that can be used as a

## Strategies in Practice 7.1

### Intonation Exercise

#### The Missing Book

**Materials Needed**
- A chalkboard or whiteboard
- Chalk or a whiteboard marker
- Copies of "The Missing Book" script (one per student)
- Highlighters (one per student)

**Directions**
- Read the following script with your students by assigning each of them a role. (Not every student will get a role the first time, but the activity can be repeated several times until every student gets a chance to participate.)
- As each student is assigned a role, have him or her highlight the part.
- Write on the board a sentence from the script. Model a few examples of how changing the intonation can change the meaning of the sentence.
- Then have students underline the word or words they are going to place more emphasis on for their parts.
- As you read the script, focus students' attention on these changes in intonation.
- After each reading, discuss as a class the impact of intonation on the meaning of the story.

**The Missing Book**

    **Narrator:** Juan and Yamin arrive at school and go to their classroom. As Yamin is emptying his book bag, he notices that something is missing.

    **Yamin:** Juan, I cannot find my book for class. Do you know where it is?

    **Juan:** I don't know where your book is, and I did not take it.

    **Yamin:** I did not say **you** took my book from my backpack. I was just wondering if you had seen my book.

    **Juan:** No, I have not seen your book. You may want to ask Betty.

    **Yamin:** Betty, have you seen my book?

    **Betty:** I did not see your book, and I did not take it either.

    **Yamin:** I did not **say** you took my book from my backpack.

    **Betty:** Well, I did not take the book from your backpack. But I think I saw Omar by your backpack earlier.

    **Yamin:** Thanks, Betty. I will go ask Omar if he has seen my book. Omar, have you seen my book?

    **Omar:** I did not take your book from your backpack.

**Yamin:** I did not say you **took** my book from my backpack. I was just wondering if you had seen my book.

**Omar:** I saw Emily take the book from your backpack.

**Yamin:** Thanks, Omar. I will go ask Emily for my book. Emily, do you have my book?

**Emily:** No, Yamin, I do not have your book, and I did not take it from your backpack.

**Yamin:** I did not say you took my book from my backpack. Omar said that he saw you take the book from my backpack.

**Emily:** I took my book from my backpack, not yours. Your book is sitting on the desk.

**Yamin:** Oh, I thought you took **my** book from my backpack. Thanks for letting me know where my book is, Emily!

read-aloud to model how intonation can change meaning as the emphasis on certain words within a single sentence is changed.

Intonation is also used to communicate emotions, such as surprise and anger, as well as moods, such as boredom and enthusiasm (Coelho, 2004). For CLD students who come from cultures in which the outward demonstration of emotion is uncommon, such displays of feeling through speech can be surprising and even unsettling. Additionally, English intonation is often used to communicate an ironic meaning that is quite different from the literal meaning of an utterance (Coelho, 2004). For example, sarcasm often confuses CLD students. The statement "Isn't he smart!" can sound very positive when it is actually meant to be negative.

3. *Emphasizing the rhythm of language.* English speech has a rhythm that is different from that of many other languages (Coelho, 2004). In English, the beats between words are spaced evenly throughout sentences. This is largely because certain *content words* in English (words that are central to the meaning of a sentence or utterance) receive more stress when spoken. *Function words* (e.g., articles, conjunctions, and prepositions) balance out these content words to make up the rest of the sentence. Consider the following sentence: *The three branches of government in the United States are legislative, executive, and judicial.* In this example, the content words include *three, branches, government, United States, legislative, executive,* and *judicial.* These words receive the most stress when read aloud because they convey the most important ideas in the sentence. The words that remain (*the, of, in, the, are, and*) serve as function words that pull the sentence together and are not stressed as the sentence is read aloud.

Different sentences with the same number of major stresses take about the same amount of time to utter because the time between stressed syllables is the same, no matter how many minor stresses and unstressed syllables separate the major ones (Coelho, 2004). To master the rhythm of English, CLD students need repeated practice with the unstressed words and syllables that help create the language's rhythmic structure (Coelho, 2004).

## The Role of Vocabulary Knowledge

One of the key factors in developing deep constructs of fluency is the reader's ability to comprehend the words being read. Vocabulary knowledge and its role in developing deep constructs of fluency is demonstrated through the following example:

> Jose's test scores precipitated his acceptance to college and his recognition as a presidential scholar.

In this example, understanding key vocabulary words such as *precipitated* and *scholar* is necessary to understand the message of the sentence. Even words such as *acceptance* and *presidential* have specialized meanings in the context of this sentence. To read the sentence fluently and with meaning, the reader must know what each of the words means and the role it plays in the context of the sentence. When working with CLD students, explicit instruction on key vocabulary is essential for demonstrating how words are used in a text to support structure and meaning. In addition, such instruction helps CLD students move from simply decoding words to comprehending them. Without this comprehension, CLD students remain at a surface construct of fluency development.

Consider the following sentence:

> My cousin eats a lot, but she is skinny.

In this sentence, the emphasis is on the word *but* to contrast the first independent clause from the second. Unless a CLD student understands how the connector *but* influences the meaning of the first phrase, he or she will not understand the message being conveyed within the sentence—for example, that the speaker's cousin has a high metabolism or possibly that the speaker is envious that his or her cousin can eat so much and not gain weight. An idiomatic example of this same concept can be seen in the following sentence:

> She is pretty, but so what?

In this example, the idiomatic phrase *so what* influences the meaning of the sentence in a specific way, implying that beauty is not everything.

When a reader develops such proficiency at decoding text that it becomes automatic, allowing him or her to focus attention on the cognitive task of comprehending instead of decoding (LaBerge & Samuels, 1974), he or she is said to have developed automaticity. *Automaticity* is the quick and effortless identification of words (Ehri & McCormick, 1998; Kuhn & Stahl, 2000; Rasinski, 2004). The words most commonly associated with the development of automaticity are sight words, such as *a, an, and, the, of,* and *it.* These sight words are most commonly pulled from word lists such as the *Dolch word list,* a high-frequency list published by Dr. Edward William Dolch in his book *Problems in Reading* (1948). Although it was published over 50 years ago, the Dolch word list is still commonly used in schools today.

It is important to note here that sight words, while important for CLD students, may need to be given a different teaching focus. Although words such as *a, an, the, of,* and *it* may be useful for monolingual English students to know, these words do not by themselves have meaning and are difficult for CLD students to understand, especially if taught in a decontextualized way. CLD students are better served by learning high-frequency words to which meaning can be easily attached. Words such as *jump, go, like,* and *see* are words that CLD students quickly develop in their oral repertoires and therefore can be easily taught as sight (or high-frequency) words and used to develop fluency in reading without losing meaning.

CLD students who lack automaticity often have great difficulty moving past the surface constructs of fluency. Some of the more common ways educators approach automaticity development with such students include having them read lists of words from top to bottom while being timed, read flashcards with the words from the list written on individual cards, and write the words repeatedly. However, each of these strategies teaches words in isolation and does not result in the immediate transfer to text. Rather, research has found that isolated instruction on sight words actually results in decreased reading comprehension (Block & Israel, 2005).

A similar approach to automaticity instruction in schools is the use of high-frequency *word walls,* which have lists of commonly occurring words (e.g., *of, it, from, the, and, then*). Teachers post these word walls in the classroom, introduce the words to students, and provide varying degrees of repeated practice. Once again, however, research has found that when these words are taught in isolation, CLD students do not readily transfer this knowledge to text (Hudson, Lane, & Pullen, 2005).

Research suggests that for CLD students to develop automaticity with a given word, they need to have opportunities to encounter the word through repeated practice with authentic text (Kuhn & Stahl, 2000; Rasinski, 2004). Providing CLD students with extensive opportunities to read a variety of texts promotes automatic word recognition. For example, teaching younger CLD students stories that are repetitive in nature authentically supports their development of automaticity. Consider the following passage from *Brown Bear, Brown Bear, What Do You See?* (Martin & Carle, 1967):

> Brown Bear,
> Brown Bear,
> What do you see?
> I see a red bird
> looking at me.
> Red Bird,
> Red Bird,
> What do you see? (pp. 2–4)

In this short passage, CLD students are learning to automatically identify, in an authentic manner, the following words: *what, do, you,* and *see.* These words are repeated throughout the story. This newly developing automaticity is then transferable across texts. In addition, repetitive texts also help CLD students learn content-specific words, such as *brown, bear,* and *black.*

Older CLD students can learn the same skills associated with automaticity through poetry, songs, and chants. For example, jazz chants are the rhythmic expression of Standard American English as it occurs in situational contexts. These chants were developed for students learning English as a second language several decades ago (Graham, 1978). Jazz chants are catchy repetitive drills that draw attention to the rhythm and kinesthetic properties of utterances. They can be used to teach surface forms of the language and/or pragmatics. When linked to students' experiences, jazz chants can be powerful tools to help students achieve greater naturalness in English and overcome blocks in pronunciation, thereby increasing fluency. The advantages of using jazz chants are that students learn to express feelings through stress and intonation while simultaneously building a vocabulary appropriate to the familiar rituals of daily life and to expressions and phrases commonly used in English reading texts. A sample chant is included in Strategies in Practice 7.2.

One teacher offered the following insights regarding the development of automaticity through the use of authentic literature:

> *I have several different languages [spoken] in my classroom. When working with such a variety of students, it is important to practice sight words so they can read the text easier. I have found that the best way for my students to learn*

## Strategies in Practice 7.2

### Fluency Chant

#### Lesson for "Please, Can You Help Me?"

Materials Needed
- Copies of the chant (one per student)

Directions
- Pass out copies of the chant, one to each student.
- Start by explaining the situational context. In the chant, the child is gathering items needed for school. Explain the meaning of the vocabulary word *stomping*.
- Read the first line of the chant at normal speed and intonation. Have the students repeat in unison.
- Continue the simple choral repetition for each line of the chant. Stop at any point to correct pronunciation or intonation patterns. Be sure students have a copy of the chant in front of them. Repeat a line several times in chorus, as desired.
- Establish a clear, strong beat by counting, clapping, or snapping your fingers. Continue to demonstrate the beat and repeat the chant.
- Next, divide the class into two equal sections. (There is no limit to the number of students in each section.)
- Have the first section read and repeat the first line of the chant with you. Have the second section read and repeat the second line with you. Continue the pattern for each line of the chant, with your voice providing a model for the reading.
- Now conduct the chant as a two-part dialogue between the students and you. Establish a clear strong rhythm and read the first line of the chant. Have the class answer in unison by reading the second line of the chant.
- Gradually withdraw your model. Have one student group take over your reading while the second group gives the response.

### Please, Can You Help Me?

Please, can you help me?
    Sure, what do you need?
I need a coat with a scarf and gloves,
A jacket and boots for stomping through mud.
    No problem! Please, just follow me.
    I'll show you the way, so you can see.

Please, can you help me?
    Sure, what do you need?

*continued*

I need crayons and a small lunchbox,
Scissors and a backpack, shoes and socks.
No problem! Please, just follow me.
I'll show you the way, so you can see.

Please, can you help me?
Sure, what do you need?
I need bread, cheese, lettuce, and meat,
All for a sandwich with milk and a treat.
No problem! Please, just follow me.
I'll show you the way, so you can see.

Thank you for helping me!
Is there something more you need?
No, I think I am ready to go,
Ready for school and to learn and grow.
Good luck to you and best wishes then,
As you learn new things and have fun with friends.

*to recognize sight words is to practice reading them in poems, songs, chants, and picture books. After we read or sing, we go back to the text and look for those words that we see all the time and try to find out how many times we saw the same word. For example, we may count the number of times we saw the word* the. *In this way, my CLD students are learning to focus on these words and learn how to watch for them in text. It becomes a game in a way— but one that really reinforces and makes my CLD students remember these words and how they fit in stories.*

Stemming from a language experience approach, such a use of sight words in context is a more meaningful way for CLD students to develop automaticity in practice.

## Comprehension as the Key

*Comprehension* is the central element in fluency development among CLD students, for it is through the comprehension of text that CLD students are able to read fluently and interpret text. Yet it is this aspect of fluency development that often is overlooked in schools, as fluency measures traditionally focus more on the rate, accuracy, and expression with which a text is read. One elementary teacher offers this opinion about the dilemma:

*I spend so much time on "timing" the students' reading and monitoring their improvement that even the smallest gains are overlooked. When working with my CLD students, it is these small gains that need to be recognized and celebrated. For example, Juantia is one of my brightest CLD students, but she continues to struggle on the timed readings. When she is not being timed, she reads with lots of feeling and can answer questions about what it is she read. Unfortunately, none of this is reflected on her fluency assessments.*

The authors' work with CLD students has illustrated that a student's ability to read text quickly and accurately is not an accurate measure of fluency development. Reading fluency for CLD students is not at all enhanced and, in fact, may be retarded by the use of timed tests. Instead, fluency is demonstrated by the CLD student's ability to understand and interpret the words and read them in such a manner that they convey the intended message of the text. It is this deeper understanding of the text's message that enables the student to develop deep constructs of fluency. Student fluency may be more effectively enhanced by encouraging students to reread texts, rehearse intonation and phrasing, and practice methodically rather than quickly. To support CLD students in fluency development, ongoing instruction, modeling, and implementation of reading comprehension strategies is essential.

*Explicit instruction* on reading comprehension strategies helps students to think about what they are reading and understanding as they read a text. According to Irvin (1998), explicit instruction on reading comprehension strategies helps students develop *metacognition,* or the ability to think about their own thinking. To read a text fluently, CLD students need to be able to monitor their thinking and assess their understanding. By teaching CLD students how to monitor their own thinking and make corrections when understanding is not taking place, educators help students increase their level of comprehension and enhance their reading fluency.

Cognitive strategies can also be used to promote CLD students' fluency development. As previously discussed in Chapter 6, cognitive strategies guide students to manipulate the material being read mentally (as in making images) or physically (as in grouping items to be learned or taking notes) (Chamot & O'Malley, 1994, p. 61). By manipulating the material they are reading, CLD students are able to focus on specific aspects of a text that might hinder their comprehension and address them in a proactive manner.

Finally, CLD students benefit from collaboration with peers in the development of fluency. Social/affective comprehension strategies foster this type of support and interaction with others to assist student learning through cooperative learning or questioning for clarification (Chamot & O'Malley, 1994). In the authors' work with teachers across the United States, this type of learning strategy has proved the most beneficial to CLD student populations. For this reason, the remainder of this chapter will focus on specific strategies that can be used with peers and small groups to promote the development of deep constructs of fluency.

## ■ Supporting Fluency Development through Collaboration

Interactive learning groups are a valuable tool for supporting CLD students' fluency development because of the language modeling that occurs during group participation. To develop proficiency with academic language, in particular, CLD students need daily opportunities to read, write, speak, and listen in all content areas. Interactive learning groups can comprise student/student, student/teacher, or student/small group configurations. Reutzel and Cooter (2003) describe these groups as temporary and flexible, varying in membership, and based on either student interests or instructional needs.

When forming interactive learning groups to support fluency development, it is important to place CLD students strategically. In each group in which a CLD student is participating, a more proficient English-speaking reader should be included. It is with the support of English-proficient peers that CLD students learn how to appropriately pronounce and produce the prosodic elements of English. Interactive groups also help lower students' anxiety by providing CLD students with a smaller group of peers with whom to practice language.

In addition to strategically placing CLD students in interactive groups, teachers should also design engaging activities that promote fluency in meaningful ways. The following sections will discuss both interactive small-group activities and partner activities that support fluency development.

### Readers' Theater

*Readers' theater* is an activity in which students are asked to adapt text and act it out orally in the form of a play. Unlike a conventional play, however, readers' theater does not require sets, costumes, props, or memorized lines. Rather, students are allowed to read from scripts, and the drama of the play is communicated through the students' phrasing, pausing, and expressive reading of text (Griffith & Rasinski, 2004). Readers' theater benefits CLD students because it allows them to engage in purposeful and repeated practice with text as well as explicit practice and modeling of the prosodic elements of English (stress, intonation, and phrasing). This activity reinforces what has been read and learned in one context by creating opportunities for students to reread and revisit a text in another context and format so that the repetition does not become boring.

By working with a small group to perform a play, CLD students have the opportunity to see, discuss, and practice reading with all the prosodic elements in place. If a CLD student is struggling with expression and voice, a more proficient peer can model the proper way to give meaning to the words. This extended modeling and practice helps CLD students better understand and express the meaning of the text.

Readers' theater can be performed with virtually any reading material. However, when selecting texts for readers' theater, teachers should keep the following points in mind:

- Use plays with distinct characters and plots.
- Make sure the parts for CLD students clearly communicate emotion.
- Keep props to a minimum to focus more closely on promoting understanding.
- Configure groups so CLD students have access to more proficient English-speaking peers for modeling and support.

Readers' theater can also be done in a student's native language to support the transfer of fluency skills from the native language to English. There are also many commercially available readers' theater pieces. Students can even develop readers' theater from their original writing. Figure 7.1 illustrates a readers' theater script that was written by two fourth-grade CLD students. It shows how they drew from personal experiences to engage in repeated practice with text.

Mrs. Melton, a fourth-grade teacher, found that her students learned a great deal about reading with fluency and expression as a result of creating their own readers' theater. Mrs. Melton shares the following about how she uses readers' theater to promote fluency with CLD students:

*Everyone is involved in working on a script, and every student has a speaking part, but the size of the role is negotiated to reduce the affective filter in kids who don't feel comfortable performing. Students work in one of three groups to write the script. Kids decide in groups which characters they want to portray. All students have to have a speaking part. This takes three days to write. Native speakers and CLD students help each other. All students have the chance to practice reading fluently. They practice fluency when practicing for the play. Then students perform their scripts for the class.*

**■ figure 7.1**    Sample Readers' Theater

**Two People Plays**
( ) = what they are doing
_____ = name of character talking
_____ = what they are saying

## PlayOutside
(title)

| | |
|---|---|
| YeRin | do you want to go outside? |
| Emma | I have to ask my mom. |
| YeRin | Okay. |
| Emma | (Emma go to mom rom and ask.) |
| Emma | mom can I play outside? |
| YeRin | You can play ( |
| Emma | I dot know But want play. |
| YeRin | lets play. |
| Emma | lets Play Hide and sick. |
| YeRin | Ok. |
| Emma | your it |
| YeRin | Hide now! |
| Emma | (Emma is Hideing          ) |
| YeRin | (Yerin count.) 12 3456,///// |
| Emma | I'm Finish/ |
| YeRin | I'm going (yeRin is going.) |
| Emma | (Emma is gigling) |

According to Mrs. Melton, her CLD students were able to connect the text to their personal lives and experiences when doing their own readers' theater. These connections enhanced the expressive and interpretive manner in which the students performed their play.

For CLD and other students who are not performing in a readers' theater, the teacher can create a rubric they can use to analyze the delivery and interpretation of the actors in the drama. Criteria for such a rubric might include interpretation of text, expression, fluidity of reading, and communication of meaning. Figure 7.2 provides an example of this type of rubric and illustrates how peers can rate a readers' theater performance. This rubric asks students not only to rate their peers' performance but also to provide elaborate feedback for guiding the performers'

■ **figure 7.2**   Readers' Theater Response Sheet

| Actors: | Name of Play: | | | Date: |
|---|---|---|---|---|
| **Audience Response** | **Great Acting!** | **Pretty Good!** | **Needs Practice** | **Hard to Follow** |
| 1. The actors made me believe what was happening in the play. | | | | |
| 2. The actors used expression in their voices. | | | | |
| 3. The actors sounded like they were talking. | | | | |
| 4. The actors made the play interesting and fun to listen to. | | | | |
| **Star Critiques** | | | | |
| 1. What I liked best about your play was . . . | | | | |
| 2. To make the play better next time, you can . . . | | | | |
| 3. Other comments/reviews . . . | | | | |

future endeavors. An alternative feedback form for student-created, two-person plays is included in Figure 7.3.

## Choral Reading

*Choral reading* is a collaborative strategy in which a whole group reads a text aloud together (Prescott-Griffin & Witherell, 2004). Choral reading encourages

■ **f i g u r e  7.3**   Sample Readers' Theater Response Rubric

**Two Person Plays**
**Skill: to improve fluency**
**Rubric**

Partner names _____ and _____

| 1 | 2 | 3 |
|---|---|---|
| Not very good | Good | Great |

I could hear the play    1    2    ③

I understood what they were doing    1    2    ③

I thought their fluency was    1    2    ③

I thought they did very well at...

_Acting was Good and Voice was Good they rememberd very very well._

CLD students to mimic the pronunciation and rhythm of reading in English. Choral reading also provides a safeguard for language practice through repetition that reduces the affective filter for CLD students.

Mrs. Tuel, a second-grade teacher, discusses the following benefits of choral reading with her CLD students:

> *I do more choral reading as part of the beginning of lessons and find that it really motivates the children. They do not feel like it cheats them [out] of being able to read. Then when I ask them to read on their own, they do it with more ease and fluency. It isn't taking the place of individual responsibility, but supports it by helping their comfort and motivation.*

When used with CLD students, choral reading lessons emphasize key vocabulary and language structures within the text. In this way, choral reading helps students understand the overall message of the text and hear the pronunciation and prosodic elements of English. Because the teacher can direct and model language both before and during the activity, the texts used for choral reading can be more challenging than those read independently by students. After repeated practice as a whole group, the teacher can have CLD students practice choral reading the same text in small groups or with partners. By grouping students with more proficient peers during small-group choral reading exercises, the teacher can help CLD students develop the skills to read fluently and expressively.

Teachers should follow these steps to prepare CLD students for a choral reading activity:

1. Choose a text for the choral reading that can be posted at the front of the room on a "big book" or chartpaper so every student can see it. If the material is available only on a single sheet of paper or in a small book, give a copy to each student or pair of students.
2. Explicitly introduce the key vocabulary in the reading to provide students with important text signals and to increase comprehension. When pictures or illustrations accompany the text, hold a prereading discussion to support comprehension for CLD students.
3. Model the reading aloud using exaggerated expression, providing a concrete example of how to read the text expressively to convey meaning.
4. Ensure that CLD students have opportunities for repeated practice to help them apply fluency skills when reading the text in a small group, with a partner, or independently.

## Repeated Reading

*Repeated reading* activities provide CLD students with the necessary practice for developing automatic recognition of English phonemes, high-frequency words, and word patterns (Grabe, 1991; McLaughlin, 1987). Through repeated readings, CLD students increase their reading rate and accuracy, and when teachers preteach and use the words from the text throughout the lesson, CLD students develop greater comprehension.

A repeated reading can be strategically orchestrated by pairing a CLD reader with a more proficient peer. In this way, the CLD student is supported in the reading activity and has a more fluent model to emulate. If possible, a less proficient English language speaker should be matched with a more capable peer who can also provide native language support. When preparing a repeated reading, the language proficiency level of the CLD student must be kept firmly in mind. Selecting an appropriate text is essential. The text should be at or slightly above the reading level of the CLD student and at the reading level of his or her more proficient partner.

When conducting a repeated reading, the teacher should prepare both reading partners for the task. Having a prereading discussion of vocabulary terms will give students a basic understanding of the words they will encounter in the story. Discussing the story, characters, plot, and genre will help familiarize students with the basic premises of the text. Students can also complete the Paired Fluency Rubric in Figure 7.4 to provide concrete feedback to their partners after each reading.

## Sustained Partner Reading

In *sustained partner reading,* a teacher, other adult, or more proficient peer first reads a passage aloud. Doing so allows the CLD student to hear the exact expression of English conventions. The CLD student then reads the same passage aloud. As the student reads, the teacher, other adult, or more proficient peer gives guidance and encouragement. Such modeling enables the CLD student to more readily identify the proper stress, intonation, and phrasing necessary for developing deep constructs of fluency. "Big books," picture books, and poems posted on chartpaper are useful for these modeling exercises.

Sustained partner reading also provides educators with opportunities to support a student's native language by having parents or other community members share texts in the native language. In addition to promoting the transfer of prosodic knowledge, shared reading activities in the native language can help

**■ figure 7.4**   Paired Fluency Rubric

Name(s) _____   Paired Fluency Rubric

Content Objective
Reads <u>so it is fun to listen to</u>

How to score

| 1 | 2 | 3 | 4 |
|---|---|---|---|
| Hard to Follow | Easy to Follow | Fun to listen to | Read like a story teller |

<u>First Time</u>

Used punctuation (. ? !)  to make the story fun to listen to
1                (2)                    3                    4

Read all of the words correctly and smoothly
1                2                    (3)                    4

<u>Second Time</u>

Used punctuation (. ? !)  to make the story fun to listen to
1                2                    (3)                    4

Read all of the words correctly and smoothly
1                2                    (3)                    4

Comments:
He read too quiet some times.
The 2nd time was better.
I understood the story better
The 2nd time.

*continued*

■ **figure 7.4** Continued

---

Name: _____

#### Paired Fluency Rubric Follow-Up:

1. **How do you think you read?** _I read okay but not loud._

2. **What was good about your reading?** _I said each word right._

3. **What could you have improved on?** _Saying some words with more loudness._

4. **What questions do you have?** _Can I read it faster and make it fun._

5. **Do you think you read with expression to make it interesting?**
   _Sometimes, if I know the words._

6. **Draw a graph below show your plans for future reading practice.**

CLD students understand the differences in interpretation between how a text is presented in the native language and in English. These often subtle differences are difficult for CLD students to identify, let alone understand, unless they are explicitly modeled.

For example, if reading a text in Russian, the parent/community member would model the intonation patterns of the Russian language. After students have heard those distinct patterns, they would benefit from discussing how Russian intonation patterns are different from those in English. If the model is a parent of a CLD student, the student's self-esteem and pride in his or her native language may also increase through the reading activity.

## Conclusion

In this chapter, we explored the implications of surface and deep constructs of fluency for CLD students. The surface constructs of fluency include accuracy, speed, and prosody. When working with CLD students, multiple dimensions of phonemic awareness and phonics skills must be considered, including decoding, orthographic cues, and prosodic elements of language. All of these factors influence the successful development of surface constructs of fluency.

Beyond development of the surface constructs of fluency, this chapter also introduced the importance of developing deep constructs of fluency, in which comprehension is emphasized. Deep constructs of fluency are developed when CLD students are empowered to use vocabulary as the springboard to automaticity and comprehension. Explicit instruction on reading comprehension strategies also helps students think about and comprehend what they are reading and understanding as they read a text. The chapter concluded with examples of readers' theater, choral reading, repeated reading, and sustained partner reading activities that educators can use to promote CLD students' acquisition of deep constructs of fluency.

## key theories and concepts

- automaticity
- choral reading
- content words
- decoding

- deep constructs of fluency
- function words
- interactive learning groups
- intonation

- orthography
- phonological memory connections
- phrasing
- prosody
- readers' theater
- repeated reading

- semantic links
- stress
- surface constructs of fluency
- sustained partner reading
- syntactic links

## ■ professional conversations on practice

1. Consider the approach to fluency instruction dictated by the curriculum in your school. Discuss how this approach does and does not reflect the differential learning needs of your CLD students. Identify any adaptations necessary to make the curriculum better reflect the needs of your CLD students.

2. This chapter discussed deep constructs of fluency. Discuss how you might approach in your own practice the development of deep constructs of fluency, given the various backgrounds and reading proficiencies of your CLD students.

3. Discuss the strategies you currently use to promote fluency development in the classroom. Identify how you might adapt these strategies based on what you learned in this chapter.

## ■ questions for review and reflection

1. What are the key components of reading fluency?

2. Explain the role of decoding in reading fluency. Which cross-language transfer issues affect the process of decoding text for CLD students?

3. Which approach is best for teaching CLD students to develop automaticity: practicing words in isolation or practicing them in context? Why?

4. What are some examples of how orthographic features differ among languages? Why is it important to explicitly teach CLD students the orthographic features of English?

5. How do you currently teach the prosodic elements of reading? How do you differentiate this instruction to reflect the linguistic differences of CLD students?

6. How do content words and function words influence literacy development for CLD students?

7. Why is it so important to place CLD students in interactive learning groups with more proficient English-speaking peers?

**Where the Classroom Comes to Life**

Now go to the Herrera, Perez, and Escamilla MyEducationLab course at www.myeducationlab.com to:

- read and connect with the chapter Objectives;
- use the Study Plan questions to assess your comprehension of the chapter content;
- study chapter content with your Individualized Study Plan;
- engage in multimedia exercises to help you build a deeper and more applied understanding of chapter content.

- How is oral language development different from written language development in the first and second language?

- What has research suggested about effective methods for teaching writing to CLD students?

- What should teachers know about assessing the writing of CLD students from a strength-based perspective?

- What role do metacognitive strategies, cognitive strategies, and social/affective strategies play in learning to write in either a first or a second language?

- What modifications to strategies or approaches can teachers make to help CLD students learn to spell in English?

# Implications of Culture and Language in Writing

*It is axiomatic that for the culture of the teacher to be in the consciousness of the child, the culture of the child must first be in the consciousness of the teacher.*

—Leanna Trail (1994, p. 1), Aborigine teacher

Teachers today often lament that they cannot possibly know about every language group in the United States. In fact, few teachers who have been educated in the United States have had opportunities to acquire proficiency in multiple languages. While those teachers should not feel inadequate, they should take the steps needed to learn something about the particular languages and cultures of the students in their classrooms.

Moreover, the demographic data in the United States indicate that 85 percent of English language learners (ELLs) in the United States speak a common language: Spanish (NCES, 2006). Further, 95 percent of the linguistic diversity is accounted for in five language groups: Spanish, Chinese, Vietnamese, Korean, and Hmong (NCES, 2006). Given this demographic breakdown, the expectation that teachers should know something about the languages and cultures represented in their classrooms is not so daunting.

Knowledge of the languages and cultures of children in the classroom (even if English is the medium of instruction) is especially critical in writing instruction. Consider this writing from a third-grade student and the analyses that follow:

### The Best and Worst of School

May best is Tony Hay wich all de kids be layec Tony hi nis hi chr hes fud wet mi. Mai wrs is Tim Nobdy lik Tim hi hab big blud.

Here is one teacher's analysis of this writing sample:

*This student is like many ELL students in my class. No matter how hard we try, these students struggle with language interference. I can almost sense him thinking in Spanish and writing in English. He likes to write, but in spite of the fact that he has been in our school since first grade, he still does not seem to have many strategies for writing in English. It is like he guesses most of the time and makes it up as he goes along. At this rate, he will not pass the state test this year.*

An alternative interpretation offers this analysis:

*The student above is indeed typical of many ELL students. The teacher's view is that his main problems are (1) Spanish interference and (2) no strategies to help his writing in English. Contrary to the teacher's views, the child has multiple strategies, some of which are influenced by Spanish, some of which are characteristic of any child learning to write in English, and none of which are indicative of "just making it up." The issue is that this particular teacher has never had an opportunity to look at the emerging writing of an ELL child from the viewpoint of what is typical of second language learners from a strength-based perspective.*

This strength-based analysis of the child's writing is offered as a way of demonstrating that this child is not "making it up" but in fact using many strategies.

Here is the message the third-grader intended to communicate:

### The Best and Worst of School

The best thing at school is Tony. I wish all the kids could be like Tony. He is nice. He shares his food with me. The worst thing at school is Tim. Nobody likes Tim. He has big blood.

This chart shows the strategies used to translate the student's original writing into the Standard English version:

| | |
|---|---|
| Spanish phonetic system | *May* for *My*<br>*Hay* for *I*<br>*Hi* for *he*<br>*Hab* for *have* |
| Invented spelling common to monolingual English learners | *Wich* for *wish*<br>*Fud* for *food*<br>*Wet* for *with*<br>*Lik* for *like*<br>*Blud* for *blood*<br>*De* for *the* |
| Cross-linguistic use of idiomatic expression | *big blud* has been translated from the Spanish *sangrón*, which literally means "big blood" but figuratively means someone who is conceited or arrogant. |

The child's strengths in approaching this writing task include his knowledge of the Spanish phonetic system. That is, he knows something about the grapheme/phoneme relationship that words are made of sounds, that graphemes (letters) represent sounds, and that sounds go together to make words. Further, the child also knows a little about the English phonetic system and its graphophonetic system. In some cases, his invented spelling mirrors that of monolingual English children learning to write in English. Finally, this student's use of the words *big blud* indicates his knowledge of idioms. Although he translated the idiom literally instead of conceptually, this knowledge of idiomatic expression should be viewed a strength to build on when teaching writing.

While some might describe this third-grader's writing as "making it up" or writing that is done absent strategies, just the opposite is true. There is ample evidence that this child is using all of his linguistic resources to express himself in writing. Teachers should strive to reinterpret the writing behaviors of second language learners from a more strength-based perspective, rather than a deficit perspective. In addition, educators should use concrete strategies to help ELL students become better writers of English. These perspectives and strategies are the foundation of this chapter.

## ◼ Differences between Oral and Written Language Development

In a frequently used and often cited book about teaching literacy to second language learners, Peregoy and Boyle (2000) provide a nice reminder to teachers of all children that while oral language and written language are both productive language skills, they differ in several rather significant ways. The skills that allow a student to understand and/or speak English do not automatically transfer to writing. This is true for monolingual English speakers as well as for ELL students. Furthermore, being able to speak a language other than English does not guarantee being able to read and write in that language. Unless a student has had formal schooling in the non-English language, he or she may not be able to write in it. It is also worth reiterating here that some languages do not have a written orthographic system, thereby making cross-language transfer of writing skills unlikely. Oral development in one's first language occurs with relatively little explicit instruction, whereas written development requires substantial explicit instruction and practice. Table 8.1 summarizes the primary differences between oral language development and written language development.

As with reading instruction, writing instruction for CLD students cannot be assumed to be the same as that for native English speakers. This chapter will focus on teaching CLD students to write by emphasizing meaningful, functional uses of

■ **table  8.1**    Differences between Oral and Written Language Development

| Oral Language Development | Written Language Development |
|---|---|
| Every culture develops oral language. | Not every culture develops written language. |
| Every child learns the oral language of his or her community. | Not every child learns the written language of his or her community. |
| Oral language is learned with little explicit instruction. | For most children, written language is learned with extensive explicit instruction. |
| Oral language is the primary vehicle for meeting people's basic needs. | Written language is not the primary vehicle for meeting people's basic needs. |

reading and writing combined with explicit instruction. As noted by others in the field (e.g., Hamayan, 1994; Peregoy & Boyle, 2000; Richard-Amato, 1996), ELL students, especially beginning learners, should not be involved in phonics instruction in writing that isolates sounds and letters from the meaningful use of text. Rather, these skills should be developed in the context of reading and writing and learning content in ways that are student centered and meaning based. Further, teachers are encouraged to expose students to a variety of functional literacy events and to provide frequent opportunities for them to read and write.

## ■ Teaching Writing in a Second Language

Several recent syntheses of research regarding literacy instruction and CLD students have focused on reading but not on writing (August & Shanahan, 2006; Genesee, Lindholm-Leary, Saunders, & Christian, 2005; Gersten & Baker, 2000; Slavin & Cheung, 2003). Nonetheless, educators know the following:

1. Students who know how to write in their native or first language transfer their knowledge of the orthographic system from one language to another. There is bidirectional transfer from the first language to the second language and back again.
2. Some strategies that are effective for teaching monolingual English speakers to write may also be effective with CLD students.
3. CLD students have unique needs depending on their age and level of proficiency in English, and effective writing instruction takes these needs into consideration. The teaching of writing to CLD students is good teaching *plus*.

Genesee and Riches (2006) reviewed three major approaches to literacy instruction for CLD students and labeled them *direct, interactive,* and *process based.*

The researchers then examined the research base, attempting to determine which approaches are most effective for teaching CLD students. It is important to note that many studies in the review included several approaches (e.g., interactive + process) in their writing programs.

Briefly, instruction using a *direct approach* emphasizes the explicit and direct instruction of specific reading/writing skills or strategies. Like the bottom-up approach to reading discussed in Chapter 1, direct instruction in writing consists of teaching discrete subskills explicitly. An example of direct instruction is the use of weekly spelling lists that are organized around some sort of spelling principle in English, such as the consonant/vowel/consonant/vowel pattern where the first vowel is long and the final letter *e* is silent (e.g., *like, cake, lone*). Direct instruction in writing might also include a daily oral language program, in which students are given words/sentences and asked to correct misspellings and errors in punctuation and capitalization. Genesee and Riches (2006) report that there is little empirical evidence about the effects of direct instruction on writing at any grade level for CLD students.

Instruction using an *interactive approach* emphasizes learning that is mediated through interaction with other learners or more competent readers and writers (such as the teacher). A goal of interactive approaches includes not just achievement in reading and writing but also engagement and interest in reading and writing. Interactive approaches include peer-learning opportunities, cooperative learning, and gradual release of responsibility models, such as the following:

I do—you watch.

I do—you help.

You do—I help.

You do—I watch.

Interactive approaches to writing also include shared writing experiences, such as the creation of class books and other group-generated writing projects.

Genesee and Riches (2006) assert that many researchers in the field of second language acquisition advocate the use of interactive approaches, for multiple reasons. First, interactive approaches support the individualized teaching and learning that is needed in classrooms with heterogeneous learners. Further, interactive learning environments are also thought to reinforce the participant structures that are used in the homes of some CLD students and that differ from those in the mainstream U.S. culture. For example, interactive learning approaches favor group versus individual learning, collaborative versus competitive demonstrations of competence, and learning by observing versus learning by lecture. General trends that emerged from the review of research in this area indicated that reading and writing behaviors improved as a consequence of participating in interactive learning environments, especially in relation to writing instruction.

*Process approaches* stress the authentic use of written language for communication and self-expression. Process approaches deemphasize teaching the component skills and strategies of reading and writing in favor of learning through induction. In process approaches, the methods are holistic (or top down, as discussed in Chapter 1), and students are invited to engage in free-reading and -writing activities, in which communication is emphasized. Process approaches include dialogue journals, literature logs, free-reading/writing, reader's and writer's workshop, and sustained silent reading.

Theoretically, students acquire standardized reading and writing conventions by being exposed to them, not by having explicit instruction in them. While process approaches are widely used in school literacy programs, evidence for their effectiveness with CLD students is tentative at best. According to Genesee and Riches (2006), "Overall mere exposure to reading and writing conventions did not improve the students' use of them. . . . Process approaches alone are not particularly effective at promoting the acquisition of specific reading and writing skills unless provision is made for such as focus" (p. 124).

The conclusions from Genesee and Riches's (2006) review of research are particularly important for teachers of CLD students:

1. Direct instruction combined with interactive approaches produced significant gains in learning. Process approaches produced mixed results at best and no enhancement in many cases.
2. Process approaches should be a component of writing instruction for CLD students to ensure meaningfulness, authenticity, and functionality. However, process approaches need to be supplemented with direct and interactive approaches to ensure acquisition of critical subcomponents of literacy. Process approaches are not sufficient alone.
3. The most effective methods are likely those that combine approaches in strategic and purposeful ways. Direct approaches in combination with interactive approaches are likely the most effective.

Writing instruction for CLD students needs to start from the beginning in classrooms. It is not in the best interest of students to delay instruction in writing until they have achieved oral proficiency in the second language. As with reading, writing instruction can be effective in promoting and enhancing the acquisition of the other language domains (listening, speaking, and reading). Further, direct instruction in writing, if used in context and combined with interactive approaches, can be effective in teaching metalinguistic skills (i.e., knowledge about language) related to writing.

For social and academic reasons, CLD students must learn to write English with the same level of competence and proficiency as monolingual English speakers.

They must learn to write narrative stories, poems, essays, informative and research papers, and persuasive essays. They must learn to summarize information, take notes, and analyze and synthesize texts. They must learn to write for specific purposes and for specific audiences. Most of all, it is hoped that they will learn to enjoy writing as well as become competent writers.

## Discourse Patterns

In addition to all the things CLD students must learn to write in English, they must also learn how to express themselves using an English discourse pattern. *Discourse patterns* are "the patterns through which a person expresses his or her thoughts on a subject" (Herrera, Murry, & Morales Cabral, 2007, p. 132). The English discourse pattern is very linear, and academic writing in English typically has a distinct introduction, body, and conclusion. Many CLD students follow a very different discourse pattern, in which "narratives, by contrast, may seem circular, repetitious, or digressive" (Herrera, Murry, & Morales Cabral, 2007). As Kaplan (2005) notes, however, "every speaker perceives his/her language as linear and all others as non-linear" (p. 388). Figure 8.1 illustrates the idea that speakers across languages demonstrate differences in rhetorical preferences as they communicate.

Knowing about these discourse patterns can shed light on CLD students' writing, as these students may write according to the discourse pattern they use in their daily lives. To support students' acquisition of an English discourse pattern, explicit instruction on what is expected in English writing is helpful. One of the most common approaches to instruction on the written discourse pattern in English is to

■ **figure 8.1**    Directionality of Discourse Patterns

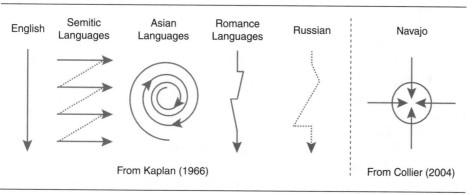

*Source:* Adapted by permission from R. B. Kaplan (1966). Cultural thought patterns in intercultural education. *Language Learning, 16*(1), 1–20, Blackwell Publishing; and C. Collier (2004). PowerPoint image. Ferndale, WA: CrossCultural Developmental Education Services.

teach students to write a five-paragraph story that includes an introduction, three supporting paragraphs, and a conclusion.

The remainder of this chapter provides specific strategies for teaching writing to CLD students using interactive and direct approaches and providing opportunities for students' acquisition of metacognitive, cognitive, and social/affective strategies. (Refer to Chapter 6 for detailed descriptions of these kinds of strategies.) Each of these strategies is centered on meaning and places students' experiences and cultures at the core of the curriculum. Some strategies encourage students to use their native languages to help structure their writing in English. Direct approaches for teaching spelling, writing conventions, and so forth are embedded in interactive activities for students at various levels of English proficiency. Finally, this chapter will discuss what teachers need to be aware of to view the emerging writing of ELL students from a strength-based perspective.

## Combined Interactive/Direct Approaches to Teaching Writing to CLD Students

As stated before, teaching writing to CLD students should not be delayed until students have reached a certain level of English proficiency. In fact, many of the methods used to teach beginning-level listening and speaking skills can easily be expanded to include the teaching of reading and writing. For example, if a teacher is using total physical response (TPR), key words can be written on the board, copied, and illustrated by students to promote reading and writing skills.

It is important to note, however, that teaching writing should always focus on creating meaning, rather than on stringing together isolated elements such as phonemes, orthographic symbols, and the like (Peregoy & Boyle, 2000; Richard-Amato, 1996). Further, the skills of listening, speaking, reading, and writing should be taught in an integrated fashion, rather than as separate entities.

### Beginning Writing

The *language experience approach (LEA)* was developed in the late 1960s and early 1970s as a means of helping native-English-speaking children learn to see reading as "talk written down" (Van Allen, 1976). LEA is an excellent tool for teaching writing to beginning writers while integrating listening, speaking, reading, and writing skills.

LEA builds on stories dictated by individual students, small groups, or the whole class. The teacher serves as a scribe and records these stories verbatim as the students dictate them. The teacher then has several options. For instance, he or she can create "big books" of the stories for students to do choral and echo reading in whole and small groups. The teacher can also create individual copies of the stories for students to read individually and/or in pairs. For reading development, the advantage of LEA is that students usually can read these stories without frustration, as they already know the meanings of the words and the story. This approach is both student centered and meaning centered, making it an authentic learning experience.

LEA also has advantages for the teaching of writing. As the teacher writes the dictated story, the students learn about the English writing system, including organization, syntax, and spellings of high-frequency and irregular words. In addition, after reading the stories, the teacher can ask students to underline their favorite words. Students can then copy these words onto note cards or put them into their own personal dictionaries. Students can also use the note cards for alphabetization tasks, as the words selected hold personal significance for them. Further, the teacher can use student-produced stories to teach English language conventions. To do this, the teacher rewrites part of a story with spelling and punctuation errors on a whiteboard. The students are then asked to correct the errors in spelling and punctuation that they see.

The People Hunt strategy, as outlined in Strategies in Practice 8.1, is one example of a listening/speaking and reading strategy that can easily be expanded to a writing activity. This activity is not only effective for beginning-level students but is also good practice for more advanced students. People Hunt exemplifies instruction using an interactive approach to teaching CLD students that integrates listening, speaking, reading, and writing and that provides opportunities for the direct teaching of grammar and language structures in context.

A second type of language experience approach used to teach writing was developed and studied over a four-year period by Hubbard and Shorey (2003). This study took place with ELL students of multiple language backgrounds who attended a school where ESL was the program model. The teacher in this study, Virginia Shorey, was a ninth-grade ESL teacher who taught ESL reading and writing. Over the years, she became concerned because many of her ESL students had reported that they could not write the stories that were most important to them because they did not know enough English. Shorey invited these students to write in their native languages first (even though she did not speak these native languages), as she felt that using the native language could be an important springboard to English.

Students who were literate in their first languages jumped at the opportunity. However, some students, such as Vinh, a Vietnamese student, were skeptical. Vinh admitted that he could only half-speak Vietnamese and half-speak English. He was concerned about his writing abilities in both languages. Shorey encouraged him to write his thoughts down, even if it meant writing partly in English and partly in Vietnamese (code switching).

As the study unfolded (Hubbard & Shorey, 2003), Shorey shared with the children that her first language was Ilocano and that she was going to try to write in Ilocano (even though it was no longer her strongest language). Shorey had used

## Strategies in Practice 8.1

### People Hunt

**Materials Needed**
- Copies of list of descriptors (one per student)
- Pens or pencils (one per student)

### Directions
- Before conducting the activity, create a list of 8 to 10 descriptors that could apply to various students in the class. Suggested attributes are as follow:

  Has shoelaces
  Hates carrots
  Wears glasses
  Is wearing black socks
  Has five letters in his or her last name
  Lives with a grandparent
  Knows two languages
  Is laughing
  Likes spaghetti
  Has a family with more than six people

- Give students a list of descriptors (one to each student), and then read the list together as a class. Make sure students understand all the vocabulary on the list.
- Tell the students to circulate in the classroom and find someone who has one of the attributes on the list. When the student finds a person with this attribute, he or she should ask that person to sign the sheet by the appropriate descriptor.
- Tell students to circulate in the room and ask each other questions for 10 to 15 minutes. (Remind students to have each person write his or her name by the corresponding attribute.)
- After 15 minutes, direct the students to sit down and then invite them to share their discoveries. Model for students how to generate sentences from their People Hunt activity—for example, "Juan lives with a grandparent" and "Khanh likes spaghetti." (This sharing activity provides an opportunity to do a grammar drill embedded in a meaningful context.)
- After students have had an opportunity to share the discoveries from their People Hunt, ask them to form pairs and compare and contrast their lists.
- Next, direct the pairs of students to write about their classmates. Each pair should write at least five sentences about their People Hunt discoveries. For beginning students, you may need to provide one or two sample sentences to get them started— for example, *Xochitl has shoelaces* and *Lee speaks two languages.* Encourage more advanced students to write more complex sentences (e.g., *María and Roberto like*

*spaghetti* and *Xochitl has shoelaces, but Qui does not*). Remind students to use capital letters to start sentences and periods to end sentences.

- After the pairs have finished writing their five sentences, invite them to read their sentences aloud to the class.

*Note:* This activity gives students experience asking questions and speaking English in a low-stress environment. If necessary, have students practice question formation before doing the activity. For example, you can guide students to ask, "Do you have shoelaces?" or "Are you wearing socks?" By doing this, you can involve students in a grammar-related drill that has been embedded in a meaningful context.

writer's workshop to teach writing, and throughout her career, she had written with her students, sharing her process and strategies. However, in this study, she decided to share with the class stories from her own childhood in the Philippines using her first language (Ilocano), which she admitted was a bit rusty. Regarding writing in Ilocano, Shorey noted:

> Like my students, I was frustrated but not discouraged because writing my stories all of a sudden opened a different world for me. . . . I kept writing no matter how difficult. . . . What did I learn from all of this? I learned not to underestimate the power of the first language. The first language is truly the language of the heart. I also learned to put aside my "Use English Only" thinking for teaching writing. . . . Using Ilocano to write and tell what is important to me validated my identity and gave me a great sense of pride. (Hubbard & Shorey, 2003, p. 55)

Shorey subsequently read her stories to her ESL students in Ilocano, and they listened and liked them, even though they did not understand the language. After Shorey read, the students asked her questions about her story. She then invited her students to do the same—to write and share their stories in their first languages as well as in English. Even those students without a well-developed writing system in their first language took up the invitation. Shorey reported that students listened intently to stories written in non-English languages, even though they did not understand all these languages. They also became more respectful of each other as people and more engaged in listening to each other while at the same time developing their skills as bilingual writers.

In short, encouraging students to write and share in their native languages did not require Shorey to know all those languages, nor did it detract from her teaching students to write in English. This use of bilingual LEA in writer's workshop in the ESL classroom enhanced the overall learning experience for students and also increased their ability to write in English. Hubbard and Shorey (2003) noted that students in this classroom became more attentive to detail in writing in both of their languages, paid more attention to word choice, and in general were more engaged in learning to write.

Culture Wheels is another strategy that provides CLD students with time to write and share their own stories as a way of motivating them to write in their second language. Culture Wheels (Gollnick & Chinn, 1983) were created as a way to have people from different racial, ethnic, and economic groups learn to reflect on their cultural experiences, write about them, and share them in multicultural classes. Although Culture Wheels originally were designed to be used by adults in classes at universities, they can easily be adapted and used to teach writing to second language learners.

Strategies in Practice 8.2 outlines the procedure for creating a Culture Wheel. It includes individual writing tasks as well as class projects using a combination of interactive and direct approaches. It allows for embedded and contextualized direct teaching of grammar and writing and is integrated in that it develops listening, speaking, and reading skills as well as writing skills.

In terms of the development of both speech and writing, Culture Wheels are appropriate for many reasons (Peregoy & Boyle, 2000; Richard-Amato, 1996). First, CLD students may have difficulty figuring out what to write about, and brainstorming exercises do not help if there is a disconnect between the cultural and experiential backgrounds of the students and the content of the class. With Culture Wheels, students have requisite background knowledge, as they are writing about themselves and their experiences. They can focus on writing because they already have ideas to write about. Culture Wheels also provide students with an opportunity to learn about clustering ideas, making maps or plans, and using graphic organizers to help with the writing process. Since generating ideas is not an issue, students can focus on the organizational structure. Likewise, students can better focus on learning the language structures needed to express what they want to say. Culture Wheels provide a wonderful beginning, intermediate, or advanced writing experience.

Students' written errors provide the perfect topics for lessons on grammar, conventions, and spelling. Because Culture Wheels are personal to students, the drafts of their Culture Wheel narratives create opportunities to revise and edit writing in a meaningful context. Furthermore, the structure provides opportunities for students to share their writing with others. Because Culture Wheels are visual, writers can easily get ideas from looking at other students' pictures and hearing other students' stories. The opportunity to interact with other students and the teacher during the creation of Culture Wheels—combined with the drawings, notes, and use of the native language—helps students compose more complex written work than personal journal entries. Culture Wheels encourage cross-cultural communication, as students from different cultural, linguistic, and ethnic groups get to know one another.

### Culture Wheels

**Materials Needed**
- Sheets of $8^1/_2'' \times 11''$ paper (several per student)
- Colored pencils, crayons, and markers (one set per student)

**Directions**
- Before beginning the activity with students, prepare your own Culture Wheel to provide a model for students to follow. Model both the wheel and the corresponding narrative; if necessary, use reduced language so all students will understand the Culture Wheel assignment. Also model how you decided which experiences were important enough to include in the Culture Wheel.
- Invite students to create their own Culture Wheels. First, have students create pie charts about six or seven inches in diameter. In each section of the chart, students should add drawings, notes, and writing in their first language to record the significant events, people, and places in their lives.
- After students have created their Culture Wheels, use the cooperative learning strategy of Think, Pair, Share to have them share the contents of their wheels in a discussion with a peer and then a small group. Solicit volunteers to share their work with the whole class.
- Return to your own Culture Wheel to model how to turn ideas from the drawings and notes into narrative sentences. Instruct students to write sentences about the content from their Culture Wheels. These sentences become the Culture Wheel narrative. The Culture Wheel narrative can consist of complex paragraphs and connected discourse or simple sentences, depending on the English proficiency of the student. (See the sample Culture Wheels and narratives from three children in the early production stage of second language acquisition at the end of this box. The narratives represent students' first drafts.)
- Return to the cooperative learning structure and invite students to read their narratives to a peer and then to a small group.
- Using the students' written language, create opportunities to directly teach English spelling and other language conventions. Students' writing can form the basis of grammar lessons and transformation exercises.
- At this point, return to your own Culture Wheel and ask students to give feedback and ask questions. Model these types of responses for students:

    I am like (<u>name of student</u>) because (<u>feedback</u>).
    I am not like (<u>name of student</u>) because (<u>feedback</u>).

- Create overhead transparencies or PowerPoint slides of all the students' Culture Wheels. Over several days or weeks, have all students share their Culture Wheels and read their culture narratives to the class.
- After the presentation of each Culture Wheel, have students write comments on a form so that the presenter gets written feedback from the class. The feedback form should include the responses modeled above and this additional prompt:

    My question is _____.

*continued*

Having to ask a question gives students a real reason to listen to the presentations of their peers and to interact in English. It is also validating for students to receive written feedback from their peers.

• As a culminating activity, organize all the students' Culture Wheels (illustrations and narratives), along with yours, and publish them as a class book. This book can be read and reread by the class.

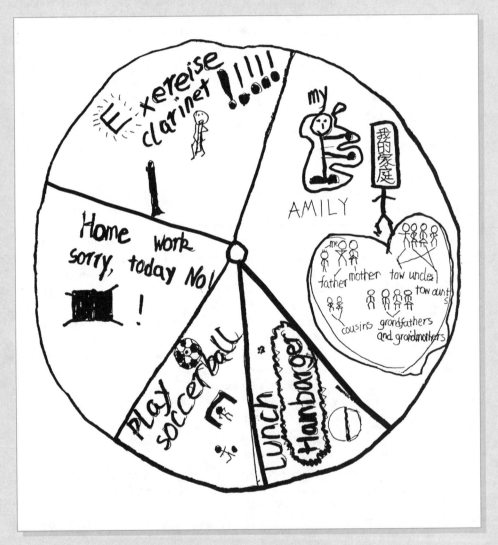

**Student Samples of Culture Wheels**

family

我一名小学生,我有一个大家庭。

I am a pupil, I have a big family.

我的家庭很大，有我爸爸妈妈姑姑姑父
表哥,表妹,和外公外婆、爷爷、奶奶 舅舅舅妈

My family is very big, have my father, mother, uncles, aunts, cousins and my old tow grandfathers, tow old grandmother.

可是只有我的舅舅、舅妈、爸爸,妈妈,和我在
这里。

Only my uncle, aunt, father, mother and me in here.

我喜欢这里,也喜欢这里的食物,我喜欢的
食物有比萨饼和汉堡包。

I like here, like here's food, I like's food is pizza and hambger.

在 这天是我踢了足球。

I play soccer in this day.

In china every day I exercise clarinet.

我在中国每天都吹黑管。

*continued*

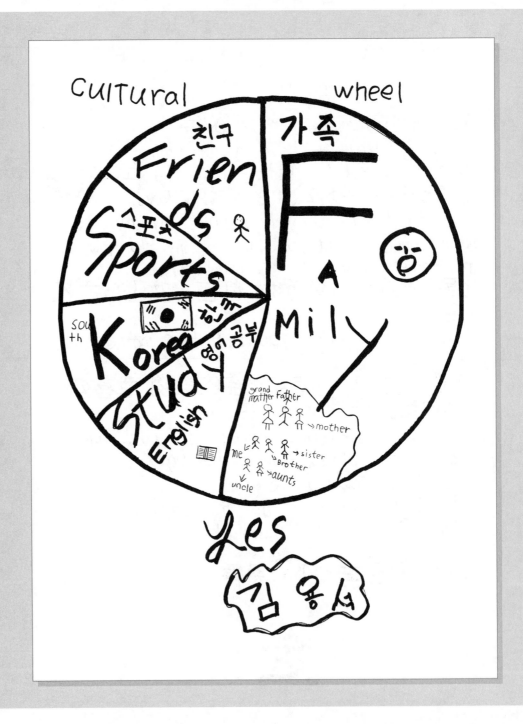

Family
My family many 5.
My gfand mother, father, mather. br
r, and me.
Ramify favolite Korea kimch.
noodle, hamberger.
Father, mather business.
I am study many Airportacademy
school go.

가족

나의 가족은 5명이다

가족은 할머니, 아버지, 어머니, 동생 그리고
나이다.

가족이 좋아하는 음식은 한국 김치
라면, 햄버거이다

나는 꼭 커서 콩큰 대학을 갈것이다.

끝 (END)

*continued*

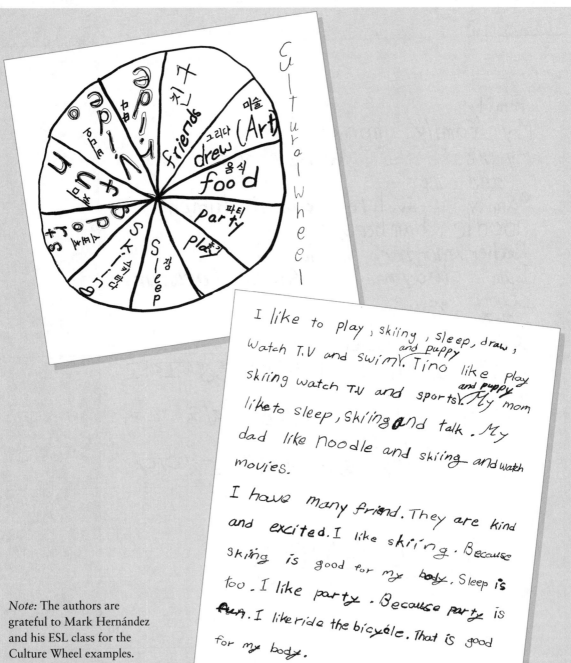

*Note:* The authors are grateful to Mark Hernández and his ESL class for the Culture Wheel examples.

## *Interactive Spelling for CLD Students*

How to teach spelling effectively to CLD students has been a common concern of teachers. Added to this concern is a lack of research providing teachers with direction in this area. However, Madrid, Canas, and Ortega-Medina (2007) demonstrated excellent results in using cooperative team peer tutoring to teach spelling to Spanish/English emerging bilingual students in the third grade. In this study, students were randomly assigned to three instructional interventions:

1. competitive team peer tutoring where individuals earned points for a team
2. cooperative team peer tutoring where students worked to earn points for participants across teams
3. teacher-led instruction where students worked alone and for themselves

The duration of the study was 15 weeks, and it utilized 150 spelling words taken from the fourth-grade basal spelling text. Students in all conditions were pretested and posttested each week on 10 spelling words.

The results of the study (Madrid et al., 2007) showed that both of the team learning conditions resulted in higher levels of correct spelling than the teacher-led intervention. However, the cooperative team peer tutoring resulted in the highest rate of correct responding. Spelling knowledge for students in the cooperative team peer tutoring increased 80.8 percent, compared with that of the competitive team peer tutoring, which increased by 67.2 percent. Spelling knowledge for students involved in teacher-led instruction increased by only 36.2 percent.

The cooperative team peer tutoring strategy was thought to be effective for several reasons (Madrid et al., 2007):

- Cooperative peer tutoring is a more culturally responsive strategy than the competitive or individual strategies that are characteristic of many U.S. classrooms.
- Cooperative peer tutoring provides more opportunities for students to use spelling words in context and with each other, thereby giving them additional practice.
- This particular strategy utilizes both interactive and direct teaching approaches that also have been found effective with CLD students.

The procedure for cooperative team peer tutoring is detailed in Strategies in Practice 8.3. It is important that children receive training in how to be tutors and tutees before trying this procedure. In the Madrid et al. (2007) study, children received five consecutive days of training, on which the teacher taught them the correct tutoring procedures. On Day 1, the teacher demonstrated the peer-tutoring procedures with the teacher assistant serving as the tutee. On Day 2, the teacher randomly chose a

## Strategies in Practice 8.3

### Cooperative Team Peer Tutoring

**Materials Needed**
- Copies of spelling list (one per student)
- Coins (one per student pair)
- Timer
- Paper and pencils for daily activities

**Time Needed**
- 20 minutes a day, five days a week

**Directions**
- On a Friday, introduce 10 new spelling words to the students. Hand out copies of the spelling list. Then pronounce each word and ask students to echo each word aloud and in unison.
- On Monday of the following week and for each day of the remainder of the week, begin the spelling session by saying the following:

   We are going to play a game with spelling words. The purpose of the game is to learn as many new spelling words as we can. The team with the most points wins.

- Randomly divide the class into teams of eight students. Further divide each team into four dyads. Tell the students that they will be with their partners for that week.
- Each day, allow 20 minutes for the spelling game. (Set the timer.) At the start of the game, have students in each dyad flip a coin to see who will be the tutor and who will be the tutee. The *tutor* will read each spelling word from the spelling list. The *tutee* will write each word while simultaneously spelling the word aloud. If the tutee misspells the word, then the tutor will slowly spell the word correctly. The tutee will then be asked to write the word consecutively three times. At this point, the tutor will give verbal reinforcement to the tutee for spelling the word correctly (e.g., "Thank-you for writing the word correctly three times."). If the dyad finishes the entire list of words before the allotted 20 minutes is over, the tutor should start over at the top of the list. Tutees are instructed to stop writing at the sound of the timer.
- On Friday, give the children a posttest on the words they have been practicing all week. Before beginning the test, ask the children to put away all books and to have only a clean sheet of paper and a pencil on their desks. Read each spelling word aloud and use it in a sentence; then repeat the word once. Allow students 10 seconds to write each word. Continue the procedure with all 10 words.
- Based on students' scores on the posttest, award points to dyads (not individuals) and their teams. Decide how to reward the dyads and teams for the points they have earned.

student to join her in front of the group. Using a word list displayed with an overhead projector, the teacher and student demonstrated how the tutoring game works, including how to perform the reinforcement procedure. On Day 3, the teacher randomly selected two students to demonstrate the tutoring procedures in front of the group. As the procedure was modeled, the teacher gave the students feedback for correct tutoring behaviors and proper use of reinforcement procedures. On Days 4 and 5, the teachers asked the children to sit with partners, and the entire group practiced peer tutoring for 20 minutes each day. A timer was used to begin and end the session.

### *Assessing the Writing of Second Language Learners*

The examples provided in this section are from research on Spanish/English bilingual students. While teachers may have multiple language groups in their classrooms, 85 percent of ELL students in the United States speak Spanish as their native language (NCES, 2006). Reporting on the emerging findings of a five-year longitudinal study, Geisler, Escamilla, Hopewell, and Ruiz (2007) examined writing samples produced by emerging bilingual English/Spanish students in grades 1 through 4. These researchers used a rubric developed by the project to examine these students' writing in English and in Spanish. The rubric centered on the writing traits of content, punctuation, and spelling. The researchers also examined the relationship between students' writing in Spanish and writing in English.

Research results demonstrated a high and positive correlation between Spanish writing and English writing in terms of content, punctuation, and overall results. Weak correlations were noted between Spanish spelling and English spelling, which is not surprising, given the differences between the orthographic systems of English and Spanish. From this study (Geisler et al., 2007) and others discussed in this text, there is ample evidence of positive cross-language transfer between English and Spanish. More importantly, however, the study yielded the following qualitative findings about the writing of emerging bilingual writers:

1. The early stages of cross-language transfer between Spanish and English are rule governed but may be misinterpreted by teachers as random strings of letters.
2. Spanish writing skills, strategies, and content served as a scaffold to English, rather than as a source of interference. For individual students, there was a nearly perfect one-to-one correspondence across languages with regard to content, form, and use of conventions.
3. Spelling errors in English were as likely to be typical of English speakers at a particular grade level as they were attributable to the use of Spanish phonology or errors related to the influence of the native language.
4. Bilingual living produces bilingual writing. Bilingual living creates the need for the use of code switching across languages that was found in student writing.

(*Code switching* is a term for students' use of their first language when writing in a second language or vice versa.)

5. In second language writing, the students' ability to express content almost always superceded conventions, indicating that the students had ideas and background knowledge. They simply may have lacked standard ways of expressing those ideas in English.

In their analysis of over 1,000 students' writing samples in English as well as in Spanish, Geisler et al. (2007) were able to demonstrate that Spanish writing serves as a scaffold to English writing. The following writing samples from a first-grade student illustrate this finding:

**Spanish Sample: *Mi animal favorito* (My Favorite Animal)**

*Las ballenas* (Whales)

*A mi me gustan las ballenas porque comen pescaditos blanditos. A mi me gustaria jugar con ellos a aventar aqua.*

(I like whales because they eat soft fish. I would like to play with them by throwing water.)

**English Sample: My Favorite Toy**

My Cat

My toy is I cat. Is e toy. I layc pley con my cat. My cat is yellow.

These two writing samples clearly show that what the student knows about forming sentences beginning with capital letters and ending with periods is transferring from Spanish to English. Further, the student is able to express approximately the same number of ideas in both languages. Although her English spelling is clearly influenced by Spanish, she has a rule-governed way to approach the task of writing in English.

Aside from cross-language transfer, bilingual writers use multiple strategies to express themselves in English and in Spanish. However, students' use of some strategies may be viewed by teachers as a sign of deficit rather than strength in writing. This is particularly true in spelling and when students code switch. The following example of student writing serves to illustrate this point:

**The Best Thing That Has Ever Happened to Me**

The firsh tiem I cam to Estados Unidos wit my family. I was hapy, I want to do alods thegs, want to play, lrn ingles. I wa na si my coins and my ent.

(The first time I came to the United States with my family I was happy.
I wanted to do a lot of things. I wanted to play and learn English. I wanted
to see my cousins and my aunt.)

This sample shows that the student clearly has ideas she wants to express about the
best thing that has ever happened to her. However, her ideas surpass her ability to
write them in standard English. Her spelling errors are a combination of Spanish-
influenced mistakes (*firsh* for *first; si* for *see; coins* for *cousins;* and *ent* for *aunt*)
and words that are commonly misspelled by monolingual English speakers (e.g.,
*tiem* for *time; wit* for *with; hapy* for *happy; thegs* for *things*). The student also uses
code switching to express herself (e.g., *Estados Unidos* for *United States; ingles* for
*English*).

Further, this child was asked to write in a second language about an experience she lived in her first language. CLD students are often asked to do this. This
phenomenon of living in simultaneous worlds with regard to language and culture
creates a situation where students must cognitively transfer the experiences lived in
one language to writing in a second. In this case, it is likely that the student's family discussed moving to the *Estados Unidos* (not the *United States*) and the need to
learn *ingles* (not *English*). Thus, this student lived the experience in Spanish and is
trying to narrate it in English.

Chapter 9 of this text discusses assessment issues in greater detail. However,
it is important for teachers to recognize that CLD students use multiple strategies
when learning to write in English, and this use of multiple strategies should be
viewed as applying a set of complex writing approximations, rather than writing
deficits. Further, understanding these complex strategies can form the basis of creating writing lessons. Teachers can use the checklist illustrated in Figure 8.2 as they
observe and analyze CLD students' strategy use.

## ■ Conclusion

Teachers are reminded of the need to begin to teach CLD students to write in English
from the minute they walk into a U.S. school. For the teaching of writing to be effective, it must be rooted in meaning and must include students' cultural experiences. All
teachers should learn something about the written orthographic systems of the non-
English languages represented in their classrooms. Moreover, they should keep in
mind that when students use conventions, phonetics, or words from their first language when writing in English, it is not a sign of interference; rather, it is a sign that
they are using rule-governed behaviors to approach the task of writing in English.

Finally, the research base on best practices for teaching writing to CLD students is sparse at best, and much work needs to be done in this area. Although

■ **figure 8.2**    Checklist of Second-Language Writing Strategies

| Second-Language Writing Strategy | Student Behavior | Teaching Strategy |
|---|---|---|
| Can get ideas down on paper in English but writing is hard to interpret | | |
| Can write in the native language and use it as a basis for writing in English | | |
| Uses concepts, rules about spelling, and so on that are appropriate in the native language | | |
| Uses approximations that monolingual English students employ in spelling | | |
| Uses code switching conceptually and/or to help get ideas on paper | | |
| Other: | | |

*Note:* Many CLD students use some or all of these strategies in their writing. Educators should note that the more strategies a student uses in any one piece of writing, the more likely his or her writing will be viewed as weak, rather than as demonstrating multiple strengths.

some of the strategies that are effective for monolingual native-English-speaking students may be effective for CLD students, many of them need to be modified. Combining interactive approaches with direct approaches seems to have some potential for teaching writing to CLD students. Teachers are encouraged to try to combine interactive and direct instruction and to modify process approaches. The potential for accelerating the language development of CLD students is great when instruction builds on the cultures and languages that students bring and allows them to interact with more proficient speakers and writers of English.

# ■ key theories and concepts

- code switching
- direct approaches
- interactive approaches
- language interference
- process approaches
- rule-governed behavior
- strength-based perspective

## ■ professional conversations on practice

1. Evaluate your current literacy program's approach to teaching writing. What are the key elements of the program? Which approaches are used? How do the strategies reflect the specific cultural and linguistic needs of your CLD students?

2. This chapter provided specific metacognitive, cognitive, and social/affective strategies for developing the writing skills of CLD students. Discuss how you might incorporate these into daily instruction and how you might expand on them.

3. Discuss the strategies you currently use to teach students to write. Identify how you might adapt these strategies for CLD students based on what you learned in this chapter.

4. Discuss how you and other teachers at your school might use the multiple strategies checklist to help teachers move from a deficit-based view to a strength-based view of second-language writing.

## ■ questions for review and reflection

1. What are the differences among direct approaches, interactive approaches, and process approaches for teaching writing?

2. What approaches are currently considered most effective for teaching writing to CLD students? Why?

3. What are some of the multiple strategies CLD students use when learning to write in a second language?

4. Why might a CLD student's use of multiple strategies cause teachers to think that he or she is a poor writer?

5. What does "living in simultaneous worlds" mean? How does this phenomenon affect the writing of CLD students?

6. What are the major differences between the acquisition of oral language and the acquisition of writing?

7. In teaching CLD students to write, why is it important to emphasize meaning rather than discrete skills?

**PEARSON**
**myeducationlab**
**Where the Classroom Comes to Life**

Now go to the Herrera, Perez, and Escamilla MyEducationLab course at www.myeducationlab.com to:

- read and connect with the chapter Objectives;
- use the Study Plan questions to assess your comprehension of the chapter content;
- study chapter content with your Individualized Study Plan;
- engage in multimedia exercises to help you build a deeper and more applied understanding of chapter content.

## critical considerations

- What are some of the drawbacks of testing CLD students' literacy skills with traditional measures?

- How can authentic assessment be used to provide the teacher with insights into the cognitive process the CLD student goes through when learning to read and write?

- What are some of the key characteristics of authentic assessment?

- Why is it important to consider the four dimensions of the CLD student biography in assessment?

- What are *formative assessments,* and how can educators use them to determine what and how CLD students are processing during instruction?

- What is the role of feedback during formative assessment, and how can it be used to extend a CLD student's connections to his or her prior experiences and background knowledge?

- How can questioning be used as a tool in reading assessment?

# Assessment beyond the Politics of High-Stakes Tests

*Assessment is a necessary evil, especially state assessments. But what we sometimes forget is that there isn't only one specific way to assess our students. Yes, we must assess our students using state, district, and building assessments, but we forget that one specific test cannot fully provide us with a clear scope of a student's ability. It only gives us a glimpse of how the student does on that given day.*

—A secondary teacher of CLD students

Of the several political issues that influence day-to-day events in U.S. classrooms, none is as attention getting as the time and energy spent on preparing students to take state-mandated tests to assess their reading progress. Every spring across the country, teachers bring instruction to a halt to weigh the fruits of their labor for the past year. What teachers have learned is that only a limited amount of information can be gained from testing CLD students using traditional state-, district-, and school-mandated standardized tests. States have failed to provide valid assessments for English language proficiency and reading specific to ELL students.

Two recent reports (Abedi, 2007; Wolf et al., 2008) document the state of assessment for second language learners and the multitude of issues that must be addressed to find assessments that demonstrate and promote these students' success in school. According to Abedi (2004), fairness demands increased efforts toward improving the quality of assessments for ELL students, especially in light of the performance gap between these students and their native-English-speaking peers. Abedi concludes that it is the inadequacies in how CLD students are taught and assessed that explain in part their gap in academic achievement.

As educators in classrooms today, teachers cannot afford to wait for state entities to provide the tools that may lead to more equitable opportunities for CLD students. This chapter will briefly present the current status of reading assessment related to the five core elements (i.e., phonemic awareness, phonics, vocabulary, comprehension, and fluency) discussed in this text and make some suggestions for authentically assessing student learning and informing teachers' practice. By taking this path while waiting for more concrete standardized assessments, teachers can provide access to reading and writing for CLD students. Truly, at this time, it is the only way teachers can move beyond a deficit perspective and advocate for what is right in assessment.

## ■ Overtested without a Foundation

The frenzy to test and get results that predict how students will do in reading is at the highest level ever. This push to segment the teaching of reading has not taken into consideration the biographies of students and has not asked about the implications of testing for students who do not speak English as their native language. For example, the DIBELS test is currently used in over 13,000 schools across the United States, but little empirical research shows how results are relevant for CLD students (Riedel, 2007). Moreover, very little thought has been given to how tests such as this may affect student motivation and engagement in reading and writing. Table 9.1 provides an overview of some of the problems associated with testing CLD students using traditional measures to predict reading and writing progress/growth. In light of these and other drawbacks, concerned educators have turned to authentic assessment to inform their understanding of CLD students' progress and achievement in reading and writing.

## ■ Authentic Assessment Defined

The use of authentic assessment during reading instruction is not a new concept (Valencia, Hiebert, & Afflerbach, 1994). After all, teachers were using observation, portfolios, checklists, informal reading inventories, and other tools to inform their instruction and assess student understanding long before standardized tests became a way of life in their classrooms. Tomlinson and McTighe (2006) have been advocating for a return to more authentic assessment for documenting what students know academically.

Assessments that are developed to provide the teacher with insights into the cognitive process that a CLD student goes through when learning to read and write will increase the chances of that student becoming a successful reader and

**table 9.1** Assessment of the Key Elements

| Assessment | Shortcomings | Recommendations |
|---|---|---|
| **Phonemic Awareness: DIBELS**<br>DIBELS is a timed test that looks for:<br>• **ISF:** Initial Sounds Fluency<br>• **PSF:** Phoneme Segmentation Fluency<br><br>The ISF Measure is a standardized, individually administered measure of phonological awareness that assesses a child's ability to recognize and produce the initial sound in an orally presented word. . . The examiner presents four pictures to the child, names each picture, and then asks the child to identify (i.e., point to or say) the picture that begins with the sound produced orally by the examiner. For example, the examiner says, "This is sink, cat, gloves, and hat. Which picture begins with /s/?" and the student points to the correct picture. The child is also asked to orally produce the beginning sound for an orally presented word that matches one of the given pictures. The examiner calculates the amount of time taken to identify/produce the correct sound and converts the score into the number of initial sounds correct in a minute.<br><br>*Source:* Taken from http://dibels.uoregon.edu/measures/isf.php | Students can lack familiarity with the pictures presented. For instance, if the examiner shows students a picture of a canoe, many students think that it is a boat and hence they say the first sound is /b/ instead of /c/. Also, often the way words are pronounced by the examiner has an effect on the students' understanding of the initial sounds. When students are in the beginning phases of language development and are being introduced to the sounds and letters, they see sounds as a whole (part of a word) rather than in isolation; therefore, it is difficult for students to present them in isolation to another person. | • Do not use this test in isolation for determining a student's level of fluency.<br>• Use this assessment as a screening tool, rather than a diagnostic tool.<br>• Once the information has been gathered on students, augment it through daily classroom observations and by providing students with opportunities to discuss sounds in their native languages.<br>• As words are presented in English, allow students to translate those words into their native languages and then discuss the different sounds in those words.<br>• Allow students to look at different objects and words in their environment and focus on the sounds in those words (e.g., *McDonald's*, *Wal-Mart*, students' own names). |

*continued*

**table 9.1**  Continued

| Assessment | Shortcomings | Recommendations |
|---|---|---|
| The **DIBELS PSF Measure** assesses a student's ability to segment three- and four-phoneme words into their individual phonemes fluently. . . . It requires the student to produce verbally the individual phonemes for each word. For example, the examiner says "sat," and the student says "/s/ /a/ /t/" to receive three possible points for the word.<br><br>*Source:* Taken from http://dibels.uoregon.edu/measures/psf.php | This test often contradicts the nature of reading development. When students are in the beginning phases of reading development and are transitioning toward fluency, it is often difficult for them to segment the sounds because they like to read them as a whole word. Often students are able to produce the beginning and the ending sound but then miss the middle sound. Teachers of ESL students are often unable to understand the variances that students show in the pronunciation. For instance, there is no /w/ sound in Hindi so when a Hindi speaker say /v/ /i/ /n/ for "win," he only gets 2 points out of 3. In this case, the teacher is not considering the difference in pronunciation; rather, he or she sees this as an inability on the part of the student to see the letter *w* correctly. So instead of modeling for the student how to make the sound /w/, the teacher starts doing letter identification for *w* with the student.<br><br>One must ask at this point if this kind of a variance should stand out when a student is pronouncing a sound other than the mainstream sound associated with the test. In most circumstances, it should. The teacher will notice the variance when engaged in meaningful, context-oriented discussions with the students. However, in the case of such tests, the tests are timed, so it is very easy for the person administering to just see this kind of a variance as an inability of students to identify the letter correctly. Furthermore, often there are | • Allow students to use words from their native languages.<br>• Understand students' reading processes. As students start developing their reading skills, remember that the skills should not be considered in isolation.<br>• Engage in meaningful, context-oriented discussions with students to hear the sounds they are pronouncing correctly and the sounds with which they are having difficulty. |

resource people in the school that conduct these assessments and there is a significant disconnect between them and the daily practice of students' language development. Much is lost between an administrator's interpretation of a student's ability and the conveying of this to the classroom teacher who works with student on a daily basis.

## Phonics: DIBELS

### Nonsense Word Fluency (NWF)

Measure asks students to produce verbally the individual letter sound of each letter or verbally produce, or read, the whole nonsense word. For example, if the stimulus word is "vaj," the student could say "/v/ /a/ /j/" or say the word "/vaj/" to obtain a total of three letter sounds correct. The student is allowed 1 minute to produce as many letter sounds as he or she can, and the final score is the number of letter sounds produced correctly in one minute. Because the measure is fluency based, students receive a higher score if they are phonologically recoding the word and receive a lower score if they are providing letter sounds in isolation. The NWF measure takes about 2 minutes to administer and has over 20 alternate forms for monitoring progress.

*Source:* Taken from http://dibels .uoregon.edu/measures/nwf.php

This is a timed test, which always adds an element of difficulty. In addition, when students are learning a new language and trying to make sense out of new words, it is hard for them to make sense out of the nonsense words presented with this type of assessment. It is important to remember that this test is designed to ascertain a student's ability to make sense of letter/sound combinations that are not in his or her permanent memory. However, the individual sounds students are able to produce are highly influenced by the language sounds they have been surrounded by since birth. Therefore, it is important not to confuse the lack of a student's ability to say a given sound with a lack of ability to understand the corresponding letter.

- In the classroom, use individual letter sounds that students can easily produce to determine their ability to work with the patterns assessed by nonsense words tests.

*continued*

**table 9.1** Continued

| Assessment | Shortcomings | Recommendations |
|---|---|---|
| **Fluency: DIBELS**<br><br>**Retell Fluency (RTF) Measure** asks a student to retell for one minute a passage that he/she read for one minute. This process is repeated with two additional passages and the score recorded is the median number of words per minute the student is able to retell.<br><br>Additional information available at http://dibels. uoregon.edu/measures/orf.php | Again, this is a timed test, which always adds a degree of difficulty. Students often are not aware of the skill of retelling. Furthermore, when students are in the initial phases of learning a new language, it is challenging for them to reflect on what they just read and do a retell using the language they are not very familiar with. | • Allow students to practice reading familiar texts with their peers.<br>• Make sure there is a wide range of books in the class library for students to read.<br>• Always remember that fluency and comprehension go hand in hand. When assessing students for fluency in reading, it is important to always ask comprehension questions that relate to the text students are reading.<br>• Allow students to listen to their own reading, as this will help them to gauge their own learning.<br>• Encourage students to use self-monitoring strategies so they can gauge their own fluency development. |
| **Comprehension: RIGBY**<br><br>Through the **RIGBY** assessment, a student's reading level is determined based on his or her comprehension skills.<br><br>Additional information available at http://rigby.harcourtachieve.com/en-US/rigby.htm | This test is very language oriented, which can often be a challenge for second language learners.<br><br>This test also leaves much to the interpretation of the tester, as this assessment includes a lot of literal and inferential questioning items. Often the inferential questions require a great deal of why and how questioning, which can be difficult for students to respond to because so much language usage is needed.<br><br>Assessing students for comprehension in isolation does not provide teachers with meaningful understanding of students' needs. | • Observe students' comprehension skills during the lesson.<br>• Incorporate activities that allow students to use mental images, retell, inferences, and so forth. |

writer in a new language. It is through daily observation and interaction with students that educators can take a more *constructivist* approach to understanding what is happening with this unique population.

*Authentic assessment* can be generally defined as having the following characteristics:

- Assessments are generally developed directly from classroom instruction, group work, and/or related classroom activities. These assessments provide an alternative to traditional assessments.
- Authentic assessments facilitate students' participation in the evaluation process.
- The measurements gained are relevant to both the teacher and the student.
- The emphasis is often placed on real-world problems, tasks, and applications that are relevant to the student and/or his or her community.

Looking beyond the traditional definition of authentic assessment toward one that encompasses a targeted emphasis on the CLD student involves consideration of the following:

- authentic assessments that observe students for both the process and the product of learning
- assessments that reflect the influence of language and culture on process and product
- assessments that build on the assets of CLD students' biographies
- authentic assessments that have preinstructional assessment as part of every lesson
- assessments that support student learning through the use of interactive grouping configurations

Thoughtful consideration and implementation of authentic assessments in reading and writing leads to a more *holistic* understanding of the gains CLD students have made during instruction. The Authentic Assessment Checklist, shown in Figure 9.1, is a simple tool teachers can use to reflect on their current use of authentic assessment with CLD students.

## Authentic Reading Assessment within a CLD Context

Each of the previous chapters has discussed the sociocultural, linguistic, academic, and cognitive dimensions of the CLD student biography as they relate to the five elements of literacy development. In this chapter, we will revisit these dimensions

■ **figure 9.1**    Authentic Assessment Checklist

The following checklist is meant to provide you with a quick tool that can be used to reflect on your use of authentic assessment in practice. **To use the checklist, simply place a check mark on any and all statements that are true about your authentic assessment tools.** After completing the checklist, assess what modifications you might incorporate based on your findings.

| **What:** What purpose does the authentic assessment serve? | ☐ Determines CLD students' native language proficiency (oral, reading, and writing).<br>☐ Explores English language growth (oral, reading, and writing).<br>☐ Identifies students' strengths (socioculturally, linguistically, academically, and/or cognitively).<br>☐ Builds upon CLD students' existing funds of knowledge (both experiential and academic) before the lesson.<br>☐ Assesses what students have learned during or after the lesson.<br>☐ Emphasizes student-constructed (rather than prescribed or regurgitated) responses that challenge and engage students while encouraging them to integrate knowledge and skills.<br>☐ Assigns a preliminary assessment of work completed on a project. |
| --- | --- |
| **How:** How will the information be used to inform instruction and improve learning? | ☐ Use before the lesson to set the stage for learning.<br>☐ Provide feedback to improve CLD student learning during the lesson.<br>☐ Redirect the lesson if needed, to increase CLD students' comprehension.<br>☐ Support the implementation of multiple grouping configurations that build on the diverse CLD student biographies represented in the class. |
| **Where:** Where does it fit in the lesson (before, during, or after)? | ☐ Use to identify the knowledge and skills CLD students bring to the lesson before it begins.<br>☐ Use to prompt and engage CLD students in tasks that promote higher-order thinking during the lesson.<br>☐ Use to empower CLD students to demonstrate their learnings in authentic ways that reflect their sociocultural, linguistic, academic, and/or cognitive assets and needs. |

*Source:* Herrera (2008), p. 32. Used with permission of KCAT/TLC, Kansas State University.

and reflect on the types of considerations and questions related to them in a discussion of authentic assessment of reading and writing.

## Sociocultural Considerations

What are the sociocultural aspects of learning to read and write? Within every family, acts of reading and writing happen that may not be considered relevant by classroom teachers. Yet these at-home literacy events help students create mental interpretations of what they read. When considering the sociocultural dimension teachers should remember the following:

- Reading, writing, and thinking involve the whole child. Teachers will be unable to build from students' early literacy experiences unless they provide the avenues and conditions necessary to ensure that these memories are made public (i.e., shared and taped) during the reading and writing process.
- CLD students may not always readily invest in the process of learning to read and write unless they can move forward and achieve something. Standardized tests often make students feel as though their reading and writing will never be at a level that is valued by the school.
- By incorporating students' so-called "funds of knowledge" (Moll, Armanti, Neff, & Gonzalez, 1992) into instruction, teachers increase the chance that students will be able to make connections between their lives and the reading and writing curriculum.

Understanding how the sociocultural background of CLD students can influence their response to reading and writing informs the teacher's selection of authentic assessment tasks. Such tasks can then provide the teacher with insight into the responses students provide during story retelling, questioning/discussion, and writing to show comprehension of a given text.

## Language as a Cultural Response

The linguistic dimension is about understanding how language develops within the family and community. In school, students are often asked to depart from known ways of asking questions, expressing thoughts and emotions, and communicating what is understood and what is needed. These known acts of language are essential to students becoming readers and writers, because they guide the child in interpreting what he or she reads and support what he or she will talk and write about.

When students' native languages are viewed from a deficit perspective and they are restricted from using the wealth of linguistic knowledge they have, educators limit the success possible during literacy tasks in school. To draw on the linguistic assets that CLD students bring to the classroom, teachers will benefit by doing the following during reading and writing activities:

- listening as students talk about what happens at home
- observing as CLD students listen for different purposes during reading instruction
- observing for levels of student motivation and engagement during reading and writing for different purposes throughout the day
- noting the linguistic variables that the CLD student must negotiate, based on his or her native language
- realizing that every act of reading and writing is a reflection of the way a CLD student comprehends, expresses, and communicates based on his or her culture and language

Language represents the culture of the CLD student. Often, little is done to explore this dimension from a sociocultural perspective. Rather, interpretation of language is based on the more formal aspects of what is required for the student to become a reader, forgetting that reading and writing are about making meaning and expressing thoughts about the world.

## Academic Considerations

During the assessment of reading and writing performance, the focus is often on linear aspects of what a CLD student knows. The information is then frequently used to target interventions that have not considered the biography of the student. More of the same information is then taught in an attempt to get the CLD student to the level where he or she will show growth on standardized tests.

Imagine if educators started to think about exploring authentic assessments from the following perspective:

- Begin by using as building blocks the academic experiences a CLD student brings from his or her background knowledge. Scaffold from the known to the unknown.
- Explore students' exposure to reading and the transfer of that knowledge to reading and writing in English.
- Maximize peers and group interaction in ways that build all levels of reading and writing, rather than isolating students based on language, reading ability, and other factors.
- Always expect that a student will perform one step beyond the level that is set, and celebrate that achievement.

If this perspective were the norm, learning to read and write in the new language would be within reach for all students, regardless of their formal reading assessment scores.

## Cognitive Pathways

Culture and language can play a large role in the way students respond to phonemic awareness tasks, story retelling, writing, and other skills that require them to think and apply what they know. Authentic assessments of CLD students that recognize the following essential considerations have a greater chance of tapping students' higher-order thinking skills and yielding insights about their current level of understanding:

- Every CLD student has developed ways of knowing and experiencing the world. By providing opportunities for the student to demonstrate how he or she has learned new content or acquired new skills, the teacher can better understand how to plan instruction that guides the student to the next level.
- Understanding that comprehension in reading has a strong link to the culture of the CLD student reminds educators to observe for interpretations of text that may not fall within the parameters of expected correct responses.

Learning to view authentic assessment from a cultural and linguistic perspective will provide new scaffolds for teachers to route and reroute students to higher levels of thinking, knowing, and applying new information both in and out of school.

## ■ Preinstructional Assessment

During *preinstructional assessment,* teachers gather information so that during instruction, they can work from the students' known (i.e., native language and existing schemas) to their unknown (i.e., new cultural and academic knowledge students will encounter in the lesson). In addition to standardized tests of English language proficiency (see Table 9.2), the following are sources of information that teachers may have available when determining which supports need to be in place to maximize time and instruction:

- standardized reading assessments
- previous school records
- student writing samples
- state- and district-mandated assessments

| Test | Purpose | Assessment Close-Up | Designations | Grade Levels | Administration |
|---|---|---|---|---|---|
| **IDEA Proficiency Test (IPT)** *Implemented across the United States* | To identify limited English proficient students and assess overall language proficiency | **Oral:** Vocabulary, comprehension, syntax, and verbal expression<br><br>**Reading:** Vocabulary, vocabulary in context, reading for understanding, reading for life skills, and language usage<br><br>**Writing:** Conventions, write a story, write your own story | **Oral:**<br>Non-English Speaker (NES)<br>Limited English Speaker (LES)<br>Fluent English Speaker (FES)<br><br>**Reading/Writing:**<br>Non-English Reader (NER)<br>Limited English Reader (LER)<br>Competent English Reader (CER) | **Oral**<br>Pre-IPT: Preschool<br>IPT I: K–6<br>IPT II: 7–12<br><br>**R/W**<br>IPT 1: 2–3<br>IPT 2: 4–6<br>IPT 3: 7–12 | Oral: 5–20 min. (individually)<br><br>Reading: 45–70 min. (group)<br><br>Writing: 25–45 min. (group) |
| **Language Assessment Scale (LAS)** *Implemented across the United States* | To determine a student's level of language proficiency compared to that of a fluent English speaker | **Oral:** Listening and speaking skills, vocabulary, listening comprehension, and oral production<br><br>**Reading:** Vocabulary, mechanics and usage, fluency, and reading for information<br><br>**Writing:** Student writes sentences and a short essay | LEPa: low R/W, mid L/S<br>LEPb: low R/W, high L/S<br>LEPc: mid R/W, mid L/S<br>LEPd: mid R/W, high L/S<br>LEPe: high R/W, mid L/S<br>FEP: high R/W, high L/S<br><br>R = Reading<br>W = Writing<br>L = Listening<br>S = Speaking | **Oral**<br>K–1<br>2–3<br>4–6<br>6–8<br>7–9+<br><br>**R/W**<br>2–3<br>4–6<br>6–8<br>7–9+ | Oral: 5–20 min. (individually)<br><br>Reading: 45 min. (group)<br><br>Writing: 45 min. (group) |

| Name | Purpose | Assessment Areas | Proficiency Levels | Tiers / Grade Levels | Timing |
|---|---|---|---|---|---|
| **ACCESS for ELLs** (Developed by the WIDA Consortium) *Implemented in Wisconsin, Delaware, Arkansas, District of Columbia, Rhode Island, Maine, New Hampshire, Vermont, Illinois, & Alabama* | Assessing Comprehension & Communication in English State-to-State for ELLs | **Assessment of 5 Content Areas Linked to Standards:** 1. Social & Instructional Language (SI) 2. English Language Arts (LA) 3. Math (MA) 4. Science (SC) 5. Social Studies (SS) *All build on the 4 language domains (listening, speaking, reading, and writing)* | **Level 1:** Entering **Level 2:** Beginning **Level 3:** Developing **Level 4:** Expanding **Level 5:** Bridging **Level 6:** Formerly ELL (Exited students) **Level 7:** Native English Speakers | **Students placed in one of 3 tiers for testing at each grade level based on their language proficiency:** Tier A Tier B Tier C **Tests by grade level:** K–2, 3–5, 6–8, 9–12 | **Listening:** 20–25 min. **Speaking:** Up to 15 min. **Reading:** 35–40 min. **Writing:** Up to 1 hour |
| **KELPA-P** *Kansas language proficiency assessment* | To determine a student's level of English proficiency in listening, speaking, reading, or writing | **Listening:** Students listen and respond to oral prompts by test administrator **Speaking:** Short answer & more detailed questions, describe what is happening in a picture/picture sequence, story retelling **Reading:** Rhyming, cloze sentences, compound words, synonyms/antonyms, definitions, facts/opinions, analogies, short reading passage **Writing:** Grammar/vocabulary, punctuation, syntax, writing essay | **Four Proficiency Level Categories** 1. Beginning 2. Intermediate 3. Advanced 4. Fluent *A differential weighting system by grade level is used to calculate scores for each of the four domains.* | **K–1** (all tests administered individually) **Listening, Speaking, Reading, & Writing** 2–3 4–5 6–8 9–12 | **Listening:** 30 min. (group) **Speaking:** 15 min. (individually) **Reading:** 40 min. (group) **Writing:** 40 min. (group) |

*Source:* Herrera (2008), pp. 64–65. Used with permission of KCAT/TLC, Kansas State University.

Information gleaned from sources such as these can then be augmented with pre-instructional authentic reading assessment tasks at the beginning of each lesson. For example, using sociocultural mind maps, as described in Strategies in Practice 9.1, is an excellent way to preassess students' knowledge prior to reading a story.

## ■ Thinking, Learning, and Formative Assessment

*Formative assessments* are tools and strategies that educators use to determine what and how students are processing the information they are being taught. This type of assessment provides opportunities for teachers to gather data during the

### Strategies in Practice 9.1

#### Sociocultural Mind Map

**Materials Needed**
- Whiteboard or chalkboard
- Markers or chalk
- Drawing materials

**Directions**
- Select a topic/critical concept from the lesson.
- Ask students to think about links they can make to the topic/critical concept from their own backgrounds and experiences.
- Have students draw and write about the links they can make to the topic/concept, creating mind maps.
- As students finish their mind maps, have them discuss their thoughts in small groups. Ensure that all students are held accountable for sharing their ideas.
- Next bring students' attention to the board, and create a class mind map of the topic/concept.
- Record everybody's thoughts on the board, starting with your own.
- Use both pictures and words as you make the mind map. (Allow students to draw.)
- Once the mind map has been completed, review it as a class, highlighting links to the topic/concept.
- During the lesson, allow students to add to their individual mind maps and encourage them to use the information to write essays, poems, persuasive arguments, and so forth.
- As an authentic assessment students can create a new individual mind maps to demonstrate their overall learning.

lesson as they observe students using their sociocultural, language, academic, and cognitive backgrounds to make sense of new content and skills. Such observation then allows teachers to modify the lesson while students are still actively engaged in learning.

Figure 9.2 elaborates on the links between the CLD student biography and formative assessment in practice. As teachers plan for using formative assessments in the classroom, they should consider the four dimensions of the CLD student biography as their roadmap for decision making. Using this roadmap should guide teachers to the best path as they provide feedback and ask questions to measure process and learning.

## Feedback in Formative Assessment

During formative assessment, feedback is provided while there is still time to reroute the student to meet the intended outcome. Feedback serves as a global

■ **f i g u r e  9 . 2**    Formative Assessments: Linking to the CLD Students' Biography

---

**Sociocultural Dimension**

- Formative assessments affirm students' learning and give them hope that they can learn academic content with the proper support.
- Formative assessments can help make explicit links to the CLD students' family by involving them in the assessment process (e.g., students might interview a family member about his or her immigration experience as part of a social studies unit on immigration).
- When multiple grouping configurations are used within formative assessment, CLD students have the opportunity to interact with peers from diverse cultural backgrounds and build links to new content.

**Linguistic Dimension**

- Formative assessments help CLD students see their growth in acquiring academic language.
- Formative assessments encourage CLD students to use English vocabulary in meaningful ways.
- Language is contextually bound and assessed within formative assessments.

**Academic Dimension**

- Formative assessments allow for ongoing monitoring of CLD students' learning throughout the lesson.
- Formative assessments help teachers see where there might be "gaps" in student learning/knowledge that need to be filled.
- Formative assessments reassure CLD students during the lesson, as they are able to monitor their own learning and see what it is they "got right."
- Formative assessments help students reach end goals.

**Cognitive Dimension**

- Formative assessments allow CLD students to demonstrate learning in multiple authentic and contextually bound ways.

---

*Source:* Herrera (2008), p. 116. Used with permission of KCAT/TLC, Kansas State University.

positioning system that provides information to students, supporting them in assessing what they currently understand and identifying the gaps that still exist in their learning (Chappuis & Chappuis, 2007/2008). Feedback serves as the scaffold CLD students may need to become aware of their own thought processes.

In making public both teacher and student thinking (e.g., through think-alouds), the student is pushed to extend learning and to make connections to his or her prior experiences and background knowledge. Feedback can be provided at multiple points while the student is engaged in learning. In addition, feedback from multiple perspectives can be ensured when the teacher plans opportunities for students to do these things:

- participate in cooperative groups that are low risk and that include students whose language and academic abilities will move the CLD student toward a deeper understanding of the lesson
- obtain written and oral feedback from the teacher, in which he or she pinpoints what the student has achieved, what can be reviewed, and which strategies might be used to fill in any gaps
- reflect on their own understanding to clarify and extend learning

Critical to providing beneficial feedback is knowing which questions to ask, when to ask them, and how to connect those questions to the culture and the language of the student. Knowing this essential information will lead teachers to ask questions that guide students to make connections between what they bring to reading and writing and what they are already learning.

## Questions as Tools in Reading Assessment

Questions are one of the most critical tools for providing effective feedback to students (Short & Echevarria, 2004/2005). Different questions promote academic dialogue between the teacher/student, student/student, and dialogue groups (as does students' self-questioning when using metacognitive strategies to understand what is being read). In formative assessment, what is gained is only as relevant as the questions teachers ask of their students throughout the lesson.

Consider the number of times during a day that students raise their hands to respond to a question the teacher has posed. What are the rest of the students thinking while one student is called on to answer the question? To move toward effective questioning, teachers should minimize hands-up questioning in reading instruction. Instead, they should think about the following:

- What kind of dialogue between students will provide the best opportunity to observe what they are thinking and learning?
- How can questions and grouping be orchestrated to increase student thinking about the material?
- What probing/scaffolding questions can be used to move students toward a deeper level of understanding?

- What questions will increase students' connections to prior experiential and academic knowledge?
- What questions will promote students' problem-solving skills?
- What questions will help students maintain their focus and increase their comprehension of the text?

Teachers are in control of what happens in their classrooms. The questions teachers choose to pose during reading and writing instruction heavily influence the academic achievement of their CLD students. Teachers who choose to go beyond hands-up questions and pose questions that reroute students to seek the correct answers are much more likely to see students meet the goals and objectives of the lesson. Figure 9.3 further elaborates on asking questions for different purposes. Teachers should strive to ask questions that move students to think beyond the facts.

■ **figure 9.3**    Beyond the Facts!

*The "formative assessment" you will gain from questioning will only be as relevant as the questions asked of your students.*

This list explores how to take CLD students beyond factual question/answer responses to more cognitively complex responses. Posing such questions allows us to access the deeper dimensions of the CLD student biography and helps students make meaningful connections to the information they are learning.

**Building on CLD Students' Sociocultural Knowledge**
- Do questions increase CLD students' connections between prior experiential/academic knowledge and new learning?
- Are questions structured in such a way that they enable CLD students to draw upon their own culture/language to make meaningful links to new content?
- Do the interactive grouping configurations used within the classroom to promote discussion and questioning encourage CLD students to share sociocultural knowledge?

**Scaffolding Student Learning**
- Are questions posed in a manner that enables the teacher to determine what students are learning?
- Can information gained from student responses help guide instruction and inform the educator as to where instruction might need to be revisited?
- Do questions inform the teacher about areas in which CLD students might need additional support?

Promoting Student Dialogue

- Does questioning engage students in rich dialogue that enhances thinking and learning?
- Is questioning structured to promote small group/partner discussions that foster problem solving?
- Are students strategically grouped based on their CLD biographies (sociocultural, linguistic, academic, and cognitive) in order to promote rich discussion and extended learning?

Building Critical-Thinking Skills

- Are questions posed that engage students in exploring deeper issues related to the topic?
- Do questions push students to think "outside the box" and critically reflect on the implications of their learning?
- Are questions posed in such a manner that they promote understanding of the concept rather than regurgitation of "facts"?

Promoting Cognitive Links

- Does questioning promote higher-order thinking skills?
- Are questions posed in such a way that they take students to the i + 1 by having them *explain the process* they used to solve a problem?

Promoting Self-Assessment

- Are students encouraged to monitor their own understanding of critical concepts by documenting questions about the content before, during, and after the lesson?
- Are students guided to ask questions of themselves so that they can monitor their own understanding/learnings?

*Source:* Herrera (2008), p. 120. Used with permission of KCAT/TLC, Kansas State University.

Preparing questions to use during a lesson involves a systematic approach to checking for understanding before, during, and after the lesson. Selecting strategies that facilitate question posing naturally as part of the lesson makes the use of questions as assessment tools much easier to integrate. Strategies in Practice 9.2 provides examples of the types of questions that can be used before, during, and after the lesson. Using questioning strategically throughout the lesson increases the teacher's understanding of what needs to be taught/retaught and what has been learned. For students, effective formative assessment can be a source of motivation, as they engage in reading and writing for multiple purposes.

## Strategies in Practice 9.2

### Sociocultural, Academic, and Cognitive (SAC) Questions

SAC questions tap into the sociocultural, academic, and cognitive skills that CLD students bring to the classroom. Just as we all have personal experiences that shape who we are and how we learn, so do our CLD students. The key is to tap into these experiences and build on them to support CLD students' academic engagement and success.

**Benefits to CLD Students**

**Before the Lesson:** *Sociocultural Questions*
- Makes CLD students' sociocultural knowledge the springboard on which learning is based.

**During the Lesson:** *Academic Questions*
- Helps CLD students learn how to articulate and monitor their own learning during the lesson.

**After the Lesson:** *Cognitive Questions*
- Allows CLD students to extend their learning by making applications that go beyond the lesson.

**Directions**

**Before the Lesson:** *Sociocultural Questions*
- Pose questions at the beginning of the lesson that tap into your CLD students' sociocultural backgrounds and experiences.
- Sample sociocultural questions include:
  - How can you connect _____ to your life?
  - Does _____ remind you of an experience you have had in your life?
  - What cultural connections can you make to _____?

**During the Lesson:** *Academic Questions*
- Questions during the lesson should uncover student learning and promote comprehension monitoring.
- Sample academic questions include:
  - What helped you understand key concepts in the lesson (e.g., the visuals, hands-on activities)?
  - What links can you make from this topic/concept to others we have learned?
  - How did you focus on key vocabulary during the lesson?
  - What would help you better understand the lesson?

**After the Lesson: Cognitive Questions**
- At the end of the lesson, cognitive questions can be used to extend student learning by prompting them to summarize key concepts and apply the concepts in future learning.
- Sample cognitive questions include:
  - What do you consider to be the most important things you learned from this lesson?
  - How might you use what you have learned to _____?
  - In what ways can you share what you have learned?

*Source:* Herrera (2008), p. 122. Used with permission of KCAT/TLC, Kansas State University.

## Student Case Studies

In this chapter, educators are challenged to look beyond standardized assessment scores and labels and implement authentic assessments, discovering the unique assets and attributes of each student that enters their classroom. For many teachers, the concept of authentic assessments is not new. However, when dealing with an entire classroom of students at different points on the spectrum, the question in many educators' minds is, How do we fit this into an already jammed curriculum?

In this section, we will present two mini–case studies to illustrate how two teachers have incorporated authentic assessment into their daily classroom practice with CLD students. These case studies highlight the interdynamics of standardized assessment and authentic assessment related to the five core elements: phonemic awareness, phonics, vocabulary, comprehension, and fluency.

### Yamin: Where Am I?

Yamin walked into Mrs. Dye's first-grade classroom in early January. He and his family had just moved to the United States from Turkey, so his father could teach at a local university. Yamin's reading assessment scores were as follow:

> DIBELS (Dynamic Indicators of Basic Early Literacy Skills)
- *Letter Naming Fluency:* Yamin was able to identify six uppercase and seven lowercase letters in English.
- *Phoneme Segmentation Fluency:* Yamin was not able to successfully segment any phonemes in English, but he was able to identify some sounds.

- *Nonsense Word Fluency:* Yamin was not able to read any of the nonsense words in English, but again, he was able to identify some sounds.
- *DIBELS Oral Reading Fluency:* Yamin was not able to read the passage, but he could pick out a few words and attempted to read them in English.

Based on these scores, the instructional support recommendation for Yamin was "Intensive—Needs substantial intervention."

Mrs. Dye is certified in English as a second language (ESL) but teaches in a sheltered classroom setting. During Yamin's first week of school, Mrs. Dye did two things. First, she searched on the Internet for some basic information about Turkey and the Turkish language. Second, she set up a meeting with Yamin's parents to learn more about his background. During a 20-minute meeting after school, Mrs. Dye learned the following things about Yamin's biography from his mother via a translator (his father was not at the meeting):

- *Socioculturally:* Yamin's mother speaks only Turkish, but his father speaks both English and Turkish. Yamin is the youngest of three children. His older brothers are in the third and fifth grades, and both speak English. This is the first time Yamin has been in the United States, but he is very excited about attending school and loves to read. His mother reads books in Turkish with him, and his brothers read him simple fairy tales in English.
- *Linguistically:* Yamin attended school for two years in Turkey and was learning some basic English skills, such as the alphabet. He also knows how to say single words in English that this brothers and father have taught him.
- *Academically:* Yamin attended school for two years in Turkey and really enjoyed school, according to his mother. He constantly asked questions, and his teachers in Turkey indicated that he was a very bright student.
- *Cognitively:* Yamin's mother described him as a very creative child who loves to draw and act.

Using the information from Yamin's preassessment scores on the DIBELS, as well as the information gained from Yamin's mother, Mrs. Dye decided to implement the following strategies with Yamin. First, she sent a blank alphabet chart home with Yamin and asked his parents to help him create a Turkish/English alphabet chart. From her Internet search, Mrs. Dye learned that Turkish uses an alphabetic writing system, so she felt the bilingual alphabet chart would support Yamin's phonemic awareness by linking the words in Turkish that started with the same letter sound as those in English. By gathering this information as a form of preassessment, Mrs. Dye worked from the known (Yamin's native language and existing schemas) to the unknown (the letter sounds in English). Since Mrs. Dye does not speak Turkish, she called Yamin's father and asked for his help learning a few words. She wrote the Turkish words phonetically as he pronounced them. During reading instruction, she used them with Yamin by emphasizing the initial sounds in vocabulary words and then having Yamin point to the same initial sound on his chart.

To support phonics development, Mrs. Dye used two forms of data. First, she looked at the letters Yamin was able to identify in English on the DIBELS Letter Naming Fluency assessment. Second, she asked Yamin to write in his writing journal (using nonlinguistic representation, as needed) about his favorite fairy tale that he knew in English. Using both sets of data, Mrs. Dye found that Yamin was able to identify and write the following letters in single English words: *b, f, m, n, p, s,* and *v.* Knowing that Yamin liked to read fairy tales in English with his older brothers, Mrs. Dye found a fairy tale that had vocabulary words that started with many of the letters Yamin already knew. She read the fairy tale with him, and then they went back to the beginning of the story and wrote down all the words that started with the letters he knew. Throughout the week, Mrs. Dye engaged Yamin in a variety of writing activities in which he practiced writing these words in meaningful contexts to build on his existing phonics skills and learn new phonics concepts.

For vocabulary development, Mrs. Dye selected eight key vocabulary words from the district-mandated curriculum story she was teaching that week. These were words that she felt were critical for Yamin to know to understand what the story was about. Mrs. Dye wrote these words (including picture cues) on a sheet of paper before beginning the story and had them translated into Turkish; she sent the list of words home with Yamin so he could practice them with his parents. When the lesson began, Mrs. Dye wrote the same vocabulary words on a piece of construction paper with the same picture cues and had Yamin write and/or draw what he knew about each word. The other students in Mrs. Dye's class did the same activity. After the students were done, Mrs. Dye paired students to share their responses. This activity allowed Mrs. Dye to see what and how Yamin was processing the meanings of the words and what additional support he might need. By pairing Yamin with another student, Mrs. Dye also made sharing a low-risk activity and provided Yamin with an opportunity to extend his understanding of the words by hearing another student's definitions.

To promote Yamin's comprehension, Mrs. Dye asked him questions about the story being read to help him make explicit connections to his prior experiences. She also used peer and small-group configurations to support Yamin's development of and practice with language in meaningful contexts. These groups were set up in such a way that Yamin had linguistic and academic support from his peers. From Mrs. Dye's observations during these activities, it was clear that Yamin's peers were engaging with him in academic dialogue that affirmed and clarified his understandings. This immediate feedback from his peers helped Yamin engage at a higher level in the lesson and become willing to risk saying and doing things in English.

For fluency, Mrs. Dye wanted to bring together Yamin's love of fairy tales and acting, so she found a short and simple readers' theater on "The Three Little Pigs" for Yamin to do with a small group of peers. Yamin was assigned the part of the wolf, as the lines were very repetitive. Multiple visual cues were incorporated into the readers' theater so that when it was rehearsed and performed, Yamin was able to understand what was being said. Mrs. Dye also sent the play home with Yamin and asked him to practice it with his brothers. When the students finally performed their play for the class, Yamin did an excellent job of reading his lines and acting out his part.

As demonstrated in this case study, Mrs. Dye used a variety of preassessments and authentic assessments to identify and build on the four dimensions of Yamin's student biography. She learned about Yamin and his family and used these insights in her instructional planning. She built on Yamin's existing funds of knowledge in his native language as well as in English, and she engaged him in grade-level tasks that incorporated content-area vocabulary. Mrs. Dye also built on Yamin's love of reading fairy tales and acting to engage him in meaningful activities such as readers' theater.

## So Yeong: Between Two Worlds

So Yeong has been in the United States for two years. She, her parents, and her younger brother emigrated from Korea to join extended family who had moved to the United States five years earlier. Since her time in the United States, So Yeong has been receiving English language support in an ESL program for one hour each day. During the rest of the schoolday, she receives instruction in a fourth-grade classroom. At the beginning of the schoolyear, her test scores were as follow:

**DIBELS (Dynamic Indicators of Basic Early Literacy Skills)**
- *DIBELS Oral Reading Fluency:* So Yeong was not able to read the entire passage because she focused on decoding the sounds within the words, which resulted in her pausing several times as she read.

- *DIBELS Retell Fluency:* So Yeong was not able to recall all the details of what she had read but remembered key facts and some additional information.

Based on these scores, the instructional support recommendation for So Yeong was "Strategic—Additional interventions."

### RIGBY Comprehension

- So Yeong was not timed on this test, so she was able to read the entire passage. Although she miscued several words, she self-corrected. When asked comprehension questions, she struggled to articulate her responses in English, although she seemed to understand what was being asked.

Ms. Jenkins is So Yeong's fourth-grade teacher. At the beginning of the schoolyear, Ms. Jenkins met with the ESL teacher to determine the type of support So Yeong was receiving when she was being pulled out of the fourth-grade classroom. The ESL teacher told Ms. Jenkins that they primarily worked on grammar and writing. Ms. Jenkins asked the ESL teacher if she could begin to preview the reading that the class was going to read to help So Yeong prepare for the lesson.

Ms. Jenkins also made a home visit. During this home visit, she learned the following things about So Yeong from her mother and father via a translator:

- *Socioculturally:* So Yeong's parents are very involved in her schooling. They are very conscious of her grades and push her to do well in school. In fact, the focus on school is so important that So Yeong's parents want her to do schoolwork most of the evening; therefore, they do not require her to do a lot of chores around the house so she can spend more time studying.
- *Linguistically:* Although So Yeong's parents do not speak English very well, they encourage So Yeong to speak only in English.
- *Academically:* In Korea, So Yeong attended school for three years. She entered the second grade in November when she moved to the United States. Her math skills are very advanced for fourth grade, but her reading skills are just below grade level.
- *Cognitively:* So Yeong is a very good at memorizing isolated facts and reciting them. However, when asked to synthesize information from texts she has read using her own words, she struggles.

Based on the standardized reading assessment scores and meetings with the ESL teacher and So Yeong's parents, Ms. Jenkins decided to take the following actions. So Yeong had already developed strong phonemic awareness and phonics skills, as evidenced by her ability to decode words in English. Although she sometimes decoded a word incorrectly, she was able to self-correct. To help So Yeong reduce the emphasis she placed on decoding every sound in each word, Ms. Jenkins placed her in a skills-based reading group, where questioning was structured to promote small-group/partner discussions that fostered the application of alternative reading strategies. These discussions and the use of alternative strategies enhanced So Yeong's phonemic awareness and phonics skills by having her explain the process she used to read short passages.

To support So Yeong's vocabulary development and to engage her in rich discussions for practice and application, Ms. Jenkins placed her in multiple types of groups; this provided her with opportunities to discuss the vocabulary words with peers in English. Ms. Jenkins also had So Yeong develop a bilingual dictionary, in which she recorded words in her native language at the same time she wrote them in English. In addition, Ms. Jenkins had So Yeong create mind maps to support her understanding and application of key vocabulary words. In her mind maps, So Yeong used visuals and words from both her native language and English to help her remember the new vocabulary words. So Yeong added to her mind maps throughout the lessons, so Ms. Jenkins used these as formative assessments to monitor So Yeong's growing understanding of the vocabulary terms.

During reading, Ms. Jenkins supported So Yeong's comprehension development by asking questions that prompted her to articulate what she understood about what she was reading, rather than restate facts. In particular, Ms. Jenkins asked So Yeong cognitive questions that extended her learning by prompting her to summarize key concepts and talk about how she might apply these concepts in future learning. Sample cognitive questions Ms. Jenkins asked included (1) Which do you consider to be the most important things you read in the story and why? (2) Can you tell me in your own words what the story was about? and (3) How might you share what you have learned with a friend?

To promote So Yeong's fluency development, Ms. Jenkins had her read with peers and university volunteers two or three times a week. When reading with her peers, So Yeong and her partner completed the Paired Fluency Rubric and the Paired Fluency Rubric Follow-Up (see Chapter 7, Figure 7.4) to document her progress. This allowed Ms. Jenkins to consider So Yeong's reading ability based on the observations of a more proficient peer. She also asked So Yeong to listen to her partner read and to complete the same rubrics for her partner's reading. The modeling by her more proficient peer provided So Yeong with examples of fluent reading as well as opportunities to observe the use of strategies that support fluent reading.

As illustrated in this case study, Ms. Jenkins used multiple forms of formative assessment to monitor So Yeong's learning. The use of these formative assessments helped Ms. Jenkins identify and address gaps in learning/knowledge. It also helped So Yeong learn how to monitor her own learning. These formative assessments were especially successful because of the ongoing questioning that Ms. Jenkins incorporated throughout the process. Such questioning prompted So Yeong to engage in rich dialogue, which enhanced her thinking and learning.

Both of the case studies presented in this chapter illustrate that when educators use CLD students' biographies as the starting point for instruction and assessment, students are empowered to demonstrate their learning in authentic ways that reflect their sociocultural, linguistic, academic, and/or cognitive assets and needs. The use of ongoing formative assessment throughout the lesson helps CLD students learn how to monitor and articulate their own learning. Questioning during the lesson extends students' learning by prompting them to use higher-order thinking skills to summarize key concepts and apply them in different contexts. All of these things used together allow CLD students to demonstrate their true potential in the classroom.

## ■ Conclusion

Formative assessment is critical in the authentic assessment of CLD students' reading and writing skills. The use of strategies that complement purposive feedback and systematic questioning promotes student motivation and engagement in reading and writing activities. Formative assessment can also provide teachers with the information on student learning that is needed for accommodating instruction. In review, teachers who implement formative assessment (1) plan strategically for before, during, and after the lesson; (2) select assessment strategies that will complement their students' biographies; (3) use questioning that promotes student talk and higher-order thinking; and (4) provide feedback that increases students' thinking and learning.

Additionally, teachers working with CLD students align lesson objectives with formative assessments to maximize time and learning opportunities. When making decisions about group configurations, teachers should consider student biographies (sociocultural, linguistic, academic, and cognitive), processes, and products. Ultimately, teaching within the current political circumstances requires teachers to ask, Do thinking and learning matter to me? If the answer is yes, formative assessment must become a regular part of teaching CLD students.

## ■ key theories and concepts

- authentic assessment
- authentic reading assessment
- feedback

- formative assessment
- questioning
- preinstructional assessment

## ■ professional conversations on practice

1. Reflect on the ways that you currently assess CLD students' reading and writing. Identify how these assessments address the four dimensions of the CLD student biography. If they do not, talk about the adaptations you think would be necessary to reflect your CLD students' biographies.

2. This chapter emphasized the role of formative assessment when assessing CLD students' literacy skills. Discuss how your program currently incorporates formative assessment and what additional types of formative assessment you might include based on what you learned in this chapter.

3. In this chapter, you learned about the role of questioning. How might you use what you learned in your own practice to move beyond hands-up questioning in your classroom?

## ■ questions for review and reflection

1. What are some key points to consider when implementing authentic assessment with CLD students?

2. How can the use of authentic assessment provide a more holistic understanding of the gains CLD students have made during instruction?

3. What are some key considerations to keep in mind when assessing the sociocultural dimensions of student learning?

4. How can teachers identify and draw on CLD students' linguistic assets to promote literacy development?

5. Why is it important to look beyond the linear aspects of assessment as it relates to the academic and cognitive dimensions of the CLD student biography?

6. What is the importance of providing feedback from multiple perspectives?

7. How can questioning be moved beyond hands-up questioning during reading assessment?

**Where the Classroom Comes to Life**

Now go to the Herrera, Perez, and Escamilla MyEducationLab course at www.myeducationlab.com to:

- read and connect with the chapter Objectives;
- use the Study Plan questions to assess your comprehension of the chapter content;
- study chapter content with your Individualized Study Plan;
- engage in multimedia exercises to help you build a deeper and more applied understanding of chapter content.

- How do educators use standards that drive literacy instruction as tools for setting the overall goals for CLD students?

- What is at the heart of the IRA/NCTE *Standards for the English Language Arts* and the TESOL *ESL Standards for Pre-K–12 Students*?

- How can instruction using a mandated curriculum be adapted yet still maintain fidelity to the CLD learner?

- How are the standards, reading programs, and CLD student biography interrelated?

- What are the key questions to ask when reflecting on literacy instruction for CLD students?

# Inclusive Literacy Instruction for CLD Students

Reading and writing, as described throughout this text, involve more than just decoding words. Rather, acquiring these skills is a holistic process that stems from the CLD student biography to the acquisition of fundamental and research-based components of literacy. To better understand the central role of the biography, take a moment to reflect on how four people from diverse backgrounds described how they became readers. Note the specific influences of each one's biography as you read.

### Japanese Immigrant Female
*My mother purchased a set of children's literature from all over the world, which was translated into my native language, Japanese. Since I was fully literate at age five, I just silently read by myself. My parents were both busy professionals when I was little, and my siblings were already teenagers then. I don't remember doing anything interactive with them in terms of literacy, except when I had to ask them what some of the unknown words meant. I basically taught myself to read, and I remember using an alphabet chart with pictures to help me.*

### Mexican American Immigrant Male
*Before I started school, my older sisters and mother would tell me stories in Spanish, which I believe prepared me for learning to read. When at school, I was interested in the stories from the books, because they reminded me of the stories that my sisters and mom would tell me. When I began to learn to read, I would bring books home from school and read them to my siblings or parents to practice my reading outside of school. My parents always checked on my progress while learning, even though they did not speak English, and even now when I visit them, my father will ask me to read him something in Spanish to make sure that I am still learning.*

### Korean Immigrant Female

*I grew up in a country where reading and academics are highly valued. Therefore, children are very motivated to learn from the time they are little. I was surrounded by family and extended family who all were very educated. We had many books in the house. I was the youngest, so learning to read was like playing a game with the other members of my family. I asked lots and lots of questions. If I even learned one new word, I received tons of praise and encouragement. Even when I just pretended to read a book (although I might only know one or two words), I was praised and complimented. Also, my older brother was already in school, so he would bring home books from school and I would sit beside him, pretending I was doing the work with him.*

### Polish Immigrant Female

*Ever since I was a small child, my parents used to read to me out loud. Everyday I would listen to "their" stories. One of my favorite stories was about an adventurous lady-bird who would fly to different places in order to discover new animals and plants. Thanks to the latter story, I was acquainted with names of flowers and insects at an early age. Soon enough, I memorized some of the tales, which allowed me to associate words with meanings. In addition, I was introduced to letters at school. Because I associated reading with my favorite childhood stories and spending time with my parents, reading was always fun for me.*

Take a moment to reflect on your own biography and how it has shaped who you are as a reader and writer. Which of the examples shared above reminds you of *your* experiences in learning how to read and write? How have your personal experiences impacted you as a reader and writer today?

In this text, much time has been devoted to examining the role of the CLD student biography in teaching students whose first language is not English to read and write. In this chapter, we explore how these biographies can be embedded in the current standards- and program-driven mandates of today's classrooms. This chapter will provide some guidance on how to align student biographies and standards. In addition, this chapter will revisit critical concepts and strategies that support teachers in modifying their daily classroom practice.

## ■ Setting the Goal: Standards-Driven Literacy Instruction

Standards serve as the starting point for planning instruction. They dictate what is going to be taught and in what sequence. Therefore, no lesson planning should begin without considering which standard is being addressed and how the lesson will be tailored to increase the chance that all students in the classroom will reach the goal.

Often, the goal may seem unattainable, given the linguistic and academic backgrounds of the students in the classroom. However, current research has shown that with thoughtful planning and instruction, teachers can address the needs of second language learners so they, too, can meet the standards (Short & Echevarria, 2004/2005). A brief overview of two of the primary sets of educational standards for language arts and ESL instruction will facilitate our discussion.

## Standards for the English Language Arts

The *Standards for the English Language Arts,* developed in 1996 by the International Reading Association (IRA) and the National Council of Teachers of English (NCTE), were intended as a guide for teachers in developing curriculum and instruction for language arts. In creating these standards, IRA and the NCTE were motivated by the following core beliefs:

1. Standards are needed to prepare students for the literacy requirements of the future as well as the present.
2. Standards can articulate a shared vision of what the nation's teachers, literacy researchers, teacher educators, parents, and others expect students to attain in the English language arts, and what we can do to ensure that this vision is realized.
3. Standards are necessary to promote high educational expectations for all students and to bridge the documented disparities that exist in educational opportunities. (IRA/NCTE, 1996, p. 2)

When exploring the implications of these standards on literacy instruction for CLD students, consider the following statement:

These standards assume that *literacy growth begins before children enter school* as they experience and experiment with literacy activities—reading and writing, and associating spoken words with their graphic representations. Recognizing this fact, these standards encourage the development of curriculum and instruction that *make productive use of the emerging literacy abilities that children bring to school.* (IRA/NCTE, 1996, p. 3, emphasis added)

Agreeing with this statement leads teachers, from the beginning of planning instruction, to consider and build on students' biographies and to recognize the importance of students' literacy backgrounds before they arrive in the classroom. This is a critical consideration when working with CLD students, whose literacy experiences are heavily embedded in their cultural and linguistic backgrounds. These students' literacy experiences, like those of their monolingual English-speaking peers, reflect the act of communication as well as an understanding of literacy within the home and community.

In addition to validating CLD students' existing literacy experiences, the *Standards for the English Language Arts* emphasize that the process of developing literacy is not based on a predetermined sequence set of skills. Rather, it builds on the understanding that "students develop language competencies in different ways and at different rates. . . . Adaptability and creativity are far more effective in the classroom than thoroughgoing applications of a single approach" (IRA/NCTE, 1996, p. 5). Therefore, IRA and the NCTE structured the standards to reflect the diverse range of students found in classrooms across the United States.

The following list presents the 12 standards identified in the IRA/NCTE *Standards for the English Language Arts*. Teachers should consider ways these standards might guide their professional practice.

1. Students read a wide range of print and nonprint texts to build an understanding of texts, of themselves, and of the cultures of the United States and the world; to acquire new information; to respond to the needs and demands of society and the workplace; and for personal fulfillment. Among these texts are fiction and nonfiction, classic and contemporary works.

2. Students read a wide range of literature from many periods in many genres to build an understanding of the many dimensions (e.g., philosophical, ethical, aesthetic) of human experience.

3. Students apply a wide range of strategies to comprehend, interpret, evaluate, and appreciate texts. They draw on their prior experience, their interactions with other readers and writers, their knowledge of word meaning and of other texts, their word identification strategies, and their understanding of textual features (e.g., sound–letter correspondence, sentence structure, context, graphics).

4. Students adjust their use of spoken, written, and visual language (e.g., conventions, style, vocabulary) to communicate effectively with a variety of audiences and for different purposes.

5. Students employ a wide range of strategies as they write and use different writing process elements appropriately to communicate with different audiences for a variety of purposes.

6. Students apply knowledge of language structure, language conventions (e.g., spelling and punctuation), media techniques, figurative language, and genre to create, critique, and discuss print and nonprint texts.

7. Students conduct research on issues and interests by generating ideas and questions, and by posing problems. They gather, evaluate, and synthesize data from a variety of sources (e.g., print and nonprint texts, artifacts, people) to communicate their discoveries in ways that suit their purpose and audience.

8. Students use a variety of technological and informational resources (e.g., libraries, databases, computer networks, video) to gather and synthesize information and to create and communicate knowledge.

9. Students develop an understanding of and respect for diversity in language use, patterns, and dialects across cultures, ethnic groups, geographic regions, and social roles.

10. *Students whose first language is not English make use of their first language to develop competency in the English language arts and to develop understanding of content across the curriculum* [emphasis added].

11. Students participate as knowledgeable, reflective, creative, and critical members of a variety of literacy communities.

12. Students use spoken, written, and visual language to accomplish their own purposes (e.g., for learning, enjoyment, persuasion, and the exchange of information). (IRA/NCTE, 1996, p. 3)

The overall vision of the *Standards for the English Language Arts,* as illustrated by these standards, is to actively engage students in rich literacy experiences and language development. Nowhere do the standards emphasize isolated skill development or decontextualized phonemic awareness exercises. Rather, they target a holistic approach to instruction that builds on the backgrounds of students. Note also that these standards recognize the need to support the native language development of students. As discussed in previous chapters, the native language of the student is central to accelerating English literacy development at all stages of second language acquisition.

## ESL Standards for Pre-K–12 Students

The *English as a Second Language (ESL) Standards for Pre-K–12 Students* were developed in 1997 by Teachers of English to Speakers of Other Languages (TESOL) as a tool for planning and thinking about developing literacy skills with students whose first language is not English. These ESL standards emphasize the following concepts:

- Language as communication.
- Language learning through meaningful and significant use.
- The individual and societal value of bi- and multilingualism.
- The role of ESOL students' native languages in their English language and general academic development.
- Cultural, social, and cognitive processes in language and academic development.
- Assessment that respects language and cultural diversity. (TESOL, 1997, p. 2)

The goals and standards of these ESL standards are as follow:

**Goal 1:** To use English to communicate in social settings
*Standards for Goal 1:* Students will:

1. Use English to participate in social interaction.
2. Interact in, through, and with spoken and written English for personal expression and enjoyment.
3. Use learning strategies to extend their communicative competence.

**Goal 2:** To use English to achieve academically in all content areas
*Standards for Goal 2:* Students will:

1. Use English to interact in the classroom.
2. Use English to obtain, process, construct, and provide subject matter information in spoken and written form.
3. Use appropriate learning strategies to construct and apply academic knowledge.

**Goal 3:** To use English in socially and culturally appropriate ways
*Standards for Goal 3:* Students will:

1. Use the appropriate language variety, register, and genre according to audience, purpose, and setting.
2. Use nonverbal communication appropriate to audience, purpose, and setting.
3. Use appropriate learning strategies to extend their sociolinguistic and sociocultural competence. (TESOL, 1997, pp. 9–10)

A review of the IRA/NCTE *Standards for the English Language Arts* and the TESOL *ESL Standards for Pre-K–12 Students* reveals that both sets highlight communication as the ultimate goal. Teaching reading and writing naturally requires teachers to contextualize their instruction based on the population they are serving during any particular year. Students' biographies dictate the accommodations educators make to the scripted reading programs found in classrooms today. Most often, the question that teachers ask at this point is, What about the limited time and materials and the sequence I am to follow everyday? Reflecting on the current requirements of the educational and sociopolitical context will help teachers solve the question of where CLD students fit into their own philosophy of what is good teaching for students whose first language is not English.

# ■ Fidelity and the CLD Learner

One of the greatest concerns in classrooms today is related to accommodations in reading and doing what the district/school reading and writing program requires of educators. "There is little room for any deviation from the program," teachers often say in response to inquiries about how they accommodate the needs of their CLD students. "The program is set, and it must be followed!"

At what expense are educators going through the motions of teaching CLD students to read and write? Should not the goal be meeting the standards and teaching the skills that lead students to become proficient readers and writers? If the latter is the goal, teachers must begin to think differently about teaching reading and writing. Reading and writing programs that are based on research must be used as solid guides that can then be examined for needed accommodations, given the population of each district, school, and classroom. When educators believe that "one size does *not* fit all," this examination becomes part of the advocacy effort they undertake to ensure equal access for all.

Understanding the research that is related to the needs of CLD students provides educators with the "weapons" to defend changes in curriculum that will lead to students' academic success. Educators must be prepared to articulate which accommodations need to be made and for what reasons. Understanding the four dimensions of the student biography, the implications they have on practice, and what the research reveals about each enables teachers to advocate for what is right for CLD students. Such knowledge also enables teachers to discuss what "fidelity to the core" was intended to mean.

Before discussing how educators can maintain fidelity to the core curriculum they are required to teach, it is important to first explore the traditional structure of these mandated curricula. Figure 10.1 presents an overview of two programs and the structure each follows. Bold type highlights those areas that target instruction related to phonemic awareness, phonics, vocabulary, comprehension, and fluency development.

As demonstrated in Figure 10.1, both programs target the development of specific skills associated with the five core elements emphasized throughout this text. Although there are some similarities between the programs, key points of distinction relate to when and how the core elements are taught. When teaching from either type of program, it is important to consider how instruction can be contextualized at each level to support CLD students' acquisition of the fundamental literacy skills they need to be academically successful.

Commercial literacy programs are very structured, so educators must find ways to adapt their existing curriculum in ways that maintain "fidelity to the core" yet better address the needs of CLD students. Table 10.1 provides tips for adapting

■ **f i g u r e  1 0 . 1**    Sample Literacy Curricula

---

**Program 1**
- Preparing to read and write (prior knowledge/building background)
- *Vocabulary* selection (preselected from story)*
- *Spelling* pretest (phonics based, not from the story)*
- *Reading strategy instruction* (e.g., predict, infer, summarize, monitor, evaluate)*
- Minilessons (e.g., *phonics review, fluency*)
- *Comprehension**
- Writing
- *Word skills and strategies**
- Building *vocabulary**
- *Spelling**
- Grammar
- Communication activities
- Cross-curricular activities

**Program 2**
- *Comprehension strategy* (using and extending what you know)*
- *Vocabulary opportunities* (preselected from story)*
- *Language study* (e.g., subjects and predicates)*
- Word structure (e.g., plurals)
- *Phonics* (e.g., soft *c* and *g*)*
- Individual needs (extended lessons that provide additional supports for various groups of students; sample groups: ESL/ELL, extra support, challenge)
- Extending the lesson (e.g., stop and respond [small group], let's write and make connections, assessment, *fluency*)*

---

*Areas that target instruction related to phonemic awareness, phonics, vocabulary, comprehension, and fluency development.

content along with a brief review of the theoretical foundation on which fundamental and research-based literacy skills are taught.

## ■ Standards, Reading Programs, and the CLD Student Biography

The CLD student biography has been highlighted throughout this text as the foundation for all decision making during planning, teaching, and assessing reading instruction. The role of the student biography in teaching phonemic awareness,

| Research-Based Skills | Key Considerations | Teacher Tips |
|---|---|---|
| Phonemic Awareness | • Phonemic awareness tasks<br>  • Phoneme isolation<br>  • Phoneme identity<br>  • Phoneme categorization<br>  • Phoneme blending<br>  • Phoneme segmentation<br>  • Phoneme deletion<br>  • Phoneme addition<br>  • Phoneme substitution | • Explore each language to identify phonemes that are specific to the native language or that may exist in English in a different position.<br>• Make phonemic awareness activities hands on and tied to cultural contexts.<br>• Actively engage students by making explicit connections to their native languages. |
| Phonics | • Cross-language transfer<br>• Contextualizing phonics<br>  • Developmental<br>  • Integrated<br>  • Application<br>  • Strategic<br>  • Peers | • Identify similarities and differences between graphophonics, syntax, and semantics in the first and second languages.<br>• Explicitly discuss and teach differences within the context of authentic literature.<br>• Modify existing phonics programs to reflect CLD students' biographies. |
| Vocabulary Development | • Approaches<br>  • Reader-based instruction<br>  • Interactive language learning<br>  • Direct instruction<br>• Teaching vocabulary within a linguistic and cultural context<br>• Instruction based on the CLD student biography<br>  • Sociocultural<br>  • Linguistic<br>  • Academic<br>  • Cognitive | • Incorporate visual cues to tap into CLD students' sensory memory.<br>• Provide students with repeated practice throughout the lesson.<br>• Allow students to demonstrate understanding of key vocabulary in their own words.<br>• Engage CLD students in authentic assessments to determine if they truly understand key vocabulary.<br>• Identify and teach a limited number of vocabulary words, making sure students can relate them to the essential meaning of the text. |
| Comprehension | • From the known to the unknown<br>  • Schematic connections in practice<br>• Metacognitve strategies<br>• Cognitive strategies<br>• Social/affective strategies | • Provide explicit and extended strategy instruction to ensure CLD students understand and can apply strategies in practice.<br>• Build on CLD students' existing skills (sociocultural, linguistic, academic, cognitive) to promote comprehension. |
| Fluency | • Deep constructs of fluency<br>  • Multiple dimensions of phonemic awareness and phonics<br>  • Vocabulary knowledge<br>  • Comprehension<br>• Supporting fluency development through collaboration | • Focus on teaching the multiple dimensions of reading fluency to move students beyond quick and accurate reading to actual comprehension.<br>• Engage CLD students in choral readings to help them hear and practice the sounds of the English language.<br>• Use readers' theater to promote repeated, meaningful practice with text. |

phonics, vocabulary, comprehension, and fluency, as well as writing, guided the discussion in each chapter and influenced assessment suggestions for these areas. Thus, this final chapter would not be complete without revisiting the dimensions of the CLD student biography and posing questions related to standards and programs for CLD students.

As authors, we like to think about reading and writing programs as materials that set the scope and sequence of what should be taught at a certain grade level, with the understanding that human potential is realized for different students at different times. What teachers do with the curriculum either provides access and promotes learning to reach that potential or shuts the door through robotic instruction. Think about the questions that follow related to each of the four dimensions as you bridge the world of standards, curricular mandates, and the CLD students you teach.

## Sociocultural Knowledge

Motivation plays an important role in CLD students' learning. When teachers work diligently to include multicultural and multilingual texts in daily instruction (and not just on holidays), they validate and motivate their CLD students through the positive recognition of their cultural identities. Ongoing validation of students' cultural and linguistic diversity helps create a true community of learners.

To assess how the sociocultural dimension of the CLD student biography is being addressed, consider the following questions:

- How has literacy instruction built on the sociocultural assets and literacy biographies that CLD students bring with them from home?
- How have CLD students been engaged in reading a wide variety of texts identified within the existing curriculum, as well as outside this curriculum, to build an understanding of themselves and other cultures?
- How have CLD students used spoken, written, and visual language to demonstrate who they are and to foster a love of reading?
- In what ways have students been engaged in literacy activities that promote communication and social interaction with their peers and teachers?

## Linguistic Knowledge

As we have discussed throughout this text, language is more than words and more than cognition; it is a basis for identity. Second language acquisition for CLD students is intertwined with knowledge of the first language (Cummins, 1981, 2000). Thus, when a teacher supports a CLD student's first-language literacy development, this support has a direct and positive impact on his or her second-language literacy development. Research has shown that the more proficient a CLD student is in the native language, the faster he or she will acquire English, as existing knowledge, concepts, and skills in the native language transfer to reinforce reading ability in a second language (Collier & Thomas, 1992; Cummins, 1989; Escamilla, 1987). As such, the more a teacher knows about a particular student's stage of second language acquisition, the better able he or she will be to plan literacy lessons that support the student's comprehension of and engagement with academic tasks.

Consider these questions:

- How is the transfer of literacy skills learned in the native language fostered to promote the acquisition of literacy skills in English?
- In what ways do CLD students use spoken and written English for personal expression and enjoyment?
- How does targeted vocabulary identified from the text address the linguistic needs of each student based on his or her stage of language acquisition?
- How do students learn how to adjust their use of spoken, written, and visual language to communicate effectively with a variety of audiences and for different purposes?

## Academic Knowledge

Academic knowledge reflects the academic experiences a CLD student has had in school. When approaching literacy instruction, teachers can first determine what academic experiences students have had; such experiences offer insights into areas of specific need. If a CLD student has had schooling in his or her native country and moves to the United States in the fourth grade, he or she will have already developed deep reservoirs of academic knowledge that can be drawn on while learning English. To support educators in first ascertaining the academic knowledge CLD students bring to the lesson and then building on that knowledge, the following questions, derived from the previously discussed standards, can serve as a valuable guide:

- How are the academic skills CLD students bring to reading identified and built on?
- How has instruction been scaffolded so that CLD students are stretched academically and learn how to read and write using grade-level content and materials?
- What types of literacy activities prompt and guide CLD students to be knowledgeable, reflective, creative, and critical members of a variety of literacy communities?
- In what ways are students exposed to a wide range of literature from many periods and in many genres to build an understanding of the multidimensional world?

## Cognitive Knowledge

For CLD students to be academically successful in acquiring grade-level literacy skills, teachers must provide them with access to grade-level content and curriculum on a daily basis. To support students in using this grade-level curriculum, teachers need to scaffold the content by previewing information before the lesson, identifying key vocabulary, and explicitly teaching reading comprehension strategies. Questions to consider include these:

- How are CLD students' existing ways of knowing identified and built on when teaching reading?
- Are reading comprehension strategies introduced and revisited throughout the lesson in ways that both build on CLD students' background knowledge and promote students' application and use of new material in meaningful contexts? How so?
- In what ways are CLD students explicitly taught a wide range of strategies designed to help them comprehend, interpret, evaluate, and appreciate texts within the existing curriculum as well as beyond?

Given the student diversity in today's classrooms and the demands that established, culturally discrete academic curricula place on teachers, the task of learning about each CLD student's biography becomes imperative for addressing his or her needs. The insights gained from such efforts will enable teachers to continually adapt these curricula to capitalize on the experiences and knowledge CLD students bring to the classroom.

## ■ Conclusion

By giving children the tools they need to decode and comprehend text, teachers have the power to shape students' lives, help them fulfill their dreams, and open up a world of opportunities. To reach the same level of academic achievement as their monolingual English-speaking peers, CLD students need to be active members of their academic world, not just passive observers.

Teachers can help make this possible. The key is to break the habits of mind that are embedded in daily instructional practices. No longer can teachers teach the same curriculum the same way, year after year. Rather, they must continually reflect on new ways to modify instruction for meeting the specific sociocultural, linguistic, academic, and cognitive needs of their CLD students. It is in the celebration of students' diversity that teachers provide them with the tools necessary not only to successfully acquire English literacy skills but also to take charge of what lies in their future.

## ■ key theories and concepts

- *ESL Standards for Pre-K–12 Students*
- *Standards for the English Language Arts*

## ■ professional conversations on practice

1. Reflect on the standards that drive your literacy instruction, and discuss the overall goals of these standards. Talk about where your CLD students fit within these standards.

2. Discuss how your current reading program structures literacy instruction. In what ways does this instruction reflect the specific linguistic and academic needs of your CLD students? If it does not, how might you use what you learned in this chapter to make the types of adaptations you believe are most critical?

3. Identify ways you will rethink how you approach literacy instruction so that the CLD student biography becomes the starting point for instruction. Specifically, discuss how you will identify and build on the sociocultural, linguistic, academic, and cognitive assets that CLD students bring.

## ■ questions for review and reflection

1. How has your view of standards and their goals changed?

2. In what ways might you use standards as a guide for what you want your students to achieve, rather than as a specific set of subskills they must acquire?

3. How can you adapt your existing curriculum to embed strategies learned throughout this text into your current instructional practice?

4. How will you begin to incorporate what you have learned about the various dimensions of the CLD student biography (i.e., sociocultural, linguistic, academic, and cognitive) and make this the starting point for instruction?

**Where the Classroom Comes to Life**

Now go to the Herrera, Perez, and Escamilla MyEducationLab course at www.myeducationlab.com to:

- read and connect with the chapter Objectives;
- use the Study Plan questions to assess your comprehension of the chapter content;
- study chapter content with your Individualized Study Plan;
- engage in multimedia exercises to help you build a deeper and more applied understanding of chapter content.

**alphabetic principle:** The ability to transfer phonological knowledge to text by linking sounds with letters.

**authentic assessment:** Refers to assessments that are generally developed directly from classroom instruction, group work, or related classroom activities that provide an alternative to traditional assessments. Authentic assessments emphasize real-world problems, tasks, or applications that are relevant to the student and his or her community. When used with CLD students, such assessments build on the assets of students' biographies.

**automaticity:** The quick, effortless identification of words that enables the reader to focus his or her attention on the cognitive task of comprehending instead of decoding.

**basic interpersonal communication skills (BICS):** The language skills needed for everyday situations and circumstances that are supported by sociocultural knowledge and nonverbal communication.

**bottom-up reading process model:** A part-to-whole model of the reading process, in which skills are mastered in a sequential order, beginning with letter recognition and ending with schema-level analysis.

**code switching:** An individual's use of his or her first language when speaking or writing in a second language, or vice versa. Code switching is born from the reality of bilingual living.

**cognates:** Words that are spelled the same (or nearly the same) in two languages and have the same meaning in both languages.

**cognitive academic language proficiency (CALP):** The language skills needed for more abstract thinking and comprehension of academic concepts and vocabulary.

**cognitive comprehension strategies:** Strategies that help the learner manipulate material being read mentally (as in visualizing) or physically (as in notetaking).

**comprehensible input:** New information the learner is able to understand because steps have been taken to accommodate his or her cognitive and linguistic assets and needs.

**culturally and linguistically diverse (CLD):** The preferred term for an individual or group of individuals whose culture or language differs from that of the dominant group.

**deep constructs of fluency:** Constructs of fluency that emphasize comprehension. Reading instruction that targets the development of deep constructs of fluency uses vocabulary as the springboard to automaticity and comprehension.

**English language learner (ELL):** An individual who is in the process of acquiring English as an additional language. This term is used in this text when discussing instruction and learning processes unique to second-language learners. However, *CLD* is the preferred term, because it emphasizes both the cultural and linguistic assets a student brings to the classroom.

**formative assessment:** Refers to assessments used to gather data during the lesson as students are observed using their sociocultural, language, academic, and cognitive backgrounds to make sense of new content and skills. Resulting insights enable the teacher to modify the lesson while students are still actively engaged in learning.

**grapheme:** An individual letter in a written word.

**graphophonic cueing system:** A reading support system that includes both visual and sound knowledge in addition to knowledge of correspondences between letters and sounds.

**interactive reading process model:**   A model of the reading process that defines the reader's role as a constructor of meaning, whereby the reader simultaneously makes schematic connections *and* decodes letters and words, thus moving fluidly between the skills and processes of whole-to-part and part-to-whole models.

**intonation:**   Characteristic patterns of rising and falling pitch in spoken language.

**metacognitive comprehension strategies:** Strategies that help the learner think about his or her own thinking. Such strategies enable a reader to take corrective action and more effectively engage with the text when reading comprehension begins to decline.

**phoneme:**   An individual sound within a spoken word.

**phoneme addition:**   A phonemic awareness task that requires students to make a new word by adding a phoneme to an existing word.

**phoneme blending:**   A phonemic awareness task that requires students to listen to a sequence of separately spoken phonemes and then combine them to form a word.

**phoneme categorization:**   A phonemic awareness task that requires students to recognize the one word in a series that sounds odd.

**phoneme deletion:**   A phonemic awareness task that requires students to recognize the word that remains when a phoneme is removed from the larger original word.

**phoneme identity:**   A phonemic awareness task that requires students to recognize, identify, and match the same sound in a series of different words.

**phoneme isolation:**   A phonemic awareness task that requires students to isolate the individual phonemes in a word.

**phoneme segmentation:**   A phonemic awareness task that requires students to segment a word into its constituent phonemes.

**phoneme substitution:**   A phonemic awareness task that requires students to replace one phoneme for another in a word, thereby forming a new word.

**phonemic awareness:**   The ability to hear, identify, and manipulate the individual sounds (phonemes) within spoken words.

**phonetics:**   The sound system of a given language.

**phonics:**   A way of teaching students to read and write by emphasizing the relationship between the sounds of a language and their symbols.

**phonological awareness:**   The ability to separate sentences into words and words into syllables.

**phrasing:**   The rhythm with which a text is read, as exemplified by prosodic cues.

**prosody:**   The rhythmic and tonal aspects of speech that create the music of oral language.

**schema:**   Connections that enable an individual to categorize and retain knowledge of objects, events, and situations in his or her memory. Each person's schema is directly impacted by his or her background knowledge and prior experiences.

**semantic cueing system:**   A reading support system that includes a reader's background knowledge and other context clues in a sentence or passage.

**social/affective comprehension strategies:** Strategies that use interaction with others as a vehicle for lowering the learner's anxiety about academic concepts and tasks, providing opportunities to share perspectives, and enhancing comprehension through opportunities for questioning and clarification.

**sociopsycholinguistic view:**   A view of reading that defines phonemic awareness as a component of the graphophonic cueing system, which is one of three language cueing systems readers use to make sense of text.

**stages of second language acquisition:**   The stages learners go through when developing second-language proficiency and literacy skills. Krashen's five stages of second language acquisition are preproduction, early production, speech emergence, intermediate fluency, and advanced fluency.

**stress:**   The degree of force with which a syllable is uttered.

**surface constructs of fluency:**   The constructs of fluency, including accuracy, speed, and prosody, that traditionally are emphasized in reading instruction and assessment.

**syntactic cueing system:**   A reading support system that includes the grammar of a language, or the patterns and rules that govern how words can and cannot be put together in a sentence.

**top-down reading process model:**   A whole-to-part model of the reading process, in which schematic connections to text are the starting point for the development of specific skills at the discourse, sentence, word, and letter levels.

**word recognition view:**   A view of reading that sees it as primarily a process of identifying words. As such, reading is broken down into component parts (i.e., phonemic awareness skills, names/sounds of letters, phonics rules, sight words, structural analysis skills) that are taught systematically.

Abedi, J. (2004). The No Child Left Behind Act and English language learners: Assessment and accountability issues. *Educational Researcher, 33*(1), 4–14.

Abedi, J. (Ed.). (2007). *English language proficiency assessment in the nation: Current status and future practice.* Davis, CA: University of California, School of Education.

Aboff, M. (2006). *India ABCs: A book about the people and places of India.* Bloomington, MI: Picture Window Books.

Abu-Rabia, S. (1995). Multicultural and problematic social contexts and their contribution to L2 learning. *Language, Culture and Curriculum, 8*(2), 183–199.

Ada, A. F. (2001). *Gathering the sun: An alphabet in Spanish and English.* New York: Harper-Collins.

Ada, A. F. (2003). *A magical encounter: Latino children's literature in the classroom* (2nd ed.). Boston: Allyn & Bacon.

Adams, M. J. (1990). *Beginning to read: Thinking and learning about the print.* Cambridge, MA: MIT Press.

Adams, M. J. (1991). Why not phonics and whole language? In W. Ellis (Ed.), *All language and the creation of literacy* (pp. 40–53). Baltimore, MD: Orton Dyslexia Society.

Allington, R. L. (2001). *What really matters for struggling readers: Designing research-based programs.* New York: Longman.

Altman, I. (1993). Dialectics, physical environments, and personal relationships. *Communication Monographs, 60,* 26–34.

Altman, L. J. (1993). *Amelia's road.* New York: Lee & Low.

Anderson, N. J. (1999). *Exploring second language reading: Issues and strategies.* Boston: Heinle and Heinle.

Antunez, B. (2002). *The preparation and professional development of teachers of English language learners.* ERIC Digest (ERIC Document Reproduction Service no. ED477724). Washington, DC: ERIC Clearinghouse on Teaching and Teacher Education.

Armbruster, B. B., Lehr, F., & Osborn, J. (2001). *Put reading first: The research building blocks for teaching children to read—Kindergarten through grade 3.* Jessup, MD: National Institute for Literacy.

August, D., Calderón, M., & Carlo, M. (2002). *Transfer of skills from Spanish to English: A study of young learners.* Washington, DC: Center for Applied Linguistics.

August, D., Carlo, M., Dressler, C., & Snow, C. (2005). The critical role of vocabulary development for English language learners. *Learning Disabilities Research and Practice, 20*(1), 50–57.

August, D., & Hakuta, K. (Eds.). (1997). *Improving schooling for language minority students: A research agenda.* Washington, DC: National Academy Press.

August, D., & Shanahan, T. (Eds.). (2006). *Developing literacy in second-language learners: Report of the national literacy panel on language-minority children and youth.* Mahwah, NJ: Lawrence Erlbaum.

Beck, I. L. (2006). *Making sense of phonics: The hows and whys.* New York: Guilford Press.

Beck, I. L., McKeown, M. G., & Kucan, L. (2002). *Bringing words to life: Robust vocabulary instruction.* New York: Guilford Press.

Bernhardt, E. (2003). Challenges to reading research from a multilingual world. *Reading Research Quarterly, 28*(1), 112–117.

Blachowicz, C., & Fisher, P. (1996). *Teaching vocabulary in all classrooms.* Englewood Cliffs, NJ: Merrill.

Block, C. C., & Israel, S. E. (2005). *Reading first and beyond*. Thousand Oaks, CA: Corwin Press.

Bradshaw, G. L., & Anderson, J. R. (1982). Elaborative encoding as an explanation of levels of processing. *Journal of Verbal Learning and Verbal Behavior, 21*, 165–174.

Brock, C. H., & Raphael, T. E. (2005). *Windows to language, literacy, and culture: Kids in sight*. Newark, DE: International Reading Association.

Brown, A. L. (1980). Metacognitive development of reading. In R. J. Spiro, B. C. Bruce, & W. F. Brewer (Eds.), *Theoretical issues in reading comprehension* (pp. 453–481). Hillsdale, NJ: Erlbaum.

Buehl, D. (2001). *Classroom strategies for interactive learning* (2nd ed.). Newark, DE: International Reading Association.

Bunting, E. (1992). *The wall*. New York: Clarion Books.

Burns, B. (1999). *The mindful school: How to teach balanced reading and writing*. Arlington Heights, IL: SkyLight Training and Publishing.

Burns, M. S., Griffin, P., & Snow, C. E. (Eds.). (1999). *Starting out right: A guide to promoting children's reading success*. Washington, DC: National Academy Press.

Calderón, M., August, D., Slavin, R., Duran, D., Madden, N., & Cheung, A. (2005). Bringing words to life in classrooms with English language learners. In E. Hiebert & M. L. Kamil (Eds.), *Teaching and learning vocabulary: Bringing research to practice* (pp. 115–136). Mahwah, NJ: Erlbaum.

Carlo, M., August, D., McLaughlin, B., Snow, C. E., Dressler, C., Lippman, D. N., Lively, T. J., & White, C. E. (2004). Closing the gap: Addressing the vocabulary needs of English language learners in bilingual and mainstream classrooms. *Reading Research Quarterly, 39*, 188–215.

Carlson, L. M. (1998). *Sol a sol: Bilingual poems*. New York: Henry Holt.

Cave, K. (2004). *W is for world: A round-the-world ABC*. London, England: Frances Lincoln.

Chall, J. (1967). *Learning to read: The great debate*. New York: McGraw-Hill.

Chamot, A. U., & O'Malley, J. (1994). The cognitive academic learning approach: A model for linguistically diverse classrooms. *Elementary School Journal, 96*, 259–273.

Chappuis, S., & Chappuis, J. (2007/2008, December/January). The best value in formative assessment. *Educational Leadership, 66*(4), 14–19.

Chard, D., Vaughn, S., & Tyler, B. (2002). A synthesis of research on effective interventions for building reading fluency with elementary students with learning disabilities. *Journal of Learning Disabilities, 35*, 386–406.

Chiappe, P., & Siegel, L. S. (1999). Phonological awareness and reading acquisition in English and Punjabi-speaking Canadian children. *Journal of Educational Psychology, 91*, 20–28.

Cisero, C. A., & Royer, J. M. (1995). The development and cross-language transfer of phonological awareness. *Contemporary Educational Psychology, 20*, 275–303.

Clay, M. M. (1993). *An observation survey of early literacy achievement*. Portsmouth, NH: Heinemann.

Coelho, E. (2004). *Adding English: A guide to teaching in multilingual classrooms*. Toronto, Canada: Pippin.

Coerr, E. (1991). *Sadako and the thousand paper cranes*. New York: Puffin Books.

Collier, C. (2004). PowerPoint image. Ferndale, WA: CrossCultural Developmental Education Services.

Collier, V. P. (1987). Age and rate of acquisition of second language for academic purposes. *TESOL Quarterly, 21*, 617–641.

Collier, V. P., & Thomas, W. P. (1989). How quickly can immigrants become proficient in school English? *Journal of Educational Issues of Language Minority Students, 5,* 26–38.

Collier, V. P., & Thomas, W. P. (1992). A synthesis of studies examining long-term language minority student data on academic achievement. *Bilingual Research Journal, 16*(1–2), 187–212.

Collier, V. P., & Thomas, W. P. (1997, December). *School effectiveness for language minority students.* National Clearinghouse for Bilingual Education (NCBE), Resource Collection Series, no. 9. Retrieved May 10, 2008, from http://www.ncela.gwu.edu/ncbepubs/resource/effectiveness/thomas-collier97.pdf

Collier, V. P., & Thomas, W. P. (1999a). Making U.S. schools effective for English language learners, Part 1. *TESOL Matters, 9*(4), 1, 6.

Collier, V. P., & Thomas, W. P. (1999b). Making U.S. schools effective for English language learners, Part 2. *TESOL Matters, 9*(5), 1, 6.

Collier, V. P., & Thomas, W. P. (1999c). Making U.S. schools effective for English language learners, Part 3. *TESOL Matters, 9*(6), 1, 10.

Comeau, L., Cormier, P., Grandmaison, E., & Lacroix, D. (1999). A longitudinal study of phonological processing skills in children learning to read in a second language. *Journal of Educational Psychology, 91,* 29–43.

Cooper, J. D. (1986). *Improving reading comprehension.* Boston: Houghton Mifflin.

Cooper, J. D., & Kiger, N. D. (2001). *Literacy assessment helping teachers plan instruction.* Boston: Houghton Mifflin.

Cooper, J. D., & Pikulski, J. J. (1997). *Teacher's assessment handbook.* Boston: Houghton Mifflin.

Cooter, R. B. (2004). *Perspectives on rescuing urban literacy education: Spies, saboteurs, and saints.* Mahwah, NJ: Erlbaum.

Cummins, J. (1979). Linguistic interdependence and the educational development of bilingual children. *Review of Educational Research, 49*(2), 222–251.

Cummins, J. (1981). The role of primary language development in promoting educational success for language minority students. In C. F. Leyba (Ed.), *Schooling and language minority students: A theoretical framework* (pp. 3–49). Los Angeles: California State University at Los Angeles, Evaluation, Dissemination and Assessment Center.

Cummins, J. (1989). Language and affect: Bilingual students at home and at school. *Language Arts, 66,* 29–43.

Cummins, J. (1991a). Interdependence of first- and second-language proficiency in bilingual children. In E. Bialystok (Ed.), *Language processing in bilingual children* (pp. 70–89). Cambridge, England: Cambridge University Press.

Cummins, J. (1991b). Empowering minority students: A framework for intervention. In M. Minami & B. P. Kennedy (Eds.), *Language issues in literacy and bilingual/multicultural education* (pp. 372–390). Reprint Series no. 22, Harvard Educational Review. Cambridge, MA: Harvard Educational Review.

Cummins, J. (1991c). Language development and academic learning. In L. Malavé & G. Duquette (Eds.), *Language, culture and cognition* (pp. 161–175). Clevedon, England: Multilingual Matters.

Cummins, J. (1996). *Negotiating identities: Education for empowerment in a diverse society.* Los Angeles: California Association for Bilingual Education.

Cummins, J. (2000). This place nurtures my spirit: Creating contexts of empowerment in linguistically diverse schools. In R. Phillipson (Ed.), *Rights to language: Equity, power and education* (pp. 249–258). Mahwah, NJ: Erlbaum.

Cummins, J. (2001). *Language, power, and pedagogy: Bilingual children in the crossfire.* Philadelphia: Multicultural Matters.

Cunningham, P. M. (2005). *Phonics they use: Words for reading and writing* (4th ed.). Boston: Allyn & Bacon.

Cunningham, P. M., Moor, S. A., Cunningham, J. W., & Moore, D. W. (1995). *Reading and writing in elementary classrooms: Strategies and observations* (3rd ed.). White Plains, NY: Longman.

Cushenbery, D. C. (1985). *Improving reading skills in the content area.* Springfield, IL: Charles C. Thomas.

Dahl, K. L., Scharer, P. L., Lawson, L. L., & Grogan, P. R. (2001). *Rethinking phonics: Making the best teaching decisions.* Portsmouth, NH: Heinemann.

Darling-Hammond, L., & Sclan, E. M. (1996). Who teaches and why: Dilemmas of building a profession for 21st century schools. In J. Sikula, T. J. Buttery, & E. Guyton (Eds.), *Handbook of research on teacher education* (2nd ed., pp. 67–101). New York: Macmillan.

Davis, F. B. (1994). Fundamental factors of comprehension in reading. *Psychometrika, 9*(3), 185–197.

Dolch, E. W. (1945). *A manual for remedial reading.* Champaign, IL: Garrard Press.

Dolch, E. W. (1948). *Problems in reading.* Champaign, IL: Garrard Press.

Duffelmeyer, F. A. (1985). Teaching word meaning from an experience base. *Reading Teacher, 39,* 6–9.

Duffy, G. G. (1993). Rethinking strategy instruction: Four teachers' development and their low achievers' understandings. *Elementary School Journal, 93,* 231–247.

Durgunoglu, A. Y., Nagy, W. E., & Hancin-Bhatt, B. J. (1993). Cross-language transfer of phonological awareness. *Journal of Educational Psychology, 85*(3), 453–465.

Durgunoglu, A. Y., & Oney, B. (1999). A cross-linguistic comparison of phonological awareness and word recognition. *Reading and Writing, 11,* 281–299.

Durgunoglu, A. Y., & Verhoeven, L. (1998). *Literacy development in a multilingual context: A cross-cultural perspective.* Mahwah, NJ: Erlbaum.

Durkin, D. (1979). What classroom observations reveal about reading comprehension. *Reading Research Quarterly, 14,* 518–544.

Durkin, D. (2004). *Teaching them to read* (6th ed.). Boston: Allyn & Bacon.

Ehri, L., & McCormick, S. (1998). Phases of word learning: Implications for instruction with delayed and disabled readers. *Reading and Writing Quarterly, 14,* 135–163.

Escamilla, K. (1987). *English proficiency to future achievement in reading English as a second language.* Doctoral dissertation, University of California, Los Angeles, School of Education.

Escamilla, K. (1993). Integrating Mexican-American history and culture into the social studies classroom. In L. E. Gronlund (Ed.), *Striving for excellence: The National Education Goals* (Vol. II, pp. 53–54). Washington, DC: Educational Resources Information Center.

Escamilla, K. (1998). *Teacher's perceptions of English and Spanish assessments in a Spanish/English bilingual program.* Paper presented at the annual conference of the Colorado Association for Bilingual Education, Breckenridge, CO.

Escamilla, K. (2004). *The psychological and emotional aspects of bilingualism: It's more than verbs.* Keynote address given at the Dual Language Pre-Conference Institute, National Association for Bilingual Education, Albuquerque, NM.

Farstrup, A., & Samuels, S. J. (Eds.). (2002). *What research has to say about reading instruction.* Newark, DE: International Reading Association.

Fisher, F., & Frey, N. (2007). *Checking for understanding: Formative assessment techniques for your classroom.* Alexandria, VA: Association for Supervision and Curriculum Development.

Flannery, D. D., & Hayes, E. (2001). Challenging adult learning: A feminist perspective. In V. Sheared & P. A. Sissel (Eds.), *Making space: Merging theory and practice in adult education* (pp. 29–41). Westport, CT: Bergin and Garvey.

Flesch, R. (1956). *Why Johnny can't read*. Newark, NJ: Popular.

Flood, J., Hasbrouck, J. E., Hoffman, J. V., Lapp, D., Medearis, A. S., Paris, S., et al. (2001). *Phonics practice reader 1*. New York: McGraw-Hill.

Fox, B. J. (2000). *Word identification strategies: Phonics from a new perspective* (2nd ed.). Upper Saddle River, NJ: Prentice-Hall.

Fox, B. J. (2003). *Word recognition activities: Patterns and strategies for developing fluency*. Upper Saddle River, NJ: Prentice-Hall.

Fox, B. J. (2005). *Phonics for the teacher of reading* (9th ed.). Upper Saddle River, NJ: Prentice-Hall.

Freeman, D. E., & Freeman, Y. S. (1998). *ESL/EFL teaching: Principles for success*. Portsmouth, NH: Heinemann.

Freeman, D. E., & Freeman, Y. S. (2000). *Teaching reading in multilingual classrooms*. Portsmouth, NH: Heinemann.

Freeman, D. E., & Freeman, Y. S. (2002). *Closing the achievement gap: How to reach limited formal schooling and long term English-learners*. Portsmouth, NH: Heinemann.

Freeman, D. E., & Freeman, Y. S. (2004). *Essential linguistics: What you need to know to teach reading, ESL, spelling, phonics, and grammar*. Portsmouth, NH: Heinemann.

Freeman, D. E., & Freeman, Y. S. (2007). *English language learners: The essential guide*. New York: Scholastic.

Freire, P. (1970). *Pedagogy of the oppressed*. New York: Herder and Herder.

Garan, E. M. (2002). *Resisting reading mandates: How to triumph with the truth*. Portsmouth, NH: Heinemann.

García, E. (2002). *Student cultural diversity: Understanding and meeting the challenge*. Boston: Houghton Mifflin.

García, E., & González, R. (1995). Issues in systemic reform for culturally and linguistically diverse students. *College Record, 96*(3), 418–431.

García, G. E., & Nagy, W. (1993). Latino students' concept of cognates. In D. Leu & C. Kinzer (Eds.), *Examining central issues in literacy research, theory, and practice* (Forty-Second Yearbook of the National Reading Conference) (pp. 367–373). Chicago: National Reading Conference.

García, G. G. (Ed.). (2003). *English learners: Reaching the highest level of English literacy*. Rowland Heights, CA: International Reading Association.

Geisler, D., Escamilla, K., Hopewell, S., & Ruiz, O. (2007). *Transitions to biliteracy: Focus on writing*. Paper presented at the annual conference of the American Education Research Association (AERA), Chicago, IL.

Genesee, F., Lindholm-Leary, K., Saunders, W., & Christian, D. (Eds.). (2006). *Educating English language learners: A synthesis of research evidence*. New York: Cambridge University Press.

Genesee, F., & Riches, C. (2006). Literacy: Instructional issues. In F. Genesee, K. Lindholm-Leary, W. Saunders, & D. Christian (Eds.), *Educating English language learners: A synthesis of research evidence* (pp. 109–175). New York: Cambridge University Press.

Gersten, R., & Baker, S. (2000). What we know about effective instructional practices for English language learners. *Exceptional Children, 66*, 454–470.

Gipe, J. P. (2006). *Multiple paths to literacy: Assessment and differentiated instruction for diverse learners*. Boston: Allyn & Bacon.

Gollnick, D., & Chinn, P. (1983). *Multicultural education in a pluralistic society*. St. Louis: C.V. Mosby.

Gonzalez-Bueno, M. (2001). Pronunciation teaching component in SL/FL education programs: Training teachers to teach pronunciation. *Applied Language Learning, 12*(2), 133–146.

Goodman, K. (1982). *Language and literacy: The selected writings of Kenneth S. Goodman*. Boston: Routledge & Kegan Paul.

Grabe, W. (1991). Current developments in second language reading research. *TESOL Quarterly, 25*(3), 375–406.

Graham, C. (1978). *Jazz chants for children.* New York: Oxford University Press.

Graves, M. F., & Prenn, M. C. (1986). Costs and benefits of various methods of teaching vocabulary. *Journal of Reading, 29*(7), 596–602.

Greenwood, S. (2002). Making words matter: Vocabulary study in the content areas. *Clearing House, 75*(5), 258–263.

Gregory, E. (1996). *Making sense of a new world: Learning to read in a second language.* London, England: Paul Chapman.

Griffith, L. W., & Rasinski, T. V. (2004). A focus on fluency: How one teacher incorporated fluency with her reading curriculum. *Reading Teacher, 58*(2), 126–137.

Gunning, T. G. (2000). *Phonological awareness and primary phonics.* Boston: Allyn & Bacon.

Gunning, T. G. (2002). *Assessing and correcting reading and writing difficulties* (2nd ed.). Boston: Allyn & Bacon.

Hamayan, E. (1994). Language development of low literacy students. In F. Genesee (Ed.), *Educating second language children* (pp. 166–199). Cambridge: Cambridge University Press.

Harris, T. L., & Hodges, R. E. (Eds.). (1995). *The literacy dictionary: The vocabulary of reading and writing.* Newark, DE: International Reading Association.

Harste, J. C., & Burke, C. L. (1977). A new hypothesis for reading teacher research: Both teaching and learning of reading are theoretically based. In P. D. Pearson (Ed.), *Reading: Theory, research, and practice* (Twenty-Sixth Yearbook of the National Reading Conference) (pp. 32–40). New York: Mason.

Harvey, S., & Goudvis, A. (2000). *Strategies that work: Teaching comprehension to enhance understanding.* York, ME: Stenhouse.

Hayes, J. (2001). *El Cucuy: A Bogeyman Cuento.* El Paso, TX: Cinco Puntos Press.

Heath, S. B. (1983). *Ways with words: Language, life, and work in communities and classrooms.* Cambridge, England: Cambridge University Press.

Heilman, A. W. (2002). *Phonics in proper perspective* (9th ed.). Upper Saddle River, NJ: Prentice-Hall.

Heilman, A. W., Blair, T. R., & Rupley, W. H. (1998). *Principles and practices of teaching reading* (9th ed.). Columbus, OH: Merril/Prentice Hall.

Helman, L. (2004). Building on the sound system of Spanish: Insights from the alphabetic spellings of English language learners. *The Reading Teacher, 57,* 452–460.

Helman, L. A. (2005). Spanish speakers learning to read in English: What a large-scale assessment suggest about their progress. In B. Maloch, J. Hoffman, D. Schallert, C. Fairbanks, & J. Worthy (Eds.), *54th yearbook of the National Reading Conference* (pp. 211–226). Oak Creek, WI: National Reading Conference.

Herrera, S. (2001). *Classroom strategies for the English language learner: A practical guide for accelerating language and literacy development.* Manhattan, KS: MASTER Teacher.

Herrera, S. (2007a). *By teachers, with teachers, for teachers: ESL methods course module.* Manhattan, KS: KCAT/ TLC.

Herrera, S. (2007b). *By teachers, with teachers, for teachers: ESL methods DVD series.* Manhattan, KS: KCAT/ TLC.

Herrera, S. (2008). *By teachers, with teachers, for teachers: ESL assessment course module.* Manhattan, KS: KCAT/ TLC.

Herrera, S., & Murry, K. (2004). Accountability by assumption: Implications of reform agendas for teacher preparation. *Journal of Latinos and Education, 5*(3), 189–207.

Herrera, S., & Murry, K. (2005). *Mastering ESL and bilingual methods: Differentiated instruction for culturally and linguistically diverse (CLD) students.* Boston: Allyn & Bacon.

Herrera, S. G., Murry, K. G., & Morales Cabral, R. (2007). *Assessment accommodations for classroom teachers of culturally and linguistically diverse students.* Boston: Allyn & Bacon.

Hoyt, L. (2005). *Spotlight on comprehension: Building a literacy of thoughtfulness.* Portsmouth, NH: Heinemann.

Hubbard, R., & Shorey, V. (2003). Worlds beneath the words: Writing workshop with second language learners. *Language Arts, 81*(1), 52–61.

Hudson, R. F., Lane, H. B., & Pullen, P. C. (2005). Assessment and instruction in reading fluency: Often neglected, yet essential for skilled reading. *Reading Teacher, 54,* 702–714.

International Reading Association (IRA). (2002). *Evidence-based reading instruction: Putting the National Reading Panel report into practice.* Newark, DE: Author.

International Reading Association (IRA)/National Council of Teachers of English (NCTE). (1996). *Standards for the English language arts.* Newark, DE: Author.

Irvin, J. W. (1998). *Reading and the middle school student.* Boston: Allyn & Bacon.

Irwin, J. W. (1986). *Teaching reading comprehension processes.* Englewood Cliffs, NJ: Prentice-Hall.

Jesness, J. (2004). *Teaching English language learners K–12: A quick-start guide for the new teacher.* Thousand Oaks, CA: Corwin Press.

Johnson, D. D., & Baumann, J. F. (1984). Word identification. In P. D. Pearson (Ed.), *Handbook for reading research* (pp. 583–608). New York: Longman.

Kaplan, R. B. (1966). Cultural thought patterns in intercultural education. *Language Learning, 16*(1), 1–20.

Kaplan, R. (2005). Contrastive rhetoric. In E. Hinkel (Ed.), *Handbook of research in second language teaching and learning* (pp. 375–391). Mahwah, NJ: Lawrence Erlbaum.

Keene, E. L., & Zimmerman, S. (1997). *Mosaic of thought: Teaching comprehension in a reader's workshop.* Portsmouth, NH: Heinemann.

Kenner, C. (2000). *Home pages: Literacy links for bilingual children.* Staffordshire, England: Trentham Books.

Kole, N. (2003). *Native-language supported reading instruction: A VALID framework.* Unpublished doctoral dissertation, Kansas State University, Manhattan, KS.

Krashen, S. D. (1987). *Principles and practice in second language acquisition.* New York: Prentice-Hall.

Krashen, S. D. (2002). Does transition really happen? Some case histories. *Multilingual Educator, 3*(1), 50–54.

Krashen, S. D., & Terrell, T. (1983). *The natural approach: Language acquisition in the classroom.* Oxford, England: Pergamon Press.

Kuder, J., & Hasit, C. (2002). *Enhancing literacy for all students.* New York: Prentice-Hall.

Kuhn, M. R., & Stahl, S. A. (2000). *Fluency: A review of developmental and remedial practices.* Ann Arbor, MI: Center for the Improvement of Early Reading Achievement.

LaBerge, D., & Samuels, S. J. (1974). Towards a theory of automatic information processing in reading. *Cognitive Psychology, 6,* 293–323.

Leslie, L., & Caldwell, J. (1995). *Qualitative reading inventory—II.* New York: HarperCollins.

Leu, D. J., & Kinzer, C. K. (2003). *Effective literacy instruction, K–8: Implementing best practice* (5th ed.). Columbus, OH: Prentice-Hall.

*Libro del maestro: Recursos para la planificacion y la ensenanza* (4th ed.). (1997). Boston: Houghton Mifflin.

Lionni, L. (1975). *A color of his own.* New York: Pantheon Books.

Luke, A., & Freebody, P. (1999). A map of possible practices: Further notes on the four resources model. *Practically Primary, 4*(2), 5–8.

Lundberg, I., Frost, J., & Peterson, O. (1988). Effectiveness of an extensive program for stimulating phonological awareness in preschool children. *Reading Research Quarterly, 23*(3), 263–284.

Lyon, G. R. (1998). Why reading is not a natural process. *Educational Leadership, 32*(4), 13–18.

Madrid, D., Canas, M., & Ortega-Medina, M. (2007, January/February). Effects of team competition versus team cooperation in class-wide peer tutoring. *Journal of Educational Research, 100*(3), 155–161.

Maria, K. (1990). *Reading comprehension instruction: Issues and strategies*. Parkton, MD: York Press.

Martin, B., Jr., & Carle, E. (1967). *Brown bear, brown bear, what do you see?* New York: Henry Holt and Company.

Marzano, R. J. (2004). *Building background knowledge for academic achievement: Research on what works in schools*. Alexandria, VA: Association for Supervision and Curriculum Development.

Marzano, R. J., Hagerty, P. J., Valencia, S. W., & DiStefano, P. P. (1987). *Reading diagnosis and instruction: Theory into practice*. Englewood Cliffs, NJ: Prentice-Hall.

McLaughlin, M. W. (1987). Learning from experience: Lessons from policy implementation. *Education Evaluation and Policy Analysis, 9*(2), 171–178.

McNeil, L. M. (2000). *Contradictions of school reform: Educational costs of standardized testing*. New York: Routledge.

Meyer, R. J. (2002). Phonics exposed: *Understanding and resisting systematic direct intense phonics instruction*. Mahwah, NJ: Erlbaum.

Moll, L. C. (2001). Through the mediation of others: Vygotskian research on teaching. In V. Richardson (Ed.), *Handbook of research on teaching* (4th ed., pp. 111–129). Washington, DC: American Educational Research Association.

Moll, L. C., Armanti, C., Neff, D., & Gonzalez, N. (1992). Funds of knowledge for teaching: Using a qualitative approach to connect homes and classrooms. *Theory into Practice, 31*(2), 132–141.

Moll, L. C., & Dworin, J. E. (2006). Guest editor's introduction. *Journal of Early Childhood Literacy, 6*(3), 234–240.

Mora, P. (1994). *Listen to the desert/Oye al desierto*. New York: Macmillan.

Nagy, W. E. (1988). *Teaching vocabulary to improve reading comprehension*. Rowland Heights, CA: International Reading Association.

Nagy, W. E., García, G., Durgunoglu, A., & Hacin-Bhatt, B. (1993). Spanish–English bilingual children's use and recognition of cognates in English reading. *Journal of Reading Behavior, 25*(3), 241–259.

Nagy, W. E., Herman, P. A., & Anderson, R. C. (1985). Learning words from context. *Reading Research Quarterly, 20*, 233–253.

Narvaez, D. A. (2002). Does reading moral stories build character? *Educational Psychology Review, 14*(2), 155–171.

National Center for Educational Statistics (NCES). (2001). *Teacher preparation and professional development: 2000*. Retrieved July 14, 2004, from http://nces.ed.gov/pubs2001/2001088.pdf

National Center for Educational Statistics (NCES). (2002). *1999–2000 schools and staffing survey: Overview of the data for public, private, public charter and Bureau of Indian Affairs elementary and secondary schools*. Washington, DC: U.S. Department of Education, Office of Educational Research and Improvement.

National Center for Education Statistics (NCES). (2006). *The condition of education 2006: Indicator 7: Language minority school age children*. Washington, DC: U.S. Department of Education, Institute of Education Sciences. Retrieved May 10, 2008, from http://nces.ed.gov/programs/coe/2006/pdf07_2006.pdf

National Education Association (NEA). (2003). *Status of the American public school teacher 2000–2001*. Washington, DC: Author.

National Institute of Child Health and Human Development (NICHHD). (2000). *Report of the National Reading Panel: Teaching children to read—An evidence-based assessment of the scientific research literature on reading and its implications for reading instruction* (NIH Publication no. 00-4769). Washington, DC: U.S. Government Printing Office.

National Reading Panel (NRP). (2000). *Report of the National Reading Panel: Teaching children to read. Reports of the subgroups* (NIH Publication no. 00-4754). Washington DC: U.S. Government Printing Office.

Neelands, J., & Goode, T. (2000). *Structuring drama work: A handbook of available forms in theatre and drama.* Cambridge, England: Cambridge University Press.

Nunan, D. (1999). *Second language teaching and learning.* Boston: Heinle and Heinle.

Ogbu, J. U. (1980). *Children's acquisition of discourse and narrative skills among the Igbus of Nigeria: The role of folklore.* Unpublished manuscript, University of Delaware, Newark, DE.

Paris, S. G., Lipson, M. Y., Wixson, K. K. (1983). Becoming a strategic reader. *Contemporary Educational Psychology, 8,* 293–316.

Paulson, E., & Freeman, A. (2003). *Insight from the eyes: The science of effective reading instruction.* Portsmouth, NH: Heinemann.

Pearson, P. D. (1984). *Handbook of reading research.* New York: Longman.

Peregoy, S. F., & Boyle, O. F. (2000). *Reading, writing, and learning in ESL: A resource book for K–12 teachers* (3rd ed.). New York: Longman.

Peregoy, S. F., & Boyle, O. F. (2005). *Reading, writing, and learning in ESL: A resource book for K–12 teachers* (4th ed.). Boston: Allyn & Bacon.

Perez, B. (1998). *Sociocultural contexts of language and literacy.* Mahwah, NJ: Erlbaum.

Perez, B. (2003). *Becoming biliterate: A study of two-way bilingual immersion education.* Mahwah, NJ: Erlbaum.

Pikulski, J. J., & Chard, D. J. (2005). Fluency: Bridge between decoding and reading comprehension. *Reading Teacher, 58*(6), 510–519.

Pinnell, G. S., & Scharer, P. L. (2003). *Teaching for comprehension in reading, grades K–2.* New York: Teaching Resources/Scholastic.

Powell, P. H. (2003). *Zinnia: How the corn was saved.* Flagstaff, AZ: Salina Bookshelf.

Prescott-Griffin, M. L., & Witherell, N. (2004). *Fluency in focus: Comprehension strategies for all young readers.* Portsmouth, NH: Heinemann.

Pressley, M., & Block, C. C. (2002). Summing up: What comprehension instruction could be. In C. C. Block & M. Pressley (Eds.), *Comprehension instruction: Research-based best practices* (pp. 383–392). New York: Guilford Press.

Raphael, T. E., Florio-Ruane, S., Kehus, M., George, M., Hasty, N., & Highfield, K. (2001). Thinking for ourselves: Literacy learning in a diverse teacher inquiry network. *The Reading Teacher, 54*(6), 506–607.

Rasinski, T. (2003). *The fluent reader: Oral reading strategies for building word recognition, fluency, and comprehension.* New York: Scholastic.

Rasinski, T. (2004, March). Creating fluent readers. *Educational Leadership, 61*(6), 46–51.

Rasinski, T., et al. (Eds.). (2000). *Teaching word recognition, spelling, and vocabulary: Strategies from* The Reading Teacher. Newark, DE: International Reading Association.

Rasinski, T., & Padak, N. (2000). *Effective reading strategies: Teaching children who find reading difficult* (2nd ed.). Upper Saddle River, NJ: Prentice-Hall.

Readence, J. E., Bean, T. W., & Baldwin, R. S. (2004). *Content area literacy: An integrated approach* (8th ed.). Dubuque, IA: Kendall/Hunt.

Reutzel, D. R., & Cooter, R. B., Jr. (2000). *Teaching children to read: Putting the pieces together.* Upper Saddle River, NJ: Prentice-Hall.

Reutzel, D. R., & Cooter, R. B., Jr. (2003). *Strategies for reading assessment and instruction: Helping every child succeed* (2nd ed.). Upper Saddle River, NJ: Prentice-Hall.

Reutzel, D. R., & Cooter, R. B., Jr. (2005). *The essentials of teaching children to read.* Upper Saddle River, NJ: Prentice- Hall.

Reyes, S. A. (2001). Two-way bilingual immersion programs: Toward a more inclusive agenda in bilingual education. *Mid-Western Educational Researcher 2001 Theme Issue on Bilingual Education, 14*(4), 13–21.

Richard-Amato, P. A. (1996). *Making it happen: Interaction in the second language classroom: From theory to practice* (2nd ed.). White Plains, NY: Longman.

Riedel, B. W. (2007). The relation between DIBELS, reading comprehension, and vocabulary in urban first-grade students. *Reading Research Quarterly, 42*(4), 546–567.

Rigby Literacy. (2005). *Reading workshop: Teacher's guide.* Austin, TX: Harcourt Supplemental.

Rodríguez, A. (1988). Research in reading and writing in bilingual education and English as a second language. In A. Ambert (Ed.), *Bilingual education and English as a second language: A research handbook 1986–1987* (pp. 61–117). New York: Garland.

Rodríguez, T. A. (2001). From the known to the unknown: Using cognates to teach English to Spanish speaking literates. *Reading Teacher, 54*(8), 744–746.

Rosenblatt, L. M. (2002). *La literature como exploracion (espacias para la lectura).* Bel Air, CA: Fondo de Cultura Economica USA.

Rousseau, M. K., Tam, B. K. Y., & Ramnarain, R. (1993). Increasing reading proficiency of language minority students with speech and language impairments. *Education and Treatment of Children, 16*, 254–271.

Rumelhart, D. E. (1980). Schemata: The building blocks of cognition. In R. J. Spiro, B. C. Bruce, & W. F. Brewer (Eds.), *Theoretical issues in reading comprehension* (pp. 33–58). Hillsdale, NJ: Erlbaum.

Rutherford, W. E. (1987). *Second language grammar: Learning and teaching.* London, England: Longman.

Rycik, M. T., & Rycik, J. A. (2007). *Phonics and word identification: Instruction and intervention, K–8.* Upper Saddle River, NJ: Prentice-Hall.

Samuels, S. J., & Farstrup, A. E. (Eds.). (2006). *What research has to say about fluency instruction.* Newark, DE: International Reading Association.

Say, A. (1993). *Grandfather's journey.* Boston, MA: Houghton Mifflin.

Schon, I., Hopkins, K. D., & Vojir, C. (1984). The effects of Spanish reading emphasis on the English and Spanish reading abilities of Hispanic high school students. *Bilingual Review/Revista Bilingüe, 11*, 33–39.

Schwarzer, D. (2001). *Noa's ark: One child's voyage into multiliteracy.* Portsmouth, NJ: Heinemann.

Scillion, D. (2003). *P is for passport: A world alphabet.* Chelsea, MI: Sleeping Bear Press.

Searfoss, L. W., Readence, J. E., & Mallette, M. H. (2001). *Helping children learn to read: Creating a classroom literacy environment.* Boston: Allyn & Bacon.

Sejnost, R., & Thiese, S. (2001). *Reading and writing across content areas.* Arlington Heights, IL: Skylight Professional Development.

Short, D., & Echevarria, J. (2004/2005). Teacher skills to support English language learners. *Educational Leadership, 62*, 8–13.

Skutnabb-Kangas, T. (1975). *Om tvåspråkighet och skolframgång [On bilingualism and school achievement].* Åbo: Svenska Litteratursällskapet i Finland. Nämnd för samhällsforskning, Forskningsrapport nr 20.

Slavin, R., & Cheung, A. (2003). *Effective reading programs for English language learners.* Washington, DC: Center for Research on the Education of Students Placed at Risk.

Snow, C. (1990). Rationales for native language instruction: Evidence from research. In A. Padilla, H. Fairchild, & C. Valadez (Eds.),

*Bilingual education: Issues and strategies* (pp. 60–74). Newbury Park, CA: Sage.

Snow, C. E., Burns, S. M., & Griffin, P. (Eds.). (1998). *Preventing reading difficulties*. Washington DC: National Academy Press.

So, S. (2004). *C is for China*. London, England: Frances Lincoln.

Spellings, M. (2005). *Academic gains of English language learners prove high standards, accountability paying off*. Presentation at the fourth annual Celebrate Our Rising Stars Summit: From Essential Elements to Effective Practice, Washington, DC.

Spinelli, C. G. (1998). *Issues in the application of aptitude-achievement discrepancy as a criteria for classifying students learning disabled*. ERIC Digest (ERIC Document Reproduction Service no. ED427468). Washington, DC: ERIC Clearinghouse on Teaching and Teacher Education.

Stahl, S. A. (1999). *Vocabulary development*. Cambridge, MA: Brookline Books.

Stahl, S. A., Duffy-Hester, A. M., & Stahl, K. A. (1998). Everything you wanted to know about phonics (but were afraid to ask). *Reading Research Quarterly, 33*, 338–355.

Stephens, E. C., & Brown, J. E. (2000). *A handbook of content literacy strategies: Seventy-five practical reading and writing ideas*. Norwood, MA: Christopher-Gordon.

Teachers of English to Speakers of Other Languages (TESOL). (1997). *ESL standards for pre-K–12 students*. Bloomington, IL: Pantagraph.

Thomas, W. P., & Collier, V. P. (1997). *School effectiveness for language minority students* (NCBE Resource Collection Series no. 9). Washington, DC: National Clearinghouse for Bilingual Education.

Tomlinson, C. A., & McTighe, J. (2006). *Integrating differentiated instruction and understanding by design*. Alexandria, VA: Association for Supervision and Curriculum Development.

Tompkins, G. (1986). *Language arts: Patterns of practice*. Englewood Cliffs, NJ: Prentice-Hall.

Tompkins, G. (2004). *Fifty literacy strategies: Step by step*. Upper Saddle, NJ: Prentice-Hall.

Trail, L. (1994). *Making reading meaningful for language minority students*. Paper presented at the annual conference of the National Association for Bilingual Education, Los Angeles, CA.

U.S. Census Bureau. (2006). *American community survey*. Washington, DC: Author. Available at www.census.gov/acs/www/index.html.

U.S. Department of Education (USDE). (2002). *Survey of the states' limited English proficient students & available educational programs and services 1999–2000 summary report*. Washington, DC: National Clearinghouse for English Language Acquisition and Language Instruction Educational Programs.

Vacca, J. L., Vacca, R. T., & Gove, M. K. (1995). *Reading and learning to read*. New York: HarperCollins.

Vacca, J. L., Vacca, R. T., & Gove, M. K. (2000). *Reading and learning to read* (4th ed.). White Plains, NY: Longman.

Vacca, J. L., Vacca, R. T., Gove, M. K., Burkey, L., Lenhart, L., & McKeon, C. (2006). *Reading and learning to read*. Toronto, Canada: Pearson.

Valencia, S. W., Hiebert, E. H., & Afflerbach, P. (Eds.). (1994). *Authentic reading assessment: Practices and possibilities*. Newark, DE: International Reading Association.

Van Allen, R. (1976). *Language experience activities*. Boston: Houghton Mifflin.

Vaughn, S., & Linan-Thompson, S. (2004). *Research-based methods of reading instruction*. Alexandria, VA: Association for Supervision and Curriculum Development.

Vygotsky, L. S. (1962). *Thought and language.* Cambridge, MA: MIT Press.

Vygotsky, L. S. (1978). *Mind in society.* Cambridge, MA: Harvard University Press.

Weill, C. (2007). *ABeCedarios: Mexican folk art, ABCs in Spanish and English.* El Paso, TX: Cinco Puntos.

Wells, R., & Yoshi. (1992). *A to zen: A book of Japanese culture.* New York: Simon & Schuster.

White, E. B. (1952). *Charlotte's web: A story about friendship.* Boston: HarperCollins.

Williams, J. D., & Snipper, G. C. (1990). *Literacy and bilingualism.* White Plains, NY: Longman.

Wolf, M. K., Kao, J., Griffin, N., Herman, J., Bachman, P., Chang, S., & Farnsworth, T. (2008). *Issues in assessing English language learners: English language proficiency measures and accommodation uses—Practice Review* (Report no. 732, part 2 of 3). Los Angeles: National Center for Research on Evaluation, Standards, and Student Testing (CRESST)/Center for the Study of Evaluation (CSE).

Wong-Fillmore, L. (2000). Loss of family languages: Should educators be concerned? *Theory into Practice, 39*(4), 203–210.

Zwiers, J. (2004/2005). The third language of academic English. *Educational Leadership, 62*(4), 60–63.

## Photo Credits

p. xx, LLC Vstock/IndexOpen; p. 18, Bob Daemmrich Photography; p. 40, Robert Harbison; p. 66, Robert Harbison; p. 102, Bob Daemmrich Photography; p. 132, Bob Daemmrich Photography; p. 164, PhotoDisc/Getty Images; p. 190, Corbis RF; p. 216, Bob Daemmrich Photography; p. 246, PhotoDisc/Getty Images.

## Text Credits

Page 50: Excerpt from *Listen to the Desert/Oye al desierto* by Pat Mora. Text copyright © 1994 by Pat Mora. Reprinted by permission of Clarion Books, an imprint of Houghton Mifflin Harcourt Publishing Company. All rights reserved.

Pages 51–52: Excerpted from *India ABCs: A Book about the People and Places of India* by Marcie Aboff. Text copyright © 2006 by Picture Window Books. Reprinted by permission of Coughlan Companies.

Page 80: Excerpted from *Zinnia: How the Corn Was Saved* by Patricia Hruby Powell. Text copyright © 2003 by Patricia Hruby Powell. Reprinted by permission of Salina Bookshelf.

Page 81: Reprinted with permission from *McGraw-Hill Reading: Phonics Practice Reader 1* by MacMillan/McGraw-Hill. Text copyright © 2001 by McGraw-Hill School Division, a Division of the Educational and Professional Publishing Group of The McGraw-Hill Companies. Reprinted by permission of The McGraw-Hill Companies.

Pages 89 and 90: Excerpt from *Grandfather's Journey* by Allen Say. Copyright © 1993 by Allen Say. Reprinted by permission of Houghton Mifflin Harcourt Publishing Company. All rights reserved.

Page 174: Excerpted from *Brown Bear, Brown Bear, What Do You See?* by Bill Martin Jr and Eric Carle. Text copyright © 1967 by Holt, Rinehart and Winston; renewed 1995 by Bill Martin Jr; Text copyright © 2004 by the Estate of Bill Martin Jr. Reprinted by permission of Henry Holt and Company, LLC.